AF669756

NGOs and Disaster Management

ABOUT THE BOOK

A non-government organization has been defined as any non-profit, voluntary citizen's group, which is organized on a local, national or international level. However the diversity in task, goal and activities, strains any simple definition of NGO. The disaster management framework can be defined as different elements of the disaster cycle, which is composed of actions before disaster, actions immediately after disaster and long-term recovery process after disaster. Although it is more or less similar to different types of disasters, in the current discussion, specific emphasis will be given to the earthquake disasters. In disaster situations, a quick rescue and relief mission is inevitable, however considerable damage can be minimised if adequate preparedness levels are achieved. Indeed, it has been noticed in the past that as and when attention has been given to adequate preparedness measures, the loss to life and property has considerably reduced. Preparedness measures such as training of role players including the community, development of advanced forecasting systems, effective communications and above all a well-networked institutional structure involving the government organisations; academic and research institutions, the armed forces and the NGOs would greatly contribute to the overall disaster management of the region. The government's recent policy changes too reflect the changing approach from rescue and relief to preparedness. The book can be used as a ready reckoner/reference material for enlightening on the topics of concern for and NGO. The checklists, forms, specimens and formats can be used to a great extent.

ABOUT THE AUTHOR

Rajesh Kumar did his M.A. in Mass Communication and at present working with SAHARA TV for last 20 years and has wide experience in the sphere to which pertains to. He is highly qualified and has presented a number of programmes. He has published several articles.

NGOs and Disaster Management

Rajesh Kumar

AMIGA PRESS. INC
Delhi -110051

AMIGA PRESS INC.
H.O :- 28-A, Indra Park,
Chander Nagar, Delhi :- 110051 (India)
Tel :- 011-22504028, +91-98736-57000
Email :- amigapress@gmail.com
amigaeditorial@gmail.com
amigapub@gmail.com
Website :- www.amigapress.co.in

This edition is published by Amiga Press Inc.

ISBN : 978-93-87295-45-2

Copyright© Reserved
First Published 2019

All rights reserved, no part of this publication may be reproduced, stored in a retrieval system or transmitted in any form or by any means, electronic, mechanical, photocopying, recording or otherwise without the prior written permission of the publisher or the copyright holder.

This book contains information obtained from authentic and highly regarded sources. Reasonable efforts have been made to publish reliable data and information, but the author's, editor/s and publisher cannot assume responsibility for the validity of all materials or the consequences of their use. The author/s, editor/s and publishers have attempted to trace and acknowledge the copyright holders of all materials reproduced in this publication and apologize to copyright holders, if permission and acknowledgements to publish in the form have not been taken. If any copyright material has not been acknowledge please write and let us know so we may rectify it, in subsequent reprints.

Publisher's note: Presentations, Logos (the way they are written/ Presented), in this book are under the copyright of the publisher and hence, if copied/resembled the copier will be prosecuted under the law.

Printed and bound by Replika Press Pvt. Ltd.

Preface

A non-government organization has been defined as any non-profit, voluntary citizen's group, which is organized on a local, national or international level. However the diversity in task, goal and activities, strains any simple definition of NGO.

The disaster management framework can be defined as different elements of the disaster cycle, which is composed of actions before disaster, actions immediately after disaster and long-term recovery process after disaster. Although it is more or less similar to different types of disasters, in the current discussion, specific emphasis will be given to the earthquake disasters.

Disaster literally means 'Catastrophe', 'Calamity', or 'Aapada'. The Second Wednesday of every October during the Decade was observed as "World Disaster Reduction Day". National Day for Disaster Reduction was observed on 11th October. Theme for the year 2000 was "Community Participation and Public Awareness". The United Nations observed the Nineties as the "International Decade For Natural Disaster Reduction" (IDNDR), in order to focus on International Initiatives for minimizing the adverse impact of natural calamities particularly in the developed countries like India. The period of 1970 alone accounted for death of over 1 million persons and destruction of property over 46 billion dollars by Cyclones, Hurricanes, Tornados, Earthquakes, Floods and other disasters. In Past Century more than 10 million people have died due to Floods, Earthquakes and Tropical Storms.

Hazards are routinely divided into natural or man-made, although complex disasters, where there is no single root cause, are more common in developing countries. A specific disaster may spawn a secondary disaster that increases the impact. A classic example is an earthquake that causes a tsunami, resulting in coastal flooding.Hazards are routinely divided into natural or man-made, although complex disasters, where there is no single root cause, are more common in developing countries. A specific disaster may spawn a secondary disaster that increases the impact. A classic example is an earthquake that causes a tsunami, resulting in coastal flooding.

Man Made Disasters as a result of Toxic Chemicals; Explosions, Fire Incidents; High Rising Building's Collapse; And Hazardous Waste etc. have been the cause of many deaths and casualties. The increase in Chemical Processes and Manufacturing Industry inevitably carries the risk of accidents.

Enrico Fermi and his associates in the year 1944 at the University of Chicago developed the First Atomic Reactor and when proved that chain reaction was in fact a reality the world was introduced to new and terrifying dimensions, in the cause and scope of disasters. The Nuclear Bomb was dropped in Hiroshima and Nagasaki in 1945, since then the threat of Nuclear War is ever increasing. Increasing Nuclear Power Plants the world over inevitably carries the risk of accidents like manifested in the Three Mile Island and Chernobyl.

A non-government organization has been defined as any non-profit, voluntary citizen's group, which is organized on a local, national or international level (UN, 2000). However the diversity in task, goal and activities, strains any simple definition of NGO. It can be stated that the NGO include a wide range of groups, which act independent of government, and characterized by preliminary humanitarian activities, with focus on the citizen's need and demand. The term of NGO varies from county to country, e.g., while in the USA, it is often called as a 'private voluntary organization', in the African countries, it is often termed as 'voluntary development organization'. Although the universities and research organizations may be non-governmental, this directive refers principally to the private organizations, that pursue activities to relieve suffering, promote the interest of poor, protect the environment, provide basic social services, or undertake community development.

This is a reference book. All the matter is just compiled and edited in nature, taken from the various sources which are in public domain.

The book can be used as a ready reckoner/reference material for enlightening on the topics of concern for and NGO. The checklists, forms, specimens and formats can be used to a great extent.

—Editor

Contents

1

Role of NGOs

Non-Governmental Organizations (NGOs) are becoming increasingly important in the field of development. NGOs are a very important link between people at the grassroots, civil society and the state. They are diverse both in terms of organisational form, structure and culture and in terms of the issues they cover. Their involvement is not only seen in the implementation of governmental programmes but also in the process of formulation of public policies, and even in the enforcement of social legislation.

This unit will discuss Non-Governmental Organisations, their objectives, community support, projects and innovations and monitoring and evaluation with a view to understand their roles and responsibilities in the present context. According to Gangrade (2001) voluntary sector has always played an important role in society from time immemorial. The concept and approach in voluntary work has undergone many changes from time to time. From pure charity, relief and welfare oriented approach this sector has in recent times suitably modelled and equipped itself to meet the development needs of society. There is hardly any field which is not now touched by NGO sector/ voluntary sector. The NGOs have acquired an important position in various fields at the national and international levels. In 1994., at the Cairo International Conference on Population and Development, Governments unanimously endorsed, through the programme of action, the need to promote an effective partnership between all levels of Government and the full range of non-governmental organisations, and local community groups in the discussion and decisions on the design, implementation, coordination, monitoring and evaluation of programmes relating to population, development and environment. In the Cairo Conference a call was made to the governments and donors to ensure that NGOs are able to maintain their capacities. In our country, the role of NGOs in various fields such as education, health, culture and social welfare has been increasingly recognised.

Hasheni (1990) is of the opinion that NGOs and their members are organised in such a manner that they appear to be participatory. There is a need to institutionalise the role of NGOs in various fields through strong policy directives and implementation of such directives must be ensured by the Government of India and State Governments. The voluntary sector earlier was confined to the role of the capacity building, awareness raising and mobilisation of the community. During present time NGOs are no longer confined to their traditional domain of health, education and welfare.

Today they are also taking up sophisticated technical assignments in various technical fields like water resources, watershed, forestry, environment, Human Immuno-Virus (HIV) or Acquired Immune Deficiency Syndrome (AIDS), drug abuse and consumer rights. Alarge number of Indian NGOs is now manned by professionals and technocrats of high caliber. Under the changing scenario competent NGOs need to be involved in all the developmental fields, including technical fields. In the age of globalization and consumerism when every field is being opened up for the industries, private sector and multi-nations, NGOs are also playing their important role especially in the field of social sector-education and health. The NGO sector has contributed significantly in finding innovative solutions to poverty, deprivation, social discrimination and social mobilisation. It also includes service delivery, training, research and advocacy. The NGO sector has been serving as an important non-political link between the people and the Government.

CONCEPT AND HISTORY

Commission of Non-Governmental Organisations (2000) defines a Non-Governmental Organisation (NGO) as any non profit, voluntary citizens' group which is organised at a local, national or international level. Task oriented and driven by people with a common interest, NGOs perform a variety of service and humanitarian functions, bring citizens' concerns to Government, advocate and monitor policies and encourage political participation through provision of information. Some are organised around specific issues, such as human rights, environment or health. Deborah (1997) specifies the role of NGOs in terms of the capacity building.

The NGO sector has often been described as extremely diverse, heterogeneous and populated by organisations with hugely varied goals, structures and motivations. It is not easy to define an NGO. It cannot be based on any legal definition, given the wide variations in laws related to NGO activities. World Bank Operational Manual (1989) defines NGOs as organisations that are entirely or largely independent of government and characterised primarily by rather than commercial. The terminology varies; for example, in the United States they are called, private voluntary organisations, and most African NGOs prefer the label, "Voluntary Development Organisations". These can beproduction related NGOs, consumer and credit cooperatives, charitable and religious associations.

NGOs vary in terms of manpower and professional staff depending upon the number of objectives they carry out. Operational NGOs contribute to the delivery of services (such as in the field of welfare), whereas in the primary aim of advocacy an NGO influences the policies of public authorities and public opinion in general Some of the characteristics shared by different NGOs are as follows:

- NGOs are independent, in particular, of government and other public authorities and of political parties or commercial organisations.
- They are accountable to their members, donors and even with the funding agencies in terms of programme planning and implementation.
- They have their own governing bodies, office bearers and the procedure for the election as per the Registrar of the Societies.
- NGOs are formed voluntarily and there is usually an element of voluntary participation in the organisation.
- NGOs are not created to generate personal profit. However, they receive grants, donations from national and international sources.
- NGOs are also called as 'voluntary organizations' or 'civil society organisations'.

A Non-Governmental Organisation is a legally constituted organisation created by private persons or organisations with no participation or representation of any government. In cases in which NGOs are funded totally or partially by governments, the NGO maintains its non-government status insofar as it excludes representatives from membership in the organisation.

Globalization during the 20th century gave rise to the importance of NGOs. IVGOs have evolved to emphasize humanitarian issues, developmental aid and sustainable development. Aprorninent example of this is the 'World Social Forum' which is a rival convention of World Economic Forum. The fifth World Social Forum in 2005 held in Brazil was attended by more 1000 NGOs including Indian NGOs. Registered Societies: Societies Registration Act 1860 is a Central Act for registering non-profit organisations. Almost all the states in India have adopted the Central Act for creating state level authorities for registering various types of non profit entities. According to the Act, any seven persons who subscribe to the Memorandum of Association can register a society.

The memorandum should include aims of society, its objectives, its names, addresses and occupation of the members. NGOs have a long history at the international level, dating back to mid 19" century. They were important in the anti-slavery movement and the movement of women's suffrage and reached a peak at the time of the world Disarmament Conference.

However, the phrase non-governmental organisation only came into Role of Non-Governmental popular use with the establishment of the United Nations organisation in 1945 Organisations with provisions in Article 71 of the chapter 10 of the United Nations charter, for a consultative role for organisations which are neither governmental nor the member states. The definition of International NGO is first given in resolution 288(x) in 1950 as any International organisation that is not founded by an International treaty.

The vital role of NGOs was recognised in chapter 27 of Agenda 21. An NGO can be created for public charitable purposes. There is no all India Act for setting up public Charitable Trusts. Some of the states in India have enacted the public Charitable Trust Act. An NGO can be created only under a Public Trust Act. Diane (2004) in Transfer Agents and Global Network emphasised that globalization during the 20" century gave rise the importance of NGOs. NGOs have developed to emphasize humanitarian issues, development aid and sustainable development. In the Fifth World Social Forum (2005), more than 1000 NGOs participated to discuss poverty and social issues.

A Trust can be registered in one state, but the same has the scope to operate in any number of states. Private Trusts: A private Trust created under governed by the Indian Trust Act of 1882, aims at managing assigned Trust properties for private or religious purposes. A private Trust does not enjoy the privileges and tax benefits that are available for public Trust or NGOs. 7.2.2 NGOs in India: Emergence and Role NGOs or voluntary organisations in India are shaped by a variety of factors; they have been nurtured and threatened in turn as the dominant political outlook has oscillated between liberalism and statism. Diverse in their functions and purposes, they serve primarily a vast and assorted population of informal workers. A sizeable sum from public and foreign sources is expended by this sector. And yet the sector has 'received surprisingly scanty attention from academic researchers and social analysts. Kaplan (1999) analysed the classical statement of the organisational development approach to development with particular relevance to smaller, indigenous NGOs. Population Foundation of India (1999) emphasised on encouraging the role of Indian NGOs for forming opinion of Panchayati Raj Leaders, local tradition dais, aganwadi workers and private practitioners to participate in planning and implementation. voluntary !organisations tend to be emotional and ideological rather than reflective and rational. Descriptions of voluntary organisations tend to either praise or denounce them-what is missing is an effort at understanding and interpreting them. Voluntary associations have been seen alternatively as the 'harbingers of silent revolution', 'hand maidens of global imperialism', and 'footnotes in India's development'.

If voluntarism was inspired by religion and political ideology, commitment to normative pluralism facilitated its growth. National elites, already steeped in the indigenous cultural conception of society as autonomous of the State, readily embraced normative pluralism. Their commitment has been manifested in several ways. Formally, the Constitution guarantees the right to form organisations to Indian citizens. In addition to this legal provision, certain practices and norms were developed which promoted voluntary organisations.

First, from the very outset Indian policy-makers had developed a tradition of consulting social elites and groups. Representative committees were created to secure opinions from various groups in society, and their views were solicited in formulating major domestic policies, even as a centrally planned model of development was adopted. Second, voluntary organisations were involved not only in formulating policies, but their help was also sought in implementing programmes. The Planning Commission itself had realized at the outset that the task of development was so large and so complex that the State alone would not be able to accomplish it. Accordingly, the very First Five Year Plan document had camed a plea to voluntary organisations to become involved in the task of development, mainly by implementing government programmes. Appropriate financial provisions were also made for them. Beginning with an allocation of Rs.4 crore in the First Plan, the voluntary sector has been receiving increasing amounts of public funds.

In the Eighth Plan it rose to Rs.750 crore and multiplied in subsequent plans. Finally, because of the stand of international aid agencies, an extraneous factor has also played a conducive role. In the 1970s, the philosophy and strategy of the international development community began to change. Foreign aid donors started to focus their attention on voluntary organisations as supplementary delivery vehicles for development. They began to channel large amounts of developmental aid to those organisations which worked directly for the poor instead of for the governments. This access to financial resources led to mushrooming of voluntary organisations.

The activities of voluntary organisations can be seen in a new way. Many typologies of voluntary associations have been developed, and the proposed typology makes no radical departure from them. It differs from them only in emphasising the political activities of voluntary associations. The activities can be considered under three heads; developmental, political and catalytic. Developmental, catalytic and political activities are not mutually exclusive, and most voluntary organisations pursue some combination of all three, often in conjunction with each other or as a series of successive steps. However, both voluntary associations themselves and the researchers have shied away from focusing exclusively on political activities.

Types of NGOs

Apart from NGO, alternative terms are used such as *Independent Sectol; Voluntary* Sector, Civil Society, Grassroots Orgunisation, Transnational Voluntary *Organisation, Self Help Groups* and *Non-State Actors.*

The primary purpose of an operational NGO is the design and implementation of development related projects. The primary purpose of an Advocacy NGO is to defend or promote a specific cause. As opposed to operational project management, these organisations typically try to raise awareness, acceptance and knowledge by lobbying with the government, and media advocacy activism. The small NGOs (Population Foundation of India, 1989) work at the grassroots Role of Non-governmental levels for advocacy capacity building and provide information to the community.

Organisations

Information at the grassroots level will help in generating demands at the various levels. As it is rightly stated, development is the best contraceptive. United States Agency for International Development (USAID) refers to NGO as private voluntary organisations. However, many scholars have argued that this definition is highly problematic as many NGOs are in fact state and corporates funded and manage projects with professional staff. NGOs exist for a variety of reasons, usually to further the political or social goals of their members or donors. Examples include encouraging the observance of human rights, improving the state of the natural environment, improving the welfare of the disadvantaged or representing a corporate agenda. There are a huge number of such organisations and their goals cover a broad range of political and philosophical positions. NGOs have several names and alternative tens. However, there are by and large called Non-Governmental Organisations.

Methods

NGOs also vary in their methods. Several NGOs work on education and health.. Oxfam is concerned with poverty alleviation and Prayas is corfcerned with education. Population Foundation of India marks in the areas of health and environment.

Public relations: Non-Governmental Organisations need healthy relationships with the public to meet their goals. Foundations and Charities use sophisticated public relations campaigns to raise funds and employ standard lobbying techniques with governments. Interest groups may be of political importance because of their ability to influence social and political outcomes.

Consulting: Many International NGOs have a consultative status with United Nations agencies relevant to their area of work. However, initially only 41 to 50 NGOs had consultative status, which became 3550 by 2003.

Project Management: There is an increasing awareness that management techniques are crucial to project success in non-governmental organisations. Normally, NGOs focus on the community issues and also on environment. NGOs are also working as part of International relations. They are also directly involved in local action.

Management: Diverse management styles deal with different work-cultures in an organisation. To develop the organisation, individuals have to be able to contribute in the decision making process and they need to learn by the following processes.

Staffing: All the staff of non-governmental organisations are not volunteers. Some of them are working in specific projects. organisations are not volunteers. Some of them are working in specific projects.

The NGO sector is gradually becoming an imporant employer in term of Number. Since the government sector is minimising its roles gradually increasing in the voluntary sector. For example, school health program in India earlier the government through its doctors and nurses were taking care of the health check-up of the children in primary schools. Now, this responsibility is assigned to the voluntary sector. In the case of Sarva Shiksha Abhiyan of Universalisation of Elementary Education (WE Mission), the voluntary sector is involved in enrolling and main streaming the learners of the age-group 6-14. The Sarva Shiksha Abhiyan is operating in each state. There are several methods through which NGOs operate in their respective areas. Staffing pattern and their capacity building is very important.

Legal Status

While creating an NGO, its objects are defined in the deed of creation, viz; care of the sick, disabled, economically weak, illiterate, old, women, children, agriculture and rural development, environment, animal welfare, any other social, cultural or educational activities. The NGO may be focused on one or several activities, stated in the memorandum of association. Broadly speaking NGO is an association of persons, and that it can be created by Role of Non-Governmental one of the three modes, viz; either by i) registration under the Indian Trust Act.

Organizations

1882 (or Charitable Religious Trusts Act, 1920), or by ii) registration under Societies Registration Act, 1860, or by iii) registration with the Registration of Companies, under section 25 of the Companies Act, 1956.

Creation of an NGO as a Trust: It is the simplest and easiest mode of setting up an NGO, and thus commence charitable/social work for the purpose of public good without any fear or favour and without any motive of profit, directly or indirectly. It is a legal entity where the trustees work as per the objects and rules defined in the trust deed. The contents of the trust deed must include-the name of the trust, its address, the settler, the trustees, the beneficiaries, the objectives, the procedure to appoint remove trustees and any other condition that the settler may wish to enforce. In Chandigarh, the trust deeds are registered by the Sub-Registrar Tehsildar.

Creation of an NGO under Societies Registration Act, 1860: As mentioned in the foregoing, an association of persons has to be well organised and enjoys the status of a legal entity, to function as an NGO effectively.

The commonest mode of creation of NGO is through registration under Societies Registration Act, 1860. Such societies are established for the promotion of charitable objectives, besides the promotion of literature, science or fine arts. Some states have made minor modifications in the said Act, to enlarge the scope of societies or to give broader meaning to them. Any seven or more persons associated for any literary, scientific or charitable purpose, or for any such purpose, as is described in Section 20 of this Act, may, by subscribing their names to a memorandum of association, and filing the same with the Registrar of Societies, can form themselves into societies under this Act.

Incorporation as a non-profit company: Section 25(1) of Company Regulations, 1956: This is the least exercised option since it is expensive and cumbersome. If it is private company at least 2 members are required, if it is for public purpose, at least 7 members are required.

STRUCTURES AMONG NGOS

There is a great variety of ways in which NGOs are structured. The classic model is of a membership organization, coordinated in a geographically-defined hierarchy. Individual people work in local groups, which coordinate in provinces and then have a headquarters in the capital city for the country as a whole. Such country-wide organizations are called national NGOs. Frequently, the national NGOs combine in an international NGO, or INGO, which may consist of regional groups of countries and be capped by a global body. Not all the levels of the hierarchy need exist. Many countries are too small to have provincial structures. Smaller specialist NGOs may simply enrol individual members at the national level, without having any local branches. Occasionally, individuals are enrolled at the international level. On the other hand, in large organizations, the international level often seems relatively remote and attracts little attention, even among the NGO's own members. The group running a local family planning clinic does not necessarily know about the work of the International Planned Parenthood Federation (IPPF) at the UN World Conference on Women in Beijing. Nevertheless, such global organizations with their membership measured in millions do maintain a democratic policy-making process.

While some may hold direct elections for key posts at the national level, the responsibility to the membership at the global level is always indirect, via some international council or assembly of national representatives. It should be noted that one of the ambiguities about the term, NGO, is whether it is referring to a local, provincial, national, regional or global body. Until the early 1990s, the matter was generally straightforward in academic, news media or political discussions. The overwhelming majority of local and provincial NGOs never engaged in transnational activities. Thus NGO, by itself, usually meant a national NGO and regional or global bodies were called international NGOs. National NGOs did engage in transnational development and humanitarian activities, but, with very few exceptions, they were not, in their own right, participants in international diplomacy. When they wanted to exercise political influence at the global level, they did so through the appropriate INGO. In the 1990s, there was a great upsurge in local organizations becoming active at the global level, particularly on environmental issues, because of the Rio Earth Summit in June 1992, and on social issues, because of the Copenhagen Social Summit in March 1995.

Since then, the term INGO has not been used so much and NGO, by itself, has come to cover both national and international NGOs. As an expression of the new politics, various terms then were popularized to refer to local NGOs. Grass-roots organizations, community based organizations (CBOs), and civil society organizations (CSOs), all came into currency. There is still an ambiguity whether these newer terms cover organizations that only operate at the local level or also include local branches of national organizations. Grass-roots and community organizations clearly refer solely to the local level, but civil society has connotations of any level within a single country. Indeed, it has become quite common to refer to global civil society. Linguistic usage in the legal atmosphere at the UN used to be somewhat different. When the UN was formed, any involvement of private individuals or groups in its work constituted deviation from the norm of diplomacy being the exclusive preserve of "states". Thus, a national organization, as mentioned in Article 71 of the UN Charter, was any NGO based in a single country. No distinction was made between an organization that covered a large constituency, over the whole country, and an organization based solely in a local community or a small section of the population.

The lack of any distinction did not matter, as participation by either country-wide or more limited national NGOs was so rare in the permanent UN organs. Participation began on a small scale in the 1970s at UN conferences, on an *ad hoc* basis. When the ECOSOC rules were changed in 1996, to admit "national NGOs" to consultative status as a matter of routine, the presumption became that a national organization was a country-wide membership organization or a federation of local groups or an umbrella group, that is a coalition of NGOs operating in different fields. As is common at the UN, practice has not been consistent: a few local NGOs have been admitted as "national NGOs" to consultative status. The Rio conference also produced a term that has only been used in environmental politics at the UN. "Major Groups" refers to a system of categorizing NGOs from all levels, for the purposes of participating in UN policy-making processes. Hereafter, use of NGO alone will imply that any or all levels are included, while local, national or global will be used when the meaning must be restricted to that level. Terms such as CBOs and Major Groups will also be used in the appropriate political context. A minority of NGOs conform to the model of a global democratic hierarchy, in which any person may become a member. One variant is for the NGO to have subscribers or supporters, providing income, receiving newsletters and responding to calls for action, but not having any democratic control either over expenditure or over policy priorities for the organization. This is common among altruistic NGOs, promoting social welfare and poverty alleviation, and also among environmental NGOs. Another variant is for a specific status or participation in some activity to be a prerequisite for membership.

Thus trade unions are only open to those employed in certain occupations (sometimes very broadly defined). Similarly, professional, scientific and technical bodies are only open to people with the relevant qualification. Such organizations may then be grouped on a functional basis rather than a geographical basis, before they form national and/or international federations. Trade unions do maintain democratic decision-making structures (at least in principle, if not always in practice). However, professional, scientific and technical bodies have professional norms that override democratic norms and members may be expelled for violating the professional norms. A third variant is a religious organization.

The major religions do all have complex hierarchies, from the local faith community through to global spiritual authorities. None of them claim to be democratic: authority is based on faith, a holy text, the charisma of individuals or a hierarchical tradition. To some it will be surprising to discuss trade unions, professional bodies and religious organizations as if they are NGOs.

Indeed, the leaders of all three will usually deny they are NGOs. Nevertheless, they are treated on the same basis as NGOs throughout the UN system, with the exception of the special place for unions in the International Labour Organisation's tripartite system of governance.

Coalition-Building Among NGOs

Once NGOs do decide to influence public policy, they organize, in broad coalitions, specifically for this purpose. This means there is a large number of NGOs that bear no resemblance to the classic model of a unified hierarchy. Coalitions may take the form of umbrella INGOs, networks or caucuses. In the days when the main form of communication was by mail and even transnational telephone conversations were expensive and time-consuming to arrange, multinational coalitions generally took the form of institutional structures. Many international women's organizations, the International Council of Voluntary Agencies and the World Conservation Union are examples that date from this era. They are referred to as umbrella organizations, to signify the presence under the single umbrella of a variety of different NGOs that do not share a common identity. In the 1960s, direct transnational telephone dialing was established and air travel became sufficiently cheap for individuals to meet occasionally. Then in the 1970s the news media gradually used satellite communications, so that events in one place were shared around the world as television images. These processes encouraged the formation of looser issue-based networks of NGOs to exchange information, mobilize support and coordinate strategies. At this stage, networks still required some degree of formal organization, with enough resources being raised to pay the salary of a network administrator and associated costs for the paperwork. The International Baby Foods Action Network was the prototype, followed by similar networks on pesticides, rainforests, climate change and other questions.

The advent of e-mail and the web in the 1990s then meant that the costs of running a network dropped substantially and individual people could afford to take part in sophisticated instantaneous global communications. The number of networks increased dramatically and they no longer needed any formal structure. Once a lead organization or even a lead individual establishes technical and political communication skills, a coalition of thousands of NGOs can be formed rapidly and their influence focused on specific targets. The International Campaign to Ban Landmines, the Coalition for an International Criminal Court and Jubilee 2000 are the most spectacular examples. However, the impact of technological change should not be exaggerated. The most effective modern networks still derive their impact from being coalitions of well-organized NGOs. Although communication costs are now minimal, it is still essential to have sufficient resources at the centre, even if they are provided by a single member of the network, for at least one person to devote most or all of his/her time to servicing the network. A variant of the global network is a global caucus.

This arises when a group of NGOs come together as lobbyists at an international diplomatic event, such as a UN agenda-setting conference or a UN forum for negotiating on the formulation or implementation of a treaty. The caucus will be highly focused on achieving specific outcomes from the diplomatic process. The impression is given that such a caucus is an ad hoc grouping that only exists during the two or three weeks of the relevant diplomatic meetings. It may be accurate that the particular combination of NGOs having the particular political purpose will never meet again. However, a successful caucus will be well prepared and will carry forward procedural expertise, substantive knowledge, political status and diplomatic contacts gained in one forum through to the next forum, handling similar questions. Key organizations and key individuals provide continuity. Women's organizations and environmentalists are among the most successful operating in this way. When we consider something as loose and transient as a caucus, it is perhaps inappropriate to call it an organization. Nevertheless, structured umbrella coalitions, networks and caucuses are all handled in the same way by governments. In the UN system, all transnational actors have to accept the label "NGO", in order to participate. They may be present under the label of the coalition or of its constituents or through both routes. Umbrella INGOs have consultative status and networks usually are listed, but caucuses rarely have any formal recognition. Coalitions that focus on policy outcomes in a particular country or a particular intergovernmental organization will tend to take the form of an umbrella organization. Coalitions that focus on issues tend to take the form of a network or a caucus, with different members being active in different policy forums. In global environmental politics, there is a unique set of caucuses – the system of "Major Groups".

The term was adopted at the Earth Summit, when *Agenda 21* devoted one of its four sections to "Strengthening the Role of Major Groups". The preamble argued that "one of the fundamental prerequisites for the achievement of sustainable development is broad public participation in decision-making" and this must be done as a "real social partnership" with "individuals, groups and organizations". The aim was for the UN to move beyond the traditional reliance on the established NGOs, in two ways. Communication must reach down to individuals at the level of local communities and particular sectors of society of importance for the environment must be mobilized. The section devoted separate chapters to nine Major Groups, under the following headings.

- Strengthening the role of business and industry
- Scientific and technological community
- Strengthening the role of farmers.

The choice of these nine groups was the arbitrary and incoherent outcome of negotiations at UNCED. It was influenced by the personal concerns of Maurice Strong and by the lobbying of NGOs who were accredited to the conference. It is arbitrary to single out women but not men; the young but not the elderly; indigenous people but not other minorities; unions but not professional associations; business and industry but not commerce, finance and services; natural scientists but not social scientists; and farmers but not fishing communities. It is anomalous, but understandable, to emphasize one level of government, local authorities, when they have responsibility for all the Major Groups. Above all it is incoherent to have NGOs as one of the Major Groups, when *all* the other eight (including associations of local authorities) are represented in the UN system via the ECOSOC "arrangements for consultation with non-governmental organizations". This incoherence arises because many in the other Major Groups did not wish to be labelled as NGOs and there had to be a category to encompass environment and development NGOs.

In the Commission on Sustainable Development set up after the Earth Summit, special arrangements were made to allow for participation by all the new groups that had engaged with the UN for the first time at Rio. Any NGO that had been accredited for UNCED was allowed to apply for Roster NGO status at sessions of the CSD and later was given a special fast-track procedure for gaining full status with ECOSOC. Although the CSD is constitutionally a standard subsidiary body of ECOSOC, it has developed its own procedures for relating to NGOs. Rather than each NGO attempting to exercise its participation rights separately, the NGOs are organized into the nine Major Groups from *Agenda 21*. These categories are used both by the NGOs in their own caucusing and in the formal proceedings. In addition, the CSD has gone beyond the normal consultative arrangements to hold various types of formal, and informal, panels and seminars. Notably, each of the annual sessions starts with the appropriate Major Groups making presentations in special "stakeholder dialogues" on the different substantive agenda items for that year. In pragmatic terms, the illogicality of having NGOs as one of the nine groups of NGOs serves a useful function, in enabling any organization that does not fit elsewhere to be included. This Major Groups system has only operated in the CSD and in other processes that have been derived from UNCED.

THE GEOGRAPHICAL SPREAD OF NGOS

It used to be widely argued that NGOs were predominantly a feature of Western societies. This false proposition was derived from a mixture of ignorance, Western presumptions of their superiority in the Cold War and nationalist rhetoric from authoritarian regimes. All societies in modern times have had large numbers of NGOs at least at the local level. Under the most authoritarian regimes or in the least developed countries there are still self-help cooperative groups, community welfare associations, religious groups, professional and scientific associations, sports and recreational bodies, etc. Even Romania during the dictatorship of President Ceaucescu was host to the International Federation of Beekeepers' Associations. The presence or absence of a democratic political culture is one of the major variables determining the number of NGOs, but the size of a country, its ethnic, religious and cultural diversity, the complexity of its economy and the quality of its communication infrastructure are also of crucial importance.

Thus there are tens of thousands of NGOs in countries such as Bangladesh and India, while there are relatively few in Iceland or Finland. A particular source of controversy is the idea that the major NGOs are "Northern". Many people are still trapped by the mental prejudice that organizations have to be situated in geographical space. It might be a practical necessity for an international NGO to have a headquarters office in a particular building, but the location of the office in a North American or a European city does not convert a global NGO into a Northern NGO. Equally, the historical origins of an organization being formed in a particular country does not mean it is currently a Northern rather than a global organization. The proper criteria for assessment whether an organization is global are the location of its membership, the staffing of its headquarters, the sources of its funding and the content of its programs. An organization, such as Amnesty International, with 56 National Sections, groups in some 40 other countries, an International Secretariat from over 50 countries and an African Secretary-General is a global NGO, even if it started in Britain and has its headquarters in London. Due to the spread of democracy and the improvements in communications, many international NGOs that started in individual countries became global at the end of the twentieth century.

NGOs : Training and Development

Many NGOs recognize the need for enhancing technical skills in the area of management. In our encounters, the need for leadership development of NGO staff was not often a priority. Organizations were committed first to the constituents they served and seemed far less focused on the development of their staff. Learning occurred primarily on the job and most training was focused on job-related skills. Few organizations appear to focus much on "self actualization" for staff. This lack of personal development, stated one educator, was a factor in the high burnout rates and stagnation present in the sector. "People need rejuvenation" observed the president of a large NGO. In some cases there was skepticism that leadership could be developed and needed to be available for staff at large.

A foundation representative stated that there needs to be better validation of the value of leadership development at lower levels. Other institutions, however, voiced the perspective that leadership development had broad value based on the premise that one could enact leadership "without being in a position of authority." The skills identified for training included: identity development, self-confidence, motivation, perspective development, articulation of thoughts and public speaking, risk taking, team building and relationship development, conflict management, and building consensus. With regard to training there is also the expressed tension between being able to afford time for staff to attend programs ("only people who have no work can attend training") and the realization that self study or online programs are not adequate for learning. One individual put it this way "you can't learn leadership from a book; it is akin to reading a menu and feeling full." The existing training programs we encountered were usually delivered by independent trainers and used dialogue, role play, and group exercises to help individuals assess strengths and weaknesses, and build skills and abilities. These programs were often delivered at very low cost with basic amenities and residential options to make them affordable. A number of educational and training institutions we visited were working to do more for NGO professionals. They are planning to ramp up new offerings to provide NGO staff with ongoing professional development. Even so, these institutions admitted that it was hard to scale their operations enough to address the vast need for training in adequate measure.

Collective Capacity

The NGOs we visited had established effective models for addressing social needs and had plans for expansion. Many of the organizations, however, saw the scope of need in India to far exceed their present reach of activities. This was related to the shortage of human resources – "we need a lot more qualified people in the field" – as well as their ability to address the vast challenges alone. In many cases organizations expansion plans were linked to forming alliances with other NGO, corporate, and governmental entities. The need for collective effort was emphasized by several people with whom we spoke. We heard that there is a critical need to work constructively with governmental agencies, corporations, and funding bodies. Embedded in this was the recognition that these entities had differing agendas that were not always seen to be in the interest of the poor. Concern was expressed about corporate social responsibility being primarily about public relations than creating change. A founder of a rural NGO also voiced dissatisfaction that large NGOs had a tendency to become big bureaucracies that simply subcontracted work and did so with short attention spans – "you can't subcontract vision or passion."

We nevertheless heard expressed the need for NGOs to work together more effectively to align efforts, share learning and best practices, and consolidate their power. An older NGO mentioned that with maturity they were now less concerned that partnering with another NGO would enable the other to "steal their funding." Some educational institutions saw a role for them to play in enhancing NGO networks and the cross-sector sharing of knowledge.

Observations

There is clearly much pressure on the NGO sector to address significant challenges in India related to deep rooted poverty and rapid change. The commitment, achievements, and vision of the people at the NGOs we met were inspirational and provide much hope. Our sense is that leadership development –understood as enhancing the ability of individuals and organization to work together to envision and enact change – has a significant role to play in helping NGOs achieve their objectives.

We observe the need to do more to train staff to enhance skills and help them deal creatively with the immense challenge and opportunity that they must tackle. Furthermore this investment in individual employee development and growth will help enhance retention and reduce stagnation and frustration. The response by educational and training institutions to address this need is promising and must be further extended and supported by funders. At the same time, there is need to demonstrate the effectiveness and value of these investments in leadership development for funders. At a macro-level, it appears that a broadly recognized issue is working across sectors and boundaries in alliances and networks. There appears to be interest among corporations and NGOs to engage constructively, though the scope of these activities appears limited at present.

We see that higher education in India represents a key point at which a greater exposure to and engagement with the social sector can be established. This could serve the dual purpose of helping young people build soft skills, by taking on real challenges out of the classroom, as well helping spark interest among more individuals in choosing the NGO sector as their career path. The Centre for Creative Leadership is working to explore ways in which we can be a resource for leadership development for the NGO sector in India and beyond. As our work evolves, we look forward to reconnecting with NGOs in India to develop, test, and offer tangible approaches to address these needs.

NGOS, ASSOCIATIONS AND THE "THIRD SECTOR"

Without a doubt, the "major" work done thus far on the question of NGOs and associations comes from the English-speaking world, particularly from the United States. In France, research on this question is still rare, and it is not yet fully recognised, neither by sociologists, political scientists nor economists. Research on NGOs is essentially conducted within the framework of social economy, a relatively recent and still marginal discipline in France which includes work done on associations, foundations, cooperatives and mutual insurance companies (Archambault E).

In France, the lack of interest in this discipline is partially due to a scientific tradition that has "suffered" from the centralised State that characterises France and that has also left its mark on the social sphere (Rosanvallon P). In French political science, a noticeable distinction is made between "worthy" subjects which are linked to the State (for example, political parties, elections, etc.) and which interest researchers, and subjects that enjoy less esteem, such as associations and NGOs.

Nonetheless, it should be noted that two important studies have appeared recently: the first is dedicated to the non-profit sector in France (Archambault E), and the second to NGOs in the North and South, and their rapport with development. The latter is particularly relevant: as Northern NGOs are intervening more and more in Arab countries, it is vital to understand the nature of Northern NGOs working in countries in the South and the changes they have undergone over the past few years.

The most recent and pertinent work on NGOs produced in the English-speaking countries was done by the Johns Hopkins programme on international comparison of the non-profit sector which is conducted by the International Society for Third-Sector Research. This programme has held three international conferences and publishes the *Revue Voluntas*. The initiative is interesting on several counts: it includes all countries in the world, making a true international comparison possible without treating developing or Arab countries separately, which would have the effect of "stigmatising" them and singling them out artificially. The programme is based on the premise that non-profit organisations exist everywhere in the world and that they are active in similar areas.

Very little if anything is known about this sector because it is not included in conventions for international accounting standards; consequently international comparisons are virtually impossible. In order to make up for this gap the programme was launched in May 1990. It aims to "raise the veil on a world that has been ignored for a long time and yet continues to make significant contributions to solving human problems wherever they may be.

Today, after a re-examination of the role of the State in both industrialised and developing countries, non-profit organisations have become vectors of sociability and instruments of social change. They are also vital economic actors, and are capable of responding to emerging social needs, dealing with serious social issues and creating jobs in countries where public intervention has demonstrated its limits...".

The work of this project is based on certain theoretical hypotheses and on the following definition of the non-profit sector: these are private, non-institutional organisations (distinct from the State, administrations and local authorities); they are independent, with their own decision-making bodies and an autonomous budget; and all projects that are undertaken must be reinvested to serve the social purpose, and entail a certain degree of voluntary participation by volunteers or donors. Two other, non fundamental, criteria have been added to this definition: these organisations should not be strictly religious, and should not have a declared political aim.

In considering this definition, Alain Piveteau reflects on the specificity of the "third sector" within the framework of the opposition between the market and the State, as highlighted by economic theory. He notes that the "non-distribution of profits" is central to the definition of NGOs, and that their general features are considered to be "solidarity, unselfishness, and confidence". The specificity of development NGOs is that they are organisations of "mediation". Their main objective is the philanthropic redistribution of essentially private resources to support development.

The importance given to the "organisational" or "institutional" aspect of the non-profit sector is noteworthy. This aspect can become problematical for developing countries and Arab countries in particular, which have acquired some "informal" or "non-institutional" forms of social solidarity. The definition may be pragmatic and useful for doing work on international comparisons, but it fails to address several problems and questions that have been raised by French research, notably during the symposium on NGOs and development that was held in Bordeaux in 1997. During this symposium, the issues under discussion took into consideration the work of French sociologists who had developed new approaches to social sciences (in particular Pierre Bourdieu, Laurent Thévenot and Luc Boltanski).

How do development NGOs constitute a unique institutional category that is different from development bureaucracies? Are the characteristics of these organisations in line with the aims they proclaim? What is known of the trajectory, origins, profiles and future of those who found, direct and ainimate NGOs, of their motivations and strategies? How are their forms of action specific? Given that the "field of development NGOs" has become increasingly professional, is it not true that the directors and organisers of NGOs have now become "brokers", even entrepreneurs, of development?

NGOs have both obvious and latent functions, and they are organised and regulated places where different power plays, legitimacies, material and symbolic interests and ideologies are acted out. NGOs are the intermediaries between donors and people; consequently their "social capital" should be studied, as well as their networks of connections up and down the social ladder. NGOs are at the heart of multiple cultural entanglements and also have their own specific histories that merit examination (de Sardan P-O). In addition to its definition of the non-profit sector, research of the Johns Hopkins programme has produced certain theories concerning the "third sector". These are either socio-political or economic in nature. The socio-political theories refer to the failure of the welfare State and advance the hypothesis that the bigger the welfare State, the smaller the role of the non-profit sector. They also concern the legal and political framework, with the hypothesis that systems of common law are more favourable to the development of non-profit organisations than systems of statute law. On a sociological level, the theory is that the growth of an educated middle-class is vital for promoting an active "third sector".

The economic theories refer to the heterogeneous supply of collective goods. Non-profit organisations often provide collective goods which complement or compete with those provided by the State which tries to satisfy the average voter. Consequently, the greater the heterogeneity of society, the greater will be the needs for heterogeneous collective goods; it is that type of society that interests the non-profit sector. The latest economic theory is linked to asymmetrical information and the cost of transactions. Non-profit organisations may constitute an effective response when the market fails in cases of asymmetrical information exchange between producers and consumers (Archambault E).

Researchers of the Johns Hopkins programme have recognised the importance of the work published by the economist Edith Archambault on the non-profit sector in France. The results of this study are significant for several reasons. First of all, they reveal a discrepancy between the size of this sector and its relative invisibility in the institutional landscape. Over the past few years the author has observed a baby boom of associations. In 1990, this sector had 800,000 full-time employees, and from 1981 to 1990, employment there grew by 40%, while overall employment stagnated. Jobs in the third sector account for 4.5% of total employment, which is clearly higher than the average percentage for seven other European countries. The author notes the limits of private versus public funding. These observations also apply to French NGOs active in development in countries in the South. Because of the economic crisis, rise in xenophobia, and lower profile of Southern countries in French politics and thought, there have been fewer private donations for development NGOs, a decline in activism and little renewal in the management of French NGOs (Ryphman P).

On a different level, the practices of NGOs in the North have also undergone important changes. For example, Northern NGOs are supporting the participation of local organisations from the South which they now consider to be full-fledged actor; they are also taking into account the "real" economy and the profit principle, and encouraging economic activity; they are showing a new concern for cities (rather than for rural areas, as was the case previously); they are expressing a new interest in "the poor" as well as a desire to treat the root of the problem by promoting economic activity rather than solely its symptoms, as they had done before; and, finally, they are attentive to the distribution of basic services (healthcare, education, water) and the development of differentiated financial products. In addition, less of a distinction is now made between NGOs that deal with urgencies and those that deal with development. There is a greater effort to promote rights, and an increased interest in the new work method that aims to influence political and social choices through lobbying (Le Bris E, Reveil M, Roca P-J). Another change that has affected NGOs is their "professionalism", which can be seen as supplementing-or substituting-their preoccupations with "charity", "solidarity", "development" and urgency.

As for the mediation role of NGOs, researchers note that the classical representation mechanisms are presently in crisis, and NGOs are positioning and appointing themselves as mediators. Thus they tend to take the place of political representation, play a social role and influence the way we see the world. They have distinguished themselves from associations in general, and forced the respect for a third sector that is operating between the private and public sectors.

Other researchers feel that one should also be aware of the rapports of domination and competition that exist in the development "field", which is made up of actors who can be divided into essentially two camps, depending on what kind of capital they possess: money (donors) or knowledge (experts, research institutes and academics). One should not underestimate the "ambiguous" relationship that exists between NGOs from the North and the South, which is marked by patronage and competition, especially when Southern NGOs want to emancipate themselves and go directly to donors, bypassing Northern NGOs. However, while this situation may indeed be unequal, the behaviour of the "dominated" should not be overlooked, as it may include "ruse", manipulation and misappropriation.

This is a broad outline of the latest hypotheses that researchers have formulated on Northern NGOs operating in countries of the South. The intervention of these organisations in Arab countries represents a particular case because they are countries that have their own "non-governmental organisations" and associations. Similarly, the Arab world has its own international NGOs, notably international Islamic organisations. The most important are the International Islamic Relief Organisation founded in 1978 as a branch of the World Islamic League; the Islamic Relief Agency, founded during the 1980s and based in Khartoum; and, finally, Islamic Relief which is based in Great Britain (Bellion J).

Studies on associations in Arab countries are few. At the last conference of the *International Society for Third Sector Research* (4), only a small number of papers were dedicated to Arab countries: Egypt, Palestine, Jordan and Kuwait. It is significant that there were no studies on Arab countries with a French scientific tradition, such as Tunisia, Algeria and Morocco. Even though research has been done on NGOs in these countries, it has no international visibility because of the domination of the English language, and also because of the little attention that the French-language scientific tradition has paid to this theme. In the Near and Middle East, much research is being done in Arabic, but for obvious reasons it has not gained international recognition; it is nevertheless debated within Arabic scientific communities, namely in Egypt and Lebanon. In this context we should cite the work done by *The Arab Network for NGOs* (Shabaka), which is based in Cairo and publishes the journal *Al-Mezalla*.

In the academic domain ýÿ pending confirmation ýÿ studies on NGOs in the Arab world are very few in number. Even if there have been some Masters theses, a country like Egypt has not produced one doctoral thesis dedicated to NGOs. Most of the work is done by research centres and experts whose aims are mainly short-term, selective and empirical. Research on the issue of NGOs is at present being constituted/built up, and this conference hopes to encourage researchers to become more interested in it. One of the purposes of the round table in Cairo is specifically to review and highlight the work that has been done so far on NGOs in different Arab countries.

As NGOs are now considered to be playing a strategic role in development, it is not surprising that there is a growing interest in them. However, this cannot be the sole reason since, historically, Arab countries have experimented with the modern model of associations since the late 19th and early 20th centuries. Another reason may be that once these countries had won independence, hegemonic ýÿ if not authoritarian and repressive ýÿ politico-administrative systems were imposed. This left practically no room for the autonomous activities of associations. All the activities that had previously been conducted by autonomous organisations were taken over by the government. As a result, some countries have almost lost their tradition of autonomous associations. But the role the "third sector" may now be playing in Arab countries is too recent a phenomenon to have produced a substantial body of academic work.

"Good governance" has become an important issue not only for politics, but also for the economic and social arenas and, more generally, for development. This implies supporting and introducing more efficient measures of structural adjustment, and delegating to the private sector and to "civil society" the missions which the State had previously carried out, such as education, healthcare and, more generally, helping the disadvantaged categories of society (the poor, women, the handicapped, and abandoned children). Besides taking on these social tasks, NGOs are called upon to play an overall, fundamental role in development. Today, NGOs are already playing an active role in virtually all domains of development: they foster employment, enterprise creation, professional training, and the implementation of agricultural projects; support basic urban services (transportation, water, sewage, sanitation, parks) and the fight against pollution and corruption; they promote transparent and efficient government and administrations, as well as "advocacy societies", which defend the big social and humanitarian causes, such as human rights and the rights of women.

Judging from the work that has been done so far on this issue, are associations and NGOs in Arab countries today indeed able to live up to the official discourse, and can they meet the social needs of development, as well as the societal needs for "good governance" in these countries? At this point, it is possible give a general overview of associations in Arab countries, and describe their principal characteristic features.

COMMUNITY SUPPORT

NGOs can obtain community support in two ways.

Encouraging Local Initiatives

The Community Based Voluntary Organisations have the vital responsibilities to encourage local initiatives in terms of mobilisation and enviornment building. The local persons or the stockholders can bring about meaningful change. For example, in Targeted Intervention Program of National

AIDS Control programme (2007), each voluntary organisation has to mobilise local people. The experts while evaluating the programme has to ensure that he local persons, especially various stockholders, have been taken into confidence.

The involvement of local people should be ensured by obilization camps, street plays, awareness camps, sensitisation workshops, and also by involving the local people as volunteers. Voluntary organisations working in the field of Education, Health and on other social development issue have to involve local people in their programmes. Such initiatives need to be documented as success stories, constraints felt and lessons learnt. Voluntary organisations should function on the principles of 'for the people by the people and of the people'. Bhagidari Scheme of the Delhi Government in each Ministry is one of the examples of involving local people in Shrishakti Camps, Gender Resource Centre, and by encouraging Resident Welfare Associations in the local initiatives.

The importance of non-governmental organisations in micro/local level intervention can not be ignored. It is well known that Government agencies implement programmes which are planned at the macro level for the benefit of a large section of the population. The NGOs work in isolated pockets, on issues touching the people, at the grassroots.

Enlisting Community Support

As defined by Olivier de Sardan (2005), one of the axioms of community development is that knowledge and experience are vital sources of understanding defines. Chambers (1997) states that local knowledge transfers top down bureaucratic planning, and may even reverse deep rooted patterns of social power and hierarchy. Various examples of grassroots movements can be cited to illustrate their issues, strategies, and nature. The Chipko movement led by Chandi Prasad Bhat in the hills of Uttaranchal galvanised local villagers to protect the felling of trees until an acceptable solution was worked out with the government.

Nalini Nayak and Fr. Thomas Kocherry have mobilised coastal fish workers to protect their traditional rights and livelihood. In Madhya Pradesh, the Narmada Bachao Andolan led by Medha Patkar has resulted in sustained peaceful protest by tribals and peasants living in the Narmada Valley-primarily against displacement of tribal people and flooding of their land by a large dam project.

The Self-Employed Women's Association (SEWA), a union of women workers in Gujarat, responds to the specific needs of poor self-employed women by providing access to credit and so forth; unlike the other movements, it is not operating in the anti-state space and often "practices a politics of part autonomy from, part engagement with the state. Like the NGOs, these struggle-oriented grassroots movements also form networks to enhance their efficacy. The National Alliance for People's Movements was formed as an umbrella group of more than a hundred grassroots organisations to intervene in the process of economic and political decision making from the perspective of poor and ordinary people.

The National Front for Tribal Self-Rule (NFTSR) represents tribal movements and communities from across the country and successfully spearheaded the movement for extension of self-rule to tribal areas. In addition to these large alliances, activist organisations like the People's Union for Democratic Rights (PUDR) and People's Union for Civil Liberties (PUCL), mostly made up of educated urban progressives, have also played a significant role in supporting grassroots movements through media advocacy and judicial intervention.

The majority of the development literature makes a distinction between governmental and non-governmental organisations, particularly with respect to their different roles, functions and objectives.

The whole issue, which is associated with NGOs to work together with governmental and inter-governmental institutions, basically rests on their presumed capacity to reach the poor and on the qualities of innovation and flexibility as well as how they view their roles as an active and effective co-partner in articulating more responsibility for a better understanding of some of the macro-policy issues which go beyond the limited local environment in which they work. Nevertheless, *one of the basic* Organisations *for the recent focus on NGOs is that they are perceived as being able to accomplish-u part of the development process that national governments are not able or willing, to do.* Hence, it is generally recognised that NGOs can have a great potential impact on public policy by interacting with their governments. But it is also important to note that there are vast regional and international differences in relationship between NGOs and governments. For example, NGOs in India are supported and encouraged by the government and are registered with the government and work closely with it. Similarly, NGOs in Africa frequently need to work closely with their governments and try not to antagonise the authorities.

On the other extreme, most NGOs in Latin America have historically worked in opposition to the government. In recent years, there is a growing momentum of the emergence of NGOs in Nepal as a major collective actor in development activities, as a result of the changed political scene. Presently, the term has been in use rather quite flexibly to accommodate all the NGOs which would like to be designated as quasi-official in nature because of the close link and support they draw from government establishments.

Thus, the nature of the canvas of the NGOs in Nepal is increasingly being recognized as highly relevant to the problems of the rural and urban poor. However, as the vast majority of poor in Nepal are concentrated in rural areas, the NGOs have a special role to play as agents of change and catalysts of development in the villages, by complementing and supplementing the activities of the government and other developmental agencies.

The range and diversity of the growth of NGOs is immense, and the literature and the documentation of their activities are expanding geometrically. However, the evolutionary trends of institutionalized form of such organisations can be traced back to the late 19" and early 20" centuries, particularly in the Western World where the history of social organisation seems to have been largely influenced by the lassies faire movement on the basis of the promulgation of *the* theory relating to minimisation of State-intervention, on the one hand, and dissemination of the concept of 'Volunteerism' in a more planned and organised *way, on the other:*

The nineties was an interesting decade in the context of global priorities towards massive expansion of the NGOs, both in terms of the changing direction of the flow of aid funds sector-wise and country-wise. Indeed, social development is the broadest arena in both national as well as international context within which NGOs provide their contribution, which naturally addresses several strategic questions pertinent to prospects, constraints, weaknesses and strategic objectives to future NGO development.

Thus, community support in various arenas developed during 19" and 20" century. Since mid 1980s, NGOs have been the primary focus for localized civil society driven interventions in development and this has resulted in marked increase in the number of NGOs operating throughout the developing world.

Community Organisation: 'Community organisation' viewed from a humanitarian' approach to solve the problems of the community, is as old as society itself. But viewed as one of the methods of social work profession it is of very recent origin. There is much ambiguity and vagueness as to the precise meaning of the term 'Community Organisation'.

Murray G. Ross (1904) defines community organisation as a "process by which a community identifies its needs or objectives, gives priority to them, develops the confidence and will to work at them, finds resources-internal and external-to deal with them, and in doing so, extends and develops cooperative and collaborative attitudes and practices within the community".

In other words, community organisation is a process and a method of organising the community. Its broader definition can be: Community organisation is the process by which the social system of the community provides for integration and adaptation within the community.

This is a process which continues regardless of the work of the community organiser whose function is to initiate, nourish and develop this process. In participating in this process the community organiser should have regard for certain values relating to the forms of social change and the means by which they may be brought about. Community organisation for social welfare (or community welfare organisation) is the process of bringing about and maintaining adjustment between social welfare needs and social welfare resources in a geographical area or a special field of service.

PROJECTS AND INNOVATIONS

Project-formulation and new innovations are keys to the development of the non-governmental organishtion. The funding agencies at the National and International levels require systematic projects with new innovations. For developing projects new innovative systems, like the following, are developed by various funding agencies.

Expression of Interest: A funding agency, before asking for detailed projects, requires 'Expression of Interest' by the organisation. It deals with the physical, financial and professional capacities of the voluntary organisation. It helps the funding agency in short-listing the organisation.

Executive Summary: For developing innovative projects, an executive summary is desired by the funding agency. It incorporates several points which are scored by the funding agency.

Vision: It incorporates the vision and mission of the voluntary organisation.

Objectives/Outcomes : The long and short-term objectives of the organisation and also about the specific project for which the organisation has applied.

Activities (Proposed): The first and foremost task is to enumerate major and minor activities to be undertaken to achieve the objectives of the project.

Time Schedule/Plan or Time Budget: It is also desired by the funding agency. The activity plan should cover the following details:

Time Plan

Funding-The funding details of recurring and non-recurring expenditure. Funding should also specify the contribution of the organisation applying for the project.

Sustainability-How the programme will sustain itself if the funding is delinked or minimised.

Replicability-What are the issues or important lessons learnt to be replicated by the organisation in other areas or by other funding agency.

Documentation and Dissemination: Project planning should also specify how the process will be documented and how the findings will be disseminated. The funding agency may also provide time for the organisation to present the project proposal or may award the project on the basis of project proposal or may follow additional procedure.

Expert Visit: Some of the funding agencies have started visiting the organisation to understand and review the various capacities and physical infrastructure. The selection of the project is also done on the basis of the expert visit.

Infrastructure and Logistics: Tools and equipments for facilitating project work is also essential. The implementing agency should have the required infrastructural facilities and logistic support to carry out the project activities. Before initiating the implementation, it becomes necessary to review the existing infrastructural facilities and identify those needed in future. Proper planning is also needed to ensure logistic support.

Periodic Staff Meeting: Staff members and those who are the stockholders meet to review, plan and monitor the programme. Several funding agencies require weekly and monthly review meetings. Such meeting reviews the achievements and the future planning. Such meetings help the grassroots workers to be in tune with the objectives.

Participation of the Community Members: It is to be ensured that all the stockholders in the community are involved in the programme. Their participatory involvement helps in ensuring the success of the programme.

Field and Exposure Visits: Field visits in the project area and exposure visits by the project staff help in implementation and monitoring of the program.

MONITORING AND EVALUATION

Monitoring can be defined as a process of measuring, recording, collecting and analysing data on actual implementation of the-programme to identify any deviation from the planned operations. Monitoring can be both internal and external:

- The programme staff monitors the programme in the field by various means. For an effective monitoring system, a plan for the main programme needs to be prepared thoroughly.
- The plan should identify key result areas and how they will be measured. It should also identify linkages of inputs and outputs.
- The monitoring process should consist of the following:
- Detecting deviations from the plans.
- Diagnosing causes for deviations.
- Taking corrective action.
- For systematic implementation of any project, monitoring should be done systematically.

Evolving a System of Record Keeping: The first step in monitoring is evolving a system of record keeping. Targeted intervention project implemented by National AIDS Control programme has developed a list for monitoring regular records. It consists of following FACTS:

- F-Factual.
- A-Accurate.
- C-Concise.
- T-Timely.
- S-Simple.

External agencies may also be involved in monitoring. Qualitative and quantitative indicators may be developed for monitoring.

Community Participation: We should secure community participation in monitoring. The continuous feedback should come from the community.

Evaluation: Evaluation is a continuous process aimed at correcting and improving actions in order to render the activities more relevant and effective. This involves different aspects of implementation of a programme, its relevance, its formulation, its efficiency and effectiveness, its costs and acceptance by the community.

Evaluation is expected to identify problems and also possible solutions. Evaluation might be a continuous process or mid-term evaluation or final (summative) evaluation. The process of evaluation should cover the following points:

Ensuring Information Support

- Verify Relevance.
- Assess Adequacy.
- Review Progress.
- Assess Efficiency.
- Assess Effectiveness.
- Assess Impact.

Evaluation of a project may be mid-term or final evaluation. Mid-term evaluation helps, in analysing the progress of the project and the intervention required at that point. The final evaluation is carried out at the end of the project.

Methodology for Evaluation: The methodology of the evaluation of the programme depends upon the purpose of evaluation. For example, health programs of the Ministry of Health & Family Welfare, implemented through F non-governmental organisations are evaluated each year to recommend the continuation for the next year. It consists of the records evaluation, field-visits and focus group discussions with the various project staff and other community people.

The objective of the evaluation is decided on the basis of the programme, objectives and also the financial allocations. It involves success stories, case studies, sample field visits and evaluating the documents and also the capacities of the various staff in relation to their roles and responsibilities. Evaluation helps in the next programme planning, programme designing or using the same interventions in the ongoing programmes. Monitoring and evaluation are essential tools of the non-governmental organisations.

Human Relations and Employees' Welfare

In a technology-driven, fiercely competitive, dynamic and globalised business environment of the 21st century, providing, managing and retaining a quality work force to a corporate organization is a formidably multifaceted task that an HR professional accomplishes. Moreover, with the businesses growing by gallops across the globe and demand for seasoned HR professionals soaring high, this career has become lucrative and rewarding as handsome monetary returns are commensurate with the stimulating challenges.

Human Resource Management or Personnel Management implies the management of human resource or labour, an important input or factor of any organization or industry, apart from land and capital. The role of an HR professional involves optimally harnessing and utilizing the full potential and productivity of the manpower to the best advantage of the industry.

Human Resource Management has eventful history of change in nomenclature and nature of functions. It was known as Labour Welfare or Employee Welfare during pre-independence and immediate post independence era. In the wake of subsequent industrialization, the field grew with the influx of new inputs and technology and came to be renamed as Industrial Relations/ IR in our socialism-oriental mixed economy, run by Five-Year Plans. With the liberalization of Indian economy after 1991 and its entry in integrated world order of competitive economics under the aegis of globalization, private sector expanded at an exponential pace. Business from foreign shores infiltrated through our porous economic frontiers, new industries cropped up and older ones caught up with the pace of development. Commensurately, infused with greater knowledge and newer skills, HR was recast in the mould of a more reactive and proactive management from the former purely administrative one and acquired its current name.

HR manager's multifarious functions broadly include recruiting the right personnel, training them, providing them adequate remuneration. As the pivot of the recruitment process, he/she puts advertisements for job opportunities, screens resumes for short listing potentially right candidates, conducts interviews for selecting those with qualifications suiting the work profile and prepares offer letters specifying the terms and conditions of employment. An HR manager has to be conversant with preparing training programmes in consonance with the specific needs of the company and the job up to the six Sigma Level, currently followed by most companies. More importantly, he/she has to undertake the mammoth task of managing employees with diverse backgrounds, skill-sets and personalities by understanding their psyche, temper and professional conduct.

He/she has to devise strategies for realizing the full potential of manpower, like providing them with offers, compensation packages like esops, promotions, job change, rewards, incentives etc. Such efforts are also meant to retain employees, promote their talents, further their motivation and ensure their satisfaction. An HR manager has to be an excellent communicator to be understood well by the employees and to understand and empathise with their grievances, opinions and needs. Further, he/she has to effectively redress their grievances, and complaints and negotiate with the management and employees for an acceptable solution, in accordance with the labour laws and stipulations of agreements between company and employees. Besides, they are engaged with sundry administrative jobs like maintaining employees' records, payroll processing, calculating bonus, leave, etc.

Corporate world, though ruthlessly competitive, has to be socially responsible by helping in the socioeconomic progress of underprivileged or underdeveloped sections and promoting the general well-being. Here comes the concept of Corporate Socio-responsibility which HR manager shoulders. Besides maintaining cordial relations between employees and management, she/he has to society, by preparing and implementing programmes of social welfare like providing education, healthcare and civic amenities to a village.

This implies undertaking the construction of schools for children, or imparting professional training to the rural unemployed youth, opening charitable dispensaries for the treatment and medication of the diseased, laying roads, or arranging for sewage system, etc. The HR division thus plays active role in this area. In such a multi-faceted professional capacity, an HR manager thus acts as a strategic partner and a vital asset to the industry he is associate with. He/she has to be abreast of the developments in the organizations in particular and the business environment in general.

He/she also acts as the agent of change, staying alert to the changes in the organisation or the business environment and assiduously responding to them by making suitable customisations in the recruitment process and acclimatizing the employees to these changes. Finally, he/she acts as an advocate of employees by effectively addressing their grievances, needs and concerns.

Of late, IT (Information Technology) has been instrumental in facilitating and qualitatively improving the efficiency of the functions of HR. It has fully computerized the entire gamut of HR functions. HR info-system software packages have ensured the proper storage of the vast database of an organisation's manpower in a computer system, which can be instantly accessed with the click of a mouse.

This has rendered the extraction of data of employees easy and effortless, so that the information can aid the HR manager to assess the relative work efficiency of employees and the need for training an employee to improve certain skills. Automation of routine functions like payroll processing has spared the HR professional from the drudgery of repetitive administration jobs like payroll, gratuity, leave, etc. Therefore, given the sea change brought about in the HR functions by the rapid strides in IT, being computer savvy is the key to successful multi-tasking in HR.

Welfare includes anything that is done for the comfort and improvement of employees and is provided over and above the wages. Welfare helps in keeping the morale and motivation of the employees high so as to retain the employees for longer duration. The welfare measures need not be in monetary terms only but in any kind/forms. Employee welfare includes monitoring of working conditions, creation of industrial harmony through infrastructure for health, industrial relations and insurance against disease, accident and unemployment for the workers and their families.

Labour welfare entails all those activities of employer which are directed towards providing the employees with certain facilities and services in addition to wages or salaries.

Labour welfare has the following objectives:

1. To provide better life and health to the workers.
2. To make the workers happy and satisfied.
3. To relieve workers from industrial fatigue and to improve intellectual, cultural and material conditions of living of the workers.

The basic features of labour welfare measures are as follows:

1. Labour welfare includes various facilities, services and amenities provided to workers for improving their health, efficiency, economic betterment and social status.
2. Welfare measures are in addition to regular wages and other economic benefits available to workers due to legal provisions and collective bargaining.
3. Labour welfare schemes are flexible and ever-changing. New welfare measures are added to the existing ones from time to time.
4. Welfare measures may be introduced by the employers, government, employees or by any social or charitable agency.
5. The purpose of labour welfare is to bring about the development of the whole personality of the workers to make a better work force.

The very logic behind providing welfare schemes is to create efficient, healthy, loyal and satisfied labour force for the organization. The purpose of providing such facilities is to make their work life better and also to raise their standard of living. The important benefits of welfare measures can be summarized as follows:

- They provide better physical and mental health to workers and thus promote a healthy work environment
- Facilities like housing schemes, medical benefits, and education and recreation facilities for workers' families help in raising their standards of living. This makes workers to pay more attention towards work and thus increases their productivity.
- Employers get stable labour force by providing welfare facilities. Workers take active interest in their jobs and work with a feeling of involvement and participation.

- Employee welfare measures increase the productivity of organization and promote healthy industrial relations thereby maintaining industrial peace.
- The social evils prevalent among the labours such as substance abuse, etc. are reduced to a greater extent by the welfare policies.

Leadership and Group Dynamics

Managers and supervisors frequently face such a dilemma-standards that should be met but aren't for what seems like no apparent reason. What Jeff Lane and other managers/supervisors sometimes fail to realize is that within every organization there are often informal group pressures that influence and regulate individual behaviour.

Informal groups formulate an implicit code of ethics or an unspoken set of standards establishing acceptable behaviour In Jeff's department, the informal group may have established a norm below that set by the organization, subtly exercising control over its members regarding the amount of output.

DYNAMICS OF INFORMAL GROUPS

Often, these groups serve a counter organizational function, attempting to counteract the coercive tendencies in an organization. If management prescribes production norms that the group considers unfair, for instance, the group's recourse is to adopt less demanding norms and to use its ingenuity to discover ways in which it can sabotage management's imposed standards. Informal groups have a powerful influence on the effectiveness of an organization, and can even subvert its formal goals. But the informal group's role is not limited to resistance. The impact of the informal group upon the larger formal group depends on the norms that the informal group sets. So the informal group can make the formal organization more effective, too.

A norm is an implied agreement among the group's membership regarding how members in the group should behave. From the perspective of the formal group, norms generally fall into three categories-positive, negative, and neutral. In other words, norms either support, obstruct, or have no effect on the aims of the larger organization.

For example, it the informal group in Jeff's shop set a norm supporting high output, that norm would have been more potent than any attempt by Jeff to coerce compliance with the standard. The reason is simple, yet profound. The norm is of the group members own making, and is not one imposed upon them. There is a big motivational difference between being told what to do and being anxious to do it. If Jeff had been aware of group dynamics, he might have realized that informal groups can be either his best friend or his worst enemy. He should have been sensitive to the informal groups within his area and he should have cultivated their goodwill and cooperation and made use of the informal group leadership.

That is, he should have wooed the leadership of the informal group and enlisted the support of its membership to achieve the formal organization's aims. The final effect of his actions might have been positive or negative, depending upon the agreement or lack of it between the informal group and himself. Harnessing the power of informal groups is no easy task. The requirements include: an understanding of group dynamics and, an ability to bring about changes in informal group norms that positively reinforce the formal organization's goals. As a starting point, managers and supervisors should at least be aware of the reasons behind informal group formation and the properties and characteristics of these groups.

Formation of Informal Work Groups

Individuals are employed by an organization to perform specific functions. Although the whole person joins an organization, attention is usually focused on the partial person, the part of the individual doing the job. Because people have needs that extend beyond the work itself, informal groups develop to fill certain emotional, social, and psychological needs.

The degree to which a group satisfies its members needs determines the limits within which individual members of the group will allow their behaviour to be controlled by the group.

Sense of Belonging

Several major functions are served by informal groups. For example, the group serves as a means of satisfying the affiliation needs of its members for friendship and support. People need to belong, to be liked, to feel a part of something. Because the informal group can withhold this attractive reward, it has a tool of its own to coerce compliance with its norms.

Identity and Self Esteem

Groups also provide a means of developing, enhancing, and confirming a person's sense of identity and self-esteem. Although many organizations attempt to recognize these higher needs, the nature of some jobs-their technology and environment-precludes this from happening. The long assembly line or endless rows of desks reinforce a feeling of depersonalization.

Stress Reduction

Another function of groups is to serve as an agent for establishing and testing social reality. For instance, several individuals may share the feeling that their supervisor is a slave driver or that their working conditions are inadequate. By developing a consensus about these feelings, group members are able to reduce the anxiety associated with their jobs.

All for One, One for All

Finally, the informal group serves as a defence mechanism against forces that group members could not resist on their own. Joining forces in a small group makes the members feel stronger, less anxious, and less insecure in the face of a perceived threat. As long as needs exist that are not served by the formal organization, informal groups will form to fill the gap. Since the group fills many important needs for its members, it influences member behaviour.

Leadership of Informal Work Groups

Informal groups possess certain characteristics that, if understood, can be used to advantage. While many of these characteristics are similar to those of formal organizations, others are unique. One attribute of informal groups is rotational leadership. The informal leader emerges as the individual possessing qualities that the other members perceive as critical to the satisfaction of their specific needs at the moment; as the needs change so does the leader. Only rarely does a single individual possess all of the leadership characteristics needed to fill the various needs of the group.

Unlike the formally appointed leader who has a defined position from which to influence others, the informal leader does not possess formal power. If the informal leader fails to meet the group's expectations, he or she is deposed and replaced by another. The informal group's judgment of its leaders tends to be quicker and more cold-blooded than that of most formal groups.

Supervisory Strategies

The supervisor can use several strategies to affect the leadership and harness the power of informal groups. One quick and sure method of changing a group is to cause the leader to change one or more of his or her characteristics. Another is to replace the leader with another person.

One common ploy is to systematically rotate out of the group its leaders and its key members. Considering the rotational nature of leadership, a leader may emerge who has aims similar to the formal goals of the organization.

There are problems with this approach, however. Besides the practical difficulties of this, this strategy is blunted by the fact that group norms often persist long after the leader has left the group.

A less Machiavellian approach is for the supervisor to be alert to leaders sympathetic to the supervisor's objectives and to use them toward the betterment of the formal group's effectiveness. Still another method is to attempt to 'co-opt' informal leaders by absorbing them into the leadership or the decision-making structure of the formal group. Co-opting the informal leader often serves as a means of averting threats to the stability of the formal organization.

Remember, though, a leader may lose favour with the group because of this association with management, and group members will most likely select another leader.

INFORMAL WORK GROUP COMMUNICATION (THE GRAPEVINE)

Another characteristic of the informal group is its communications network. The informal group has communications processes that are smoother and less cumbersome than those of the formal organization. Thus its procedures are easily changed to meet the communication needs of the group.

In the informal group, a person who possesses information vital to the group's functioning or well-being is frequently afforded leadership status by its members. Also, the centrally located person in the group is in the best position to facilitate the smooth flow of information among group members.

Knowing about informal group communication the supervisor can provide a strategically placed individual with information needed by the group. This not only enhances the stature of this individual perhaps elevating him or her to a leadership position but also provides an efficient means of distributing information.

Providing relevant information to the group will also help foster harmony between the supervisor and the informal group. By winning the cooperation of informal group leaders the supervisor will most likely experience fewer grievances and better relationships.

Informal Group Cohesiveness

A third characteristic of informal groups is group cohesiveness-the force that holds a group together. Group cohesiveness varies widely based on numerous factors-including the size of the group dependence of members upon the group achievement of goals status of the group and management demands and pressures.

For example group cohesiveness increases strongly whenever the membership perceives a threat from the outside. This threat produces the high anxiety that strong group cohesiveness can help reduce.

If the supervisor presses the group to conform to a new organizational norm that Is viewed as a threat to the security needs of group members The group will become more unified in order to withstand the perceived threat. Thus management can limit its own effectiveness by helping to increase the group's cohesiveness. With the passing of the threat the group tends to lose its cohesiveness. Perhaps paradoxically the most dangerous time for group cohesion is when things are going well. Supervisors can use the factors that affect group cohesiveness to increase their own effectiveness.

Decision Making Process Involvement

For instance a supervisor can involve the informal group members in the decision-making process. Input from group members will not only reduce their feeling of alienation but also improve communication between the supervisor and subordinates thereby reducing potential conflict. Where group participation in decision making is not practical the supervisor should carefully explain the reasons to play down what might be seen as a threat to the group. In some cases the supervisor may want to increase the groups cohesiveness deliberately devising situations that put one group into competition with another. If this gambit is carefully controlled the solidarity that results may bring a higher level of performance.

The danger of this strategy is that the supervisor may be unable to control the reaction of the group. The ploy could backfire bringing competition and dissension within the group.

Informal Group Norms or Values (Unspoken Rules)

The final characteristic of informal groups is the establishment of the groups norms (values). As we discussed earlier, norms keep a group functioning as a system instead of a collection of individuals. Norms are of great importance to the informal group in controlling behaviour and measuring the performance of members. Because norm (values) violations threaten a group's existence, departures from the norm usually carry severe sanctions. The members must either conform or sever their group affiliation. The latter action is unlikely, especially if the individual values group membership to satisfy certain needs.

Two Points are Important to Note About the Norms of Informal Groups

First, where both formal and informal norms exist, the informal norms transcend the formal. At moments when norms conflict with organizational objectives, organizational effectiveness suffers.

Second, members of an informal group may be unaware that the norms of the group influence their behaviour. Norms are particularly potent because without knowing it members would not even think of acting otherwise-norms are that ingrained into their behaviour pattern.

2

Disaster Management

Recently, expert bodies have dwelt on the role of the Planning Commission and the use of plan funds in the context of disaster management. Suggestions have been made in this regard by the Eleventh Finance Commission, and also the High Powered Committee on Disaster Management.

An approach on planning for safe development needs to be set out in the light of these suggestions. This chapter reflects the considerations outlined above.

It briefly outlines the global context and the Indian experience of disasters, sets out the institutional and financial arrangements for disaster management and the response towards these in the country, looks at directions for improvement, and concludes with a strategy to facilitate planning for safe national development in the Tenth Plan period.

WHAT IS DISASTER?

Disaster is a sudden, calamitous event bringing great damage, loss, destruction and devastation to life and property. The damage caused by disasters is immeasurable and varies with the geographical location, climate and the type of the earth surface/degree of vulnerability. This influences the mental, socio-economic, political and cultural state of the affected area. Generally, disaster has the following effects in the concerned areas:

1. It completely disrupts the normal day to day life.
2. It negatively influences the emergency systems.
3. Normal needs and processes like food, shelter, health, etc. are affected and deteriorate depending on the intensity and severity of the disaster.

It may also be termed as "a serious disruption of the functioning of society, causing widespread human, material or environmental losses which exceed the ability of the affected society to cope using its own resources." Thus, a disaster may have the following main features:-

- Unpredictability
- Unfamiliarity
- Speed
- Urgency
- Uncertainty
- Threat

Thus, in simple terms we can define disaster as a hazard causing heavy loss to life, property and livelihood. *E.g.* a cyclone killing 10,000 lives and a crop loss of one crore can be termed as disaster.

TYPES OF DISASTER

Generally, disasters are of two types—Natural and Man-made. Based on the devastation, these are further classified into major/minor natural disaster and major/minor man-made disasters. Some of the disasters are listed below:

Major Natural Disasters

- Flood
- Cyclone
- Drought
- Earthquake

Minor Natural Disasters

- Cold wave
- Thunderstorms
- Heat waves
- Mud slides
- Storm

Major Man-made Disasters

- Setting of fires
- Epidemic
- Deforestation
- Pollution due to prawn cultivation
- Chemical pollution
- Wars

Minor Man-made Disasters

- Road/ train accidents, riots
- Food poisoning
- Industrial disaster/ crisis
- Environmental pollution

Risk

Risk is a measure of the expected losses due to a hazardous event of a particular magnitude occurring in a given area over a specific time period. Risk is a function of the probability of particular occurrences and the losses each would cause. The level of risk depends on:

- Nature of the Hazard
- Vulnerability of the elements which are affected
- Economic value of those elements

Vulnerability

It is defined as "the extent to which a community, structure, service, and/ or geographic area is likely to be damaged or disrupted by the impact of particular hazard, on account of their nature, construction and proximity to hazardous terrain or a disaster prone area".

Hazards

Hazards are defined as "Phenomena that pose a threat to people, structures, or economic assets and which may cause a disaster. They could be either man-made or naturally occurring in our environment." The extent of damage in a disaster depends on:

1. The impact, intensity and characteristics of the phenomenon and
2. How people, environment and infrastructures are affected by that phenomenon

Man-made Hazards

Disasters having an element of human intent, negligence, error or the ones involving the failure of a system are called man-made disasters. Man-made hazards are in turn categorised as technological or sociological. Technological hazards are results of failure of technology, such as engineering failures, transport accidents or environmental disasters. Sociological hazards have a strong human motive, such as crime, stampedes, riots and war.

With the tropical climate and unstable landforms, coupled with high population density, poverty, illiteracy and lack of adequate infrastructure, India is one of the most vulnerable developing countries to suffer very often from various natural disasters, namely drought, flood, cyclone, earthquake, landslide, forest fire, hail storm, locust, volcanic eruption, etc. Which strike causing a devastating impact on human life, economy and environment.

Though it is almost impossible to fully recoup the damage caused by the disasters, it is possible to:

(i) minimize the potential risks by developing early warning strategies

(ii) prepare and implement developmental plans to provide resilience to such disasters

(iii) mobilize resources including communication and telemedicinal services, and

(iv) to help in rehabilitation and post-disaster reconstruction.

Space technology plays a crucial role in efficient mitigation of disasters. While communication satellites help in disaster warning, relief mobilization and telemedicinal support, earth observation satellites provide required database for pre-disaster preparedness programmes, disaster response, monitoring activities and post-disaster damage assessment, and reconstruction, and rehabilitation.

The chapter describes the role of space technology in evolving a suitable strategy for disaster preparedness and operational framework for their monitoring, assessment and mitigation, identifies gap areas and recommends appropriate strategies for disaster mitigation *vis-a-vis* likely developments in space and ground segments.

THE IMPORTANCE OF DISASTER PLANS

After several close calls with hurricanes, executives at Florida Hospital in Orlando decided to rethink their disaster plans. A direct hit by a storm could, of course, endanger patients. But it could also destroy the technology that the facility depends on for medical records, clinical test results, and accounting. With strict regulations about hospital safety and the critical nature of the facility's services, nothing could be left to chance. The hospital came up with a comprehensive strategy to prepare for future disasters, reengineering how it safeguarded its digital records and reserving backup offices. "In 2004 we had what we called the hurricane trifecta—Charlie, Francis, and Jeanne," says Robert Goodman, disaster recovery coordinator for Florida Hospital. "The hurricanes got our management's attention."

Disaster planning plays an important role for businesses in ensuring they can still operate after an earthquake, a blackout, or other serious disruption. Failing to prepare can mean millions of dollars in losses and major headaches while trying to recover. As a precaution, many companies draw up what are known as business continuity plans, which provide a road map for responding to a variety of problems. The first step is invariably to identify critical assets such as manufacturing facilities, technology infrastructure, and corporate data. The next step is to figure out how to protect them—or at least minimize downtime—amid bad weather, labour strikes, or cyber-attacks. Planning should not be limited just to a company's own operations. Key partners and suppliers could also run into trouble. For example, companies are increasingly using software in the cloud—services provided by third parties from remote data centres. What if such a vendor went offline? Nearly three-quarters of all companies have a business continuity plan, according to a survey of 300 executives conducted last year by Disaster Recovery Journal, an industry publication, and consulting firm Forrester Research (FORR). Government regulations all but require such plans in critical industries like health care, energy, and finance. Technology almost always plays a prominent role. Ensuring that key computer systems operate during and after disasters has evolved into a mini-industry with armies of consultants and vendors. Shoring up technology against disruptions can be costly. Companies will spend an average 7 percent of their IT budgets on business continuity and disaster recovery this year, according to Forrester.

Al Berman, president of DRI International, a non-profit certification organization for the disaster recovery industry, says that in light of the cost, companies must set priorities. They may be able to live without access to certain software for a few days, for instance, or entire lines of business.

"Some companies say, 'We want to service our five biggest customers—and let the others go,'" Berman says. "Or they want to preserve their highest-margin business and let the other ones go." Florida Hospital, which has more than 20 facilities across central Florida, has prepared for disaster by backing up its critical records at a data centre 1,000 miles away in the Northeast. (The hospital declined to name the location for security reasons.) If its primary data centre in Orlando is taken down by a hurricane, employees will still be able to access information via the secondary facility.

SunGard, a company that specializes in disaster recovery services, operates the backup facility. In addition to storing the hospital's data, SunGard technical staff will help get the hospital's records back online if a disaster strikes. The job of restoring the data should take around four to six hours, Florida Hospital's

Goodman says. At worst, a few minutes' worth of new data may be lost after the primary servers go down, he explains. Previously the hospital relied on an unwieldy system in which it saved data to tapes and delivered them by truck to another backup facility in the Northeast. When a hurricane approached, the hospital staff would have to scramble to get 2,000 tapes ready and then wait a couple of days for them to arrive at their destination. By the time the data could be restored, it would be several days old. "You would run into a situation where you would go look up a lab order and couldn't even see that the patient was ever admitted," Goodman says.

DISASTER PLANNING SYSTEM

A disaster is an unplanned event in which the needs of the affected community outweigh the available resources. A disaster occurs somewhere in the world almost daily, but these events vary considerably in scope, size, and context. Large-scale disasters with numerous casualties are relatively unusual events. Certain widely publicized disasters, including events such as the terrorist attacks on September 11, 2001, Hurricanes Katrina and Sandy, and the Boston Marathon bombing, have focused people's attention on disaster planning and preparedness. Disasters are becoming more frequent, and the number of persons affected is also increasing. This greater morbidity is attributable not only to the greater number of events, but also to population dynamics, location, and susceptibilities. While these incidents have lead to an increase in general disaster awareness, the relative infrequency of major catastrophes affecting defined populations leads to a certain degree of complacency and underestimation of the impact of such an event. In the wake of a large-scale event, public attention focuses on disaster planning and preparedness and the resources dedicated to improving response and resiliency surge. This phenomenon has been described as "issue salience" and has then been noted to decline over time as communities return to their quotidian lives. The result of complacency is relative reluctance to devote the necessary resources for adequate disaster preparedness. Understanding the effects of a serious event on the community may indicate that the best time to propose major changes for disaster preparedness, including funding, is immediately following a widely publicized disaster, even if the event has occurred in a remote location. In the United States, large, multiple-casualty events have been rare. Only 10 disasters in US history have resulted in more than 1,000 casualties. The vast majority of events have resulted in fewer than 40 fatalities. According to data from the US Centers for Disease Control and Prevention (CDC), the September 11 attacks caused 2,819 deaths. This number is a fraction of the 44,065 deaths from motor vehicle accidents in the United States in 2002. The dramatic nature of disasters, however, with a relatively high death toll and psychological impact for a short period, can overwhelm an unprepared health and emergency response system and create chaos in the affected community and surrounding regions.

*Table : US Disasters With Greater Than 1,000 Casualties**

Year	Event	Deaths
1865	Steamship explosion	1,547
1875	Forest fire, Wisconsin	1,182
1889	Flood, Pennsylvania	>2,000
1900	Hurricane, Texas	8,000
1904	Steamship fire	1,021
1906	San Francisco earthquake	>3,000
1928	Hurricane, Florida	2,000
1941	Pearl Harbor Attack	2,403
2001	September 11 Attack	2,819
2005	Hurricane Katrina	>1,300**

*Exact death tolls can be difficult to calculate, and some of these numbers are estimates.

**Even in modern times, death tolls can be difficult to establish. Debate still exists about the actual number of people who died during Hurricane Katrina and its aftermath. An article by Brunkard et al published in*Disaster Medicine and Public Health Preparedness* in August 2008, puts the Louisiana death toll at 971 plus another 15 deaths among evacuees. An Associated Press article from 2006 claims the total number of bodies recovered from Louisiana and Mississippi was more than 1300. There is also ongoing investigation into the possibility that the storm caused deaths during subsequent months and years due to myriad causes (eg, inadequate medical care, relocation stresses).

When a disaster strikes, the general population expects public service agencies, emergency response agencies, and other branches of the local, state, or federal government to rapidly mobilize to help the injured and the broader community in general. Preservation of life and health are of paramount importance to those individuals injured in disasters. For this, among other reasons, medical professionals must be included in all phases of disaster planning as well as immediate response to these events. Medical professionals have a unique expertise and knowledge of local and regional healthcare systems, which can assist in disaster mitigation and planning. Persons affected by a disaster also rely on their skills and treatment in the immediate response to an event. Adequate preparation and planning, as well as provider and agency education and training, have become more relevant following the visibly problematic responses to many events, including the response to Hurricane Katrina.

External and Internal Planning

External planning

To the extent possible, disaster planning should incorporate formal disaster research findings. Disaster plans sometimes rely on faulty assumptions that do not prove true in actual disasters. For example, planners may logically assume that the sickest patients are transported first during a disaster, when in reality, this may not happen in many instances. Other realities that have been noted in prior events are that the initial search and rescue begins with victims and bystanders and not trained rescue teams, the majority of patients arrive to hospitals without use of the EMS system and have not been triaged or decontaminated, and there is often lack of communication between healthcare facilities and the scene. These characteristics are likely to occur in future disasters and should be incorporated into realistic disaster plans.

A disaster plan encompassing both local and regional areas must focus on the following 3 possible scenarios:

- The disaster occurs within the region and is confined and controlled with area resources.
- The disaster occurs in a neighboring region and regional assets are requested through mutual aid agreements.
- The disaster area is the region and requires state or federal assistance for an effective response.

In developing a disaster plan, leaders should remember that it is impossible to plan for all contingencies; therefore, plans must be relatively general and expandable. Most disasters that can be contained using local or regional resources have fewer than 100 fatalities and fewer than 500 casualties. Plans developed for larger-scale disasters should focus on the first 48 hours of the disaster until state and federal assistance teams can arrive and the need to address high initial fatality rates during the first 24 hours. Mutual aid agreements or contracts with other existing area resources also are important to establish before an actual incident, as well as planning for funding and reimbursement.

Incident Command System

After a series of forest fires in California in the 1970s, the Fire Fighting Resources of Southern California Organized for Potential Emergencies

(FIRESCOPE) developed the ICS concept to organize an effective response to major emergencies. Despite adequate resources, loss of life and property due to the fires was substantial. This fact was attributable to poor overall management of the incidents.

Some of the myriad flaws included multiple organizations working together at incidents who had not previously trained together, disparate organizational structures that made effective leadership challenging, an unwieldy span of control, poor coordination and resource allocation, and breakdown of intra-agency communication. ICS was designed to minimize these issues and has gained widespread use in the emergency management community.

The National Incident Management System (NIMS), which is a national guideline for managing emergency incidents, includes ICS as a critical component. The ICS structure includes 5 functional units: command, operations, logistics, planning, and finance. Most emergency operations plans include similar organizational structures that are often modified depending on normal operations. Some of the attributes of ICS are its modular structure, scalability, use of common terminology, clear chain of command, and manageable span of control.

Rehearsal

Patients and hospitals require personnel, supplies, facilities, and an incident management structure. Hospital emergency planners must take into account the scenarios previously described, including the possibility that the disaster may involve the hospital. For such rare events, aspects of hospital involvement such as mass decontamination, multiple triage and staging areas within the confines of the hospital, recall of critical personnel, and provisioning of adequate supplies and resupply must be anticipated. The ability for a healthcare facility to quickly expand its ability to treat a large influx of patients is referred to as surge capacity. In order to accommodate a surge in patients, hospitals require personnel, supplies, facilities, and an incident management structure. A goal capacity that has been advocated is to expand hospital by 20-25% within the first 24 hours.

The Joint Commission (formerly Joint Commission on Accreditation of Hospitals [JCAHO]) requires hospitals to exercise emergency operations plans periodically and to form emergency management committees. These committees should comprise key departments within the hospital, including administration, nursing, security, communications, laboratory, physician services (including but not limited to emergency medicine, general surgery, and radiology), medical records, maintenance, and engineering. Hospital emergency planners should plan using the Hospital Incident Command System (HICS), which is a modified version of the ICS and maintains many of its attributes.

The hospital emergency operations plan should include protocols and policies that meet the following needs:

- Recognition and notification
- Assessment of hospital capabilities
- Personnel recall and emergency credentialing
- Establishment of a facility control center
- Maintenance of accurate records
- Public relations
- Equipment resupply.

New, more stringent requirements for health are organizations by the Joint Commission include the requirements to integrate hospital disaster planning into community plans, to ensure that disaster programs address all phases of the disaster cycle, and to have the capability to evacuate the entire hospital staff and patients and relocate and operate from an independent facility. Evacuations of hospitals after the Northridge, California earthquake in 1994 demonstrated that large numbers of patients could be evacuated without the use of specialized equipment and in an efficient and safe manner.

Requirements concerning decontamination, policies, and training in response to terrorist activities involving chemical, biological, radiological, nuclear, and explosive agents may be strengthened in the future in response to concerns over these potential threats.

THE GLOBAL CONTEXT

There has been an increase in the number of natural disasters over the past years, and with it, increasing losses on account of urbanisation and population growth, as a result of which the impact of natural disasters is now felt to a larger extent. According to the United Nations, in 2001 alone, natural disasters of medium to high range caused at least 25,000 deaths around the world, more than double the previous year, and economic losses of around US $ 36 billion. These figures would be much higher, if the consequences of the many smaller and unrecorded disasters that cause significant losses at the local community level were to be taken into account. Devastations in the aftermath of powerful earthquakes that struck Gujarat, El Salvador and Peru;

floods that ravaged many countries in Africa, Asia and elsewhere; droughts that plagued Central Asia including Afghanistan, Africa and Central America; the cyclone in Madagascar and Orissa; and floods in Bolivia are global events in recent memory. However, what is disturbing is the knowledge that these trends of destruction and devastation are on the rise instead of being kept in check.

Natural disasters are not bound by political boundaries and have no social or economic considerations. They are borderless as they affect both developing and developed countries. They are also merciless, and as such the vulnerable tend to suffer more at the impact of natural disasters. For example, the developing countries are much more seriously affected in terms of the loss of lives, hardship borne by population and the percentage of their GNP lost. Since 1991, two-third of the victims of natural disasters were from developing countries, while just 2 per cent were from highly developed nations. Those living in developing countries and especially those with limited resources tend to be more adversely affected. With the alarming rise in the natural disasters and vulnerability per se, the world community is strengthening its efforts to cope with it. As a number of the most vulnerable regions are in India, natural disaster management has emerged as a high priority for the country. Going beyond the historical focus on relief and rehabilitation after the event, we now have to look ahead and plan for disaster preparedness and mitigation, in order that the periodic shocks to our development efforts are minimized.

THE INDIAN EXPERIENCE

Regional Vulnerabilities

Physical vulnerability relates to the physical location of people, their proximity to the hazard zone and standards of safety maintained to counter the effects. For instance, some people are vulnerable to flood only because they live in a flood prone area. Physical vulnerability also relates to the technical capacity of buildings and structures to resist the forces acting upon them during a hazard event.

The extent to which a population is affected by a calamity does not purely lie in the physical components of vulnerability, but is contextual also to the prevailing social and economic conditions and its consequential effect on human activities within a given society. Research in areas affected by earthquakes indicates that single parent families, women, handicapped people, children and the aged are particularly vulnerable social groups. The geophysical setting with unplanned and inadequate developmental activity is a cause for increased losses during disasters. In the case of India, the contribution of over-population to high population density, which in turn results in escalating losses, deserves to be noted. This factor sometimes tends to be as important as physical vulnerability attributed to geography and infrastructure alone.

The continent of Asia is particularly vulnerable to disaster strikes. Between the years 1991 to 2000 Asia has accounted for 83 per cent of the population affected by disasters globally. While the number of people affected in the rest of the world were 1,11,159, in Asia the number was 5,54,439.Within Asia, 24 per cent of deaths due to disasters occur in India, on account of its size, population and vulnerability. Floods and high winds account for 60 per cent of all disasters in India. While substantial progress has been made in other sectors of human development, there is need to do more towards mitigating the effect of disasters.

Many parts of the Indian sub-continent are susceptible to different types of disasters owing to the unique topographic and climatic characteristics. About 54 per cent of the sub-continent's landmass is vulnerable to earthquakes while about 4 crore hectares is vulnerable to periodic floods. The decade 1990-2000, has been one of very high disaster losses within the country, losses in the Orissa Cyclone in 1999, and later, the Gujarat Earthquake in 2001 alone amount to several thousand crore of Rupees, while the total expenditure on relief and reconstruction in Gujarat alone has been to the tune of Rs 11,500 crore.

Similarly, the country has suffered four major earthquakes in the span of last fifty years along with a series of moderate intensity earthquakes that have occurred at regular intervals. Since 1988, six earthquakes have struck different parts of the country. These caused considerable human and property losses. Disasters lead to enormous economic losses that are both immediate as well as long term in nature and demand additional revenues. Also, as an immediate fall-out, disasters reduce revenues from the affected region due to lower levels of economic activity leading to loss of direct and indirect taxes. In addition, unplanned budgetary allocation to disaster recovery can hamper development interventions and lead to unmet developmental targets.

Disasters may also reduce availability of new investment, further constricting the growth of the region. Besides, additional pressures may be imposed on finances of the government through investments in relief and rehabilitation work.

In the recent earthquake in Gujarat, more than 14,000 lives were lost, ten lakh houses were damaged and the asset loss has been indicated to be worth

15,000 crore. The dimensions of the damage, as evident in the tables and the diagram 7.1 emphasise the point that natural disasters cause major setbacks to development and it is the poorest and the weakest that are the most vulnerable to disasters. Given the high frequency with which one or the other part of the country suffers due to disasters, mitigating the impact of disasters must be an integral component of our development planning and be part of our poverty reduction strategy.

INSTITUTIONAL ARRANGEMENTS

The country with its federal system of Government has specific roles for the Central and State Governments. However, the subject of disaster management does not specifically find mention in any of the three lists in the 7th Schedule of the Indian Constitution, where subjects under the Central and State Governments as also subjects that come under both are specified. On the legal front, there is no enactment either of the Central or of any State Government to deal with the management of disasters of various types in a comprehensive manner.

The country has an integrated administrative machinery for management of disasters at the National, State, District and Sub-District levels. The basic responsibility of undertaking rescue, relief and rehabilitation measures in the event of natural disasters, as at present, is that of the State Governments concerned. The Central Government supplements the efforts of the States by providing financial and logistic support.

Central Level

The dimensions of response at the level of the Central Government are determined in accordance with the existing policy of financing relief expenditure and keeping in view the factors like:

(i) the gravity of a natural disaster;

(ii) the scale of the relief operation necessary; and

(iii) the requirements of Central assistance for augmenting financial resources and logistic support at the disposal of the State Government.

The Contingency Action Plan (CAP) identifies initiatives required to be taken by various Central Ministries and Public Departments in the wake of natural calamities. It sets down the procedures and determines the focal points in the administrative machinery to facilitate launching of relief and rescue operations without delay.

The Ministry of Home Affairs is the nodal Ministry for coordination of relief and response and overall natural disaster management, and the

Department of Agriculture & Cooperation is the nodal Ministry for drought management. Other Ministries are assigned the responsibility of providing emergency support in case of disasters that fall in their purview as indicated in Table 7.6. The following decision-making and standing bodies are responsible for disaster management at the Central level:

- Union Cabinet, headed by the Prime Minister.
- Empowered Group of Ministers, headed by the Deputy Prime Minister
- National Crisis Management Committee (NCMC), under the chairmanship of the Cabinet Secretary.
- Crisis Management Group (CMG): under the chairmanship of the Central Relief Commissioner comprising senior officers from the various Ministries and other concerned Departments which reviews contingency plans, measures required for dealing with a natural disaster, and co-ordinates the activities of the Central Ministries and the State Governments in relation to disaster preparedness response and relief.
- Technical Organizations, such as the Indian Meteorological Department (cyclone/earthquake), Central Water Commission (floods), Building Material and Technology Promotion Council (construction laws), Bureau of Indian Standards (norms), Defence Research & Development Organization (nuclear/biological), Directorate General Civil Defence provide specific technical support to coordination of disaster response and management functions.
- The setting up of a National Disaster Management Authority (NDMA) is being contemplated by the Ministry of Home Affairs as the proposed apex structure within the government for the purpose. Amongst other major organizational initiatives, it is proposed to:
  (a) establish a specialised and earmarked response team for dealing with nuclear/biological/chemical disasters;
  (b) establish search and rescue teams in each State;
  (c) strengthen communication systems in the North Eastern Region.

State Government

The responsibility to cope with natural disasters is essentially that of the State Government. The role of the Central Government is supportive in terms of supplementation of physical and financial resources. The Chief Secretary of the State heads a state level committee which is in overall charge of the relief operations in the State and the Relief Commissioners who are in charge of the relief and rehabilitation measures in the wake of natural disasters in their States function under the overall direction and control of the state level committee. In many states, Secretary, Department of Revenue, is also in-charge of relief. State Governments usually have relief manuals and the districts have their contingency plan that is updated from time to time.

District and Local Level

The district administration is the focal point for implementation of all governmental plans and activities. The actual day-to-day function of administering relief is the responsibility of the Collector/District Magistrate/Deputy Commissioner who exercises coordinating and supervising powers over all departments at the district level. Though it may not be a common phenomenon, there exists by and large in districts also a district level relief committee consisting of officials and non-officials.

The 73rd and 74th constitutional amendments recognise Panchayati Raj Institutions as 'Institutions of self-government'. The amendment has also laid down necessary guidelines for the structure of their composition, powers, functions, devolution of finances, regular holding of elections and reservation of seats for weaker sections including women.

These local bodies can be effective instruments in tackling disasters through early warning system, relief distribution, providing shelter to the victims, medical assistance etc.

Other than the national, state, district and local levels, there are various institutional stakeholders who are involved in disaster management at various levels in the country. These include the police and para-military forces, civil defence and home-guards, fire services, ex-servicemen, nongovernment organisations (NGOs), public and private sector enterprises, media and HAM operators, all of whom have important roles to play.

Armed Forces

The Indian Armed Forces are supposed to be called upon to intervene and take on specific tasks only when the situation is beyond the capability of civil administration. In practice, the Armed Forces are the core of the government's response capacity and tend to be the first responders of the Government of India in a major disaster. Due to their ability to organize action in adverse ground circumstances, speed of operational response and the resources and capabilities at their disposal, the Armed Forces have historically played a major role in emergency support functions such as communications, search and rescue operations, health and medical facilities, transportation, power, food and civil supplies, public works and engineering, especially in the immediate aftermath of disaster. Disaster management plans should incorporate the role expected of them so that the procedure for deploying them is smooth and quick.

External Linkages

The Government of India is a member of various international organisations in the field of disaster response and relief. While, as a policy, no requests for assistance or appeals are made to the international community in the event of a disaster, assistance offered suo moto is accepted. Linkages exist with the following organisations:

a) UN Office for Coordination of Humanitarian Affairs (UN OCHA), which has been made responsible by UN General Assembly mandate for all international disaster response.

b) United Nations Development Programme (UNDP), responsible for mitigation and prevention aspects of disaster management.

c) UN Disaster Assessment and Coordination (UNDAC) System.

Streamlining Institutional Arrangements for Disaster Response

Institutional arrangements for disaster response are the heart of disaster management systems. There is no dearth of personnel, both civilian and military, experienced in handling situations arising out of natural disasters. However, there certainly is a pressing need for improvement and strengthening of existing institutional arrangements and systems in this regard to make the initial response to a disaster more effective and professional. Most of the resources and expertise needed already exist with the Government. What needs to be streamlined is how they should be integrated, trained and deployed. Some of the areas where improvement is urgently needed are:

a) Integrated planning for disasters, including the integration of relevant Armed Forces formations into disaster management planning at all levels from District to State and Central Government.

b) Setting up of a modern, permanent national command centre or operations room, with redundant communications and data links to all State capitals. The national command centre or operations room needs to be manned on a 24-hour basis by professionals to cater for instant integrated response. There needs to be a properly equipped operations room at the State level as well.

c) Establishment of a national stand by, quick reaction team composed of experienced professionals, both military and civilian, drawn from Central and State Government staff to respond immediately by flying in a matter of hours an experienced response team to the locations when a disaster strikes. This team can be organized and run professionally on the same lines as the United Nations Disaster Assessment and Coordination (UNDAC) teams.

d) Creation of urban search and rescue capacity at all levels, by establishing a fully equipped Search and Rescue unit, as part of the fire service in all State capitals, with trained staff and modern equipment such as thermal imagers, acoustic detection devices etc. This is of immediate relevance since a major weakness exposed in the Gujarat earthquake was a lack of specialised urban search and rescue capability in India.

e) Media policy geared to handling the growing phenomenon of real time television reporting, which generates enormous political pressures on a government to respond rapidly and efficiently. This needs attention since the effect is going to increase, not decrease in future.

f) Closer interface with and better understanding of the international system for disaster response, and putting in place, systems for dealing with international assistance once it comes in e.g., customs, immigration, foreign policy implications etc. A greater appreciation is needed of the speed and automation of modern international response to a natural disaster. Closer interaction is required between the Ministry of External Affairs and the relevant international agencies concerned with disaster response.

g) Standard procedures for dealing with domestic humanitarian and relief assistance from non-government sources. Procedures and systems need to be set out to avoid confusion and ensure best utilisation of the assistance being offered, just as in the case of systems for international assistance.

h) Modern unified legislation for disaster management. In view of the current division of responsibilities between the State and Central Government into state, central and concurrent lists, there is a need to create a body of legislation dealing with response to natural disasters and other emergencies, clearly delineating responsibilities and powers of each entity and specifying what powers or actions would need to be triggered on declaration of a disaster by the Government of India or a State Government. This legislation should also incorporate the current legislation dealing with chemical emergencies that has been created by the Ministry of Environment so that all emergencies are dealt with under one law.The legislation should include clear definitions of what constitutes a disaster at a national level.

FINANCIAL ARRANGEMENTS

Financing of Relief Expenditures

The policy arrangements for meeting relief expenditure related to natural disasters are, by and large, based on the recommendations of successive finance commissions. The two main windows presently open for meeting such expenditures are the Calamity Relief Fund (CRF) and National Calamity Contingency Fund (NCCF). The Calamity Relief Fund is used for meeting the expenditure for providing immediate relief to the victims of cyclone, drought, earthquake, fire, flood and hailstorm. Expenditure on restoration of damaged capital works should ordinarily be met from the normal budgetary heads, except when it is to be incurred as part of providing immediate relief, such as restoration of drinking water sources or provision of shelters etc., or restoration of communication links for facilitating relief operations.

The amount of annual contribution to the CRF of each State for each of the financial years 2000-01 to 2004-05 is as indicated by the Finance Commission. Of the total contribution indicated, the Government of India contributes 75 per cent of the total yearly allocation in the form of a non-plan grant, and the balance amount is contributed by the State Government concerned. A total of Rs. 11,007.59 crore was provided for the Calamity Relief Fund from 2000-05.

Pursuant to the recommendations of the Eleventh Finance Commission, apart from the CRF, a National Calamity Contingency Fund (NCCF) Scheme came into force with effect from the financial year 2000-01 and would be operative till the end of the financial year 2004-05. NCCF is intended to cover natural calamities like cyclone, drought, earthquake, fire, flood and hailstorm, which are considered to be of severe nature requiring expenditure by the State Government in excess of the balances available in its own Calamity Relief Fund.

The assistance from NCCF is available only for immediate relief and rehabilitation. Any reconstruction of assets or restoration of damaged capital should be financed through re-allocation of Plan funds. There is need for defining the arrangements in this regard.

The initial corpus of the National Fund is Rs.500 crore, provided by the Government of India. This fund is required to be recouped by levy of special surcharge for a limited period on central taxes. An amount of about Rs.2,300 crore has already been released to States from NCCF. A list of items and norms of expenditure for assistance chargeable to CRF/NCCF in the wake of natural calamities is prescribed in detail from time to time.

Financing of Disaster Management

Although not specifically addressed in FiveYear Plan documents in the past, the Government of India has a long history of using funds from the Plan for mitigating natural disasters. Funds are provided under Plan schemes i.e., various schemes of Government of India, such as for drinking water, employment generation, inputs for agriculture and flood control measures etc. There are also facilities for rescheduling short-term loans taken for agriculture purposes upon certification by the District/State administration.

Central Government's assets/infrastructure are to be repaired/rectified by the respective Ministry/Department of Government of India.

Besides this, at the occurrence of a calamity of great magnitude, funds flow from donors, both local and international, for relief and rehabilitation, and in few cases for long-term preparedness/preventive measures. Funds for the latter purposes are also available from multilateral funding agencies such as the World Bank. These form part of the State Plan.

There are also a number of important ongoing schemes that specifically help reduce disaster vulnerability. Some of these are: Integrated Wasteland Development Programme (IWDP), Drought Prone Area Programme (DPAP), Desert Development Programme (DDP), Flood Control Programmes, National Afforestation & Ecodevelopment Programme (NA&ED), Accelerated Rural Water Supply Programme (ARWSP), Crop Insurance, Sampurn Grameen Rozgar Yojana (SGRY), Food for Work etc.

Various Bodies Regarding Financing Under the Plan

References have recently been made to the role of the Plan in disaster management by the High Power Committee (HPC) on Disaster Management, as well as by the Eleventh Finance Commission.

The HPC was constituted in 1999 and submitted its Report in October 2001. The HPC took an overview of all recent disasters (natural as well as manmade) in the country and identified common response and preparedness mechanisms on the basis of a series of consultations with a number of government, non-government, national and international agencies and media organisations.

An important recommendation of the Committee was that at least 10 per cent of plan funds at the national, state and district levels be earmarked and apportioned for schemes which specifically address areas such as prevention, reduction, preparedness and mitigation of disasters.

The Eleventh Finance Commission too paid detailed attention to the issue of disaster management and, in its chapter on calamity relief, came out with a number of recommendations, of which the following have a direct bearing on the Plan:

(a) Expenditure on restoration of infrastructure and other capital assets, except those that are intrinsically connected with relief operations and connectivity with the affected area and population, should be met from the plan funds on priority basis.

(b) Medium and long-term measures be devised by the concerned Ministries of the Government of India, the State Governments and the Planning Commission to reduce, and if possible, eliminate, the occurrences of these calamities by undertaking developmental works.

(c) The Planning Commission, in consultation with the State Governments and concerned Ministries, should be able to identify works of a capital nature to prevent the recurrence of specific calamities. These works may be funded under the Plan.

PLANNING FOR SAFE NATIONAL DEVELOPMENT

Development programmes that go into promoting development at the local level have been left to the general exercise of planning. Measures need also to be taken to integrate disaster mitigation efforts at the local level with the general exercise of planning, and a more supportive environment created for initiatives towards managing of disasters at all levels: national, state, district and local.

The future blue-print for disaster management in India rests on the premise that in today's society while hazards, both natural or otherwise, are inevitable, the disasters that follow need not be so and the society can be prepared to cope with them effectively whenever they occur. The need of the hour is to chalk out a multi-pronged strategy for total risk management, comprising prevention, preparedness, response and recovery on the one hand, and initiate development efforts aimed towards risk reduction and mitigation, on the other. Only then can we look forward to "sustainable development."

Preparedness Measures Information and Research Network

Disaster prevention is intrinsically linked to preventive planning. Some of the important steps in this regard are:

(a) Introduction of a comprehensive process of vulnerability analysis and objective risk assessment.

(b) Building a robust and sound information database: A comprehensive database of the land use, demography, infrastructure developed at the national, state and local levels along with current information on climate, weather and man-made structures is crucial in planning, warning and assessment of disasters. In addition, resource inventories of governmental and non-governmental systems including personnel and equipment help in efficient mobilisation and optimisation of response measures.

(c) Creating state-of-the-art infrastructure: The entire disaster mitigation game plan must necessarily be anchored to frontline research and development in a holistic mode. State-of-the art technologies available worldwide need to be made available in India for upgradation of the disaster management system; at the same time, dedicated research activities should be encouraged, in all frontier areas related to disasters like biological, space applications, information technology, nuclear radiation etc., for a continuous flow of high quality basic information for sound disaster management planning,

(d) Establishing Linkages between all knowledge-based institutions: A National Disaster Knowledge Network, tuned to the felt needs of a multitude of users like disaster managers, decision makers, community etc., must be developed as the network of networks to cover natural, manmade and biological disasters in all their varied dimensions,

Capacity Building, Training & Education

Personnel involved in the exercise have to draw upon knowledge of best practices and resources available to them. Information and training on ways to better respond to and mitigate disasters to the responders go a long way in building the capacity and resilience of the country to reduce and prevent disasters. Training is an integral part of capacity building as trained personnel respond much better to different disasters and appreciate the need for preventive measures.

The directions in this regard are:

(a) The multi-sectoral and multi-hazard prevention based approach to disaster management requires specific professional inputs. Professional training in disaster management should be built into the existing pedagogic research and education. Specialised courses for disaster management may be developed by universities and professional teaching institutions, and disaster management should be treated as a distinct academic and professional discipline, something that the American education system has done successfully. In addition to separate diploma/degree courses in disaster management, the subject needs to be discussed and taught as a specific component in professional and specialised courses like medicine, nursing, engineering, environmental sciences, architecture, and town and country planning.

(b) The focus towards preventive disaster management and development of a national ethos of prevention calls for an awareness generation at all levels. An appropriate component of disaster awareness at the school level will help increase awareness among children and, in many cases, parents and other family members through these children. Curriculum development with a focus towards dissemination of disaster related information on a sustained basis, covering junior, middle and high schools may be worked out by the different school boards in the country.

(c) Training facilities for government personnel involved in disaster management are conducted at the national level by the National Centre for Disaster Management (NCDM) at the Indian Institute of Public Administration, in New Delhi which functions as the nodal institution in the country for training, research and documentation of disasters. At the State level, disaster management cells operating within the State Administrative Training Institutes (ATIs) provide the necessary training. Presently, 24 ATIs have dedicated faculties. There is a need for strengthening specialised training, including training of personnel in disaster response.

(d) Capacity building should not be limited to professionals and personnel involved in disaster management but should also focus on building the knowledge, attitude and skills of a community to cope with the effects of disasters. Identification and training of volunteers from the community towards first response measures as well as mitigation measures is an urgent imperative. A programme of periodic drills should be introduced in vulnerable areas to enable prompt and appropriate community response in the event of a disaster, which can help save valuable lives.

Capacity building for effective disaster management therefore needs to be grounded and linked to the community and local level responders on the one hand and also to the institutional mechanism of the State and the Nation on the other.

Community Level Initiatives

The goal of any disaster management initiative is to build a disaster resistant/resilient community equipped with safer living and sustainable livelihoods to serve its own development purposes. The community is also the first responder in any disaster situation, thereby emphasising the need for community level initiatives in managing disasters. To encourage such initiatives, the following are required:

(a) Creating awareness through disaster education and training and information dissemination are necessary steps for empowering the community to cope with disasters.

(b) Community based approach followed by most NGOs and Community Based Organisations (CBOs) should be incorporated in the disaster management system as an effective vehicle of community participation.

(c) Within a vulnerable community, there exist groups that are more vulnerable like women and children, aged and infirm and physically challenged people who need special care and attention especially during disaster situations. Efforts are required for identifying such vulnerable groups and providing special assistance in terms of evacuation, relief, aid and medical attention to them in disaster situations.

Management of disasters should therefore be an interface between a community effort to mitigate and prevent disasters as also an effort from the government machinery to buttress and support popular initiatives.

Strengthening of Plan Activities

Given the pervasive nature of disasters and the widespread havoc caused by some of them, planned expenditure on disaster mitigation and prevention measures in addition to the CRF is required. The Central Sector Scheme of Natural Disaster Management Programmes has been implemented since 1993-94 by the Department of Agriculture and Cooperation with the objective to focus on disaster preparedness with emphasis on mitigation and preparedness measures for enhanced capability to reduce the adverse impact of disasters. The major activities undertaken within this scheme include the setting up of the National Centre for Disaster Management (NCDM) at the Indian Institute of Public Administration, creation of 24 disaster management faculties in 23 states, research and consultancy services, documentation of major disaster events and forging regional cooperation.

The Eighth Plan allocation of Rs 6.30 crore for this scheme was increased to Rs. 16.32 crore in the Ninth Plan. Within this scheme, NCDM has conducted over 50 training programmes, training more than 1000 people, while 24 disaster management centres with dedicated faculty have been established in the states.

Over 4000 people have been trained at the State level. In addition, some important publications and audio-visual training modules have been prepared and documentation of disaster events has been done.

Though limited in scope and outlays, the Scheme has made an impact on the training and research activities in the country. Creation of faculties in disaster management in all 28 states is proposed to be taken up in the Tenth Plan in addition to community mobilisation, human resource development, establishment of Control Rooms and forging international cooperation in disaster management.

There is also an urgent need for strengthening the disaster management pedagogy by creating disaster management faculties in universities, rural development institutes and other organisations of premier research.

Sustainability is the key word in the development process. Development activities that do not consider the disaster loss perspective fail to be sustainable. The compounded costs of disasters relating to loss of life, loss of assets, economic activities, and cost of reconstruction of not only assets but of lives can scarcely be borne by any community or nation. Therefore, all development schemes in vulnerable areas should include a disaster mitigation analysis, whereby the feasibility of a project is assessed with respect to vulnerability of the area and the mitigation measures required for sustainability. Environmental protection, afforestation programmes, pollution control, construction of earthquake resistant structures etc., should therefore have high priority within the plans.

The aim of a mitigation strategy is to reduce losses in the event of a future occurrence of a hazard. Structural mitigation may comprise construction of individual disaster resistant structures like retrofitted or earthquake-resistant buildings or creation of structures whose function is primarily disaster protection like flood control structures, dykes, levees, infiltration dams etc.

Mitigation measures on individual structures can be achieved by design standards, building codes and performance specifications.

Building codes, critical front-line defence for achieving stronger engineered structures, need to be drawn up in accordance with the vulnerability of the area and implemented through appropriate techno-legal measures. Mitigation measures need to be considered in land use and site planning activities. Constructions in hazardous areas like flood plains or steep soft slopes are more vulnerable to disasters. Necessary mitigation measures need to be built into the design and costing of development projects. Insurance is a potentially important mitigation measure in disaster-prone areas as it brings quality in the infrastructure & consciousness and a culture of safety by its insistence on following building codes, norms, guidelines, quality materials in construction etc. Disaster insurance mostly works under the premise of 'higher the risk higher the premium, lesser the risk lesser the premium', thus creating awareness towards vulnerable areas and motivating people to settle in relatively safer areas.

THE PATH AHEAD

For addressing natural calamities such as floods and drought, there already exist a number of plan schemes under which a lot is being done and can be done. State Governments need to make full use of the existing plan schemes and give priority to implementation of such schemes that will help in overcoming the conditions created by the calamity. In some cases this implies possible diversion of the funds from other schemes to those schemes the implementation of which will help meeting the situation.

There may also be need in a crisis situation for certain re-appropriations/ reallocations among the different departments. The Planning Commission will aim at responding quickly to the needs of the Central Ministries/ Departments/States in matters relating to the Plan for meeting situations arising out of natural disasters, by enabling adjustment of schemes to meet the requirements as far as possible.

A mechanism will be evolved to take expeditious decisions on proposals which involve transfer of funds from one scheme to another, or any other change which involves departure from the existing schemes/pattern of assistance, new schemes and relaxation in procedures, etc. in the case of natural disasters.

As the first responder in any disaster situation, however, each State needs to build a team, skilled personnel, make provision for specialised equipments, efficient communication network, and relevant, intelligent and easily accessible database. There is also a need to consider creation of a plan scheme in each state basically to meet the minimum requirements for strengthening communications and emergency control rooms, thereby improving coordination and response to disasters. No new institutional structures need be created in such a scheme.

In particular, with regard to major disasters, it is also necessary for disaster mitigation components to be built into all development projects. In order to save larger outlays on reconstruction and rehabilitation subsequently, a mechanism would need to be worked out for allowing components that specifically help projects coming up in highly disaster prone areas withstand the impact of natural disasters as part of approved project cost for projects financed under the Plan. The message for the Tenth Plan is that in order to move towards safer national development, development projects should be sensitive towards disaster mitigation. With the kind of economic losses and developmental setbacks that the country has been suffering year after year, it makes good economic sense to spend a little extra today in a planned way on steps and components that can help in prevention and mitigation of disasters, than be forced to spend many multiples more later on restoration and rehabilitation.

The design of development projects and the process of development should take the aspect of disaster reduction and mitigation within its ambit; otherwise, the development ceases to be sustainable and eventually causes more hardship and loss to the nation.

DISASTER MANAGEMENT IN INDIA

After independence India began a process of rapid industrialisation. It inevitably lacked some framework conditions, such as an understanding of the risks of chemical hazards. Implementation of safety procedures, including regulatory approaches, soon followed and institutions such as the National Safety Council (NSCI) were created. There was much to do.

The Bhopal disaster (1984) did much to focus more attention on the need for a holistic approach to technology disaster management, and the role of ordinary people in emergencies. The government took several important measures, with major legislative changes and stronger institutional mechanisms. It set up Crisis Groups at central, state, district and local levels. NSCI took the APELL process as a model, promoting awareness and training projects covering both hazardous materials transport and fixed installations.

India is also vulnerable to natural disasters. While well-established mechanisms for response, relief and rehabilitation were in place, major events such as the Orissa super-cyclone (1999) and the Bhuj earthquake (2001) emphasised the need for a comprehensive approach to mitigation and prevention, for natural and man-made disasters.

NSCI adopted several goals based on the APELL procedures: creating or raising public awareness of possible hazards within a community; stimulating development of cooperative plans to respond to any emergency that might occur; and encouraging accident prevention.

Implementation in this vast country followed a two-track approach of development of awareness at the national level, and in-depth implementation in selected high-risk industrial areas (HRIA—see map). We needed to gain first hand experience through pilot projects in important areas. A national Advisory Committee and Technical Core Group was set up for periodical review, guidance and technical consultation. In 2002 the first national APELL Centre opened at NSCI headquarters in Mumbai. It was the first centre of this sort in the world.

The first projects started in 1992 in six HRIAs, also drawing on international collaboration from UNEP, USAID and WEC. In 2004 an APELL sub-centre opened in Haldia (see map). A manual on cyclone emergency preparedness was prepared.

Transport issues were becoming urgent and a major new programme was based on UNEP's Trans APELL. A training module and seminars were developed for traffic police. A HAZMAT emergency van started work on a trial basis in Patalganga-Rasayani, and a broadbased programme for transporters was launched.

Several lessons may be learnt from this process. Widespread industrial development in a country like India requires comprehensive replication of the programme at local level. Sub-centres are essential, with replication programmes involving local partners. Practical experience at local level has facilitated—and has in turn been facilitated by—national legislation such as the law setting up crisis groups and safety management in general.

Crisis groups at district and local level require training and support tools (best practice, case studies, etc.) so there is an ongoing role for training organisations such as NSCI and its offshoots like NAC. Finally, the programme has pinpointed the need to treat transport as a priority issue, linking various locations in the hazardous materials chain across the country.

The experience has also aroused much interest abroad, notably in China, South Africa, Jordan and Brazil, underlining the need to share experience internationally.

Emergency prevention and preparedness is a complex issue, and industrialising countries need to address the matter as an integral part of a larger sustainable development agenda. Experience in countries such as India can do much to streamline the process elsewhere, with growing pressures to better address disaster issues.

Emergency Support Functions

Emergency Support functions (ESF's) assist and support the National, State and District Administration at the time of emergency for restoring the damaged public services and facilities of the affected area.

ESFs are the essentials of Emergency Management and comprise of various coordinating agencies, which manage and coordinate specific kinds of assistance common to all disasters types. The plan establishes an organised set-up to conduct ESF operations for any of the Natural and Man-made Disasters. It outlines an implementing framework of sharing resources and coordinating, preparedness, mitigation, response and recovery as per the requirement of a disaster situation.

It helps structure activities of concerned agencies *i.e.* primary/nodal and support agencies in an organised manner as per their capabilities, skills, resources and authorities across the state and district government.

It also attempts to unify efforts of state departments so that they are involved in emergency management comprehensively to reduce the effects of any emergency or disaster within the state. Emergency Support functions (ESF) have been constituted to support the department of Revenue (which may be renamed as 'Department of Revenue and Disaster Management', as directed by the Ministry of Home Affairs) in times of a disaster. District North has been able to accimilate ESF's from 7 line departments till date. The list of departments as per their status of submission of ESFs is as per below given table:

The Main ESFs and Their Concerned Departments

- ESFS
- Functions
- Coordinator
- Supporting Agencies
- ESF1
- Communication
- MTNL
- NIC, Police/Revenue, Wireless, HAM reps, Private telecom/mobile operators
- ESF2
- Evacuation
- DC Office
- Police, DFS, Civil Defence, NCC, Army
- ESF3
- Search & Rescue
- Delhi Fire Service
- Police, Civil Defence, NCC, Army, Health and Home Reps

- ESF4
- Law & Order
- Police
- Civil Defence & Home Guards
- ESF5
- Medical Response & Trauma Counselling
- Health Department
- CATS, DHS, Indian Red Cross, Civil defence, NSS
- ESF6
- Water Supply
- NDMC
- DC Office
- ESF7
- Relief (Food & Shelter)
- Deptt. of Food & Civil Supplies
- NDMC, CPWD, NSS, NYKS, NGOs
- ESF8
- Equipment Support, Debris/Road clearance
- DC Office
- NDMC, DDA, DMRC, CPWD
- ESF9
- Help Lines, Warning Dissemination
- Revenue
- NIC/NGO Reps
- ESF10
- Power Supply
- NDMC
- CPWD
- ESF11
- Transport
- Transport Department
- DTC, DMRC, Northern Railways, CPWD, NDMC

Status of ESFs in the District

Departments having submitted ESFs

Departments that have not submitted ESFs

- Delhi Police

- CDMO
- Irrigation and Flood Control Department
- Civil Defence
- CATS
- MCD—K.B. Zone
- MCD—City Zone
- MCD (S.P. Zone, Civil Lines Zone)
- DDA
- DJB
- PWD
- NDPL
- MRTS
- Slum and JJ Department
- Education
- Fire
- District Social Welfare Department
- Food and Civil Supplies
- Labour commissioner

DISASTER RISK MANAGEMENT

Strategies

With basis in its mandate to promote sustainable development in Latin America and the Caribbean the Bank will help the countries integrate the reduction of risk in their development planning and investments and create permanent technical and operational capacity to efficiently manage risk reduction.

With the goal to overcome the challenge of increasing risk and losses from natural hazards, the Bank will prioritize vulnerability reduction in its support to the region and it will provide financing for the prevention and mitigation of disasters resulting from natural hazards and strengthen capacities to manage risks.

This national approach is complemented by research and a regional dialogue to identify best practices and facilitate their sharing. The Plan of Action (Facing the Challenge of Natural Disasters in Latin America and the Caribbean: An IDB Action Plan. March 2000) identifies six strategic areas for Bank assistance to help countries adopt comprehensive risk management policies:

National Systems for Disaster Prevention and Response: Building national legal and regulatory frameworks and programmes that bring together the planning agencies, local governments and civil society organizations; developing national strategies for risk reduction, and assessing inter-sectoral priorities, backed by separate budgets.

Inserting Prevention into the Culture: Developing and disseminating risk information and empowering citizens and other stakeholders to take risk reduction measures.

Reducing the Vulnerability of the Poor: Supporting poor households and communities in reducing their vulnerability to natural hazards and recovering from disasters through reconstruction assistance.

Involving the Private Sector: Creating conditions for the development of insurance markets; encouraging the use of other risk-spreading financial instruments where appropriate, and designing economic and regulatory incentives for risk reduction behaviour.

Risk Information for Decision-Making: Evaluating existing risk assessment methodologies; developing indicators of vulnerability, and stimulating the production and wide dissemination of risk information.

Fostering Leadership and Cooperation in the Region: Stimulate coordinated actions and to mobilize regional resources for investments in risk mitigation.

Proposed Actions

With the goal to increase the effectiveness of the Bank's support in the identified strategic areas, the Bank is faced with the challenge to put risk management to the top of its agenda. The following list of actions provides the necessary elements to integrate risk management in the operations and activities of the Bank.

1. Creation and revision of financial mechanisms of the Bank to help the countries take and strengthen necessary measures of disaster prevention and risk management.
2. *Risk Reduction as a Component of the Banks Country Dialogue with Borrowing Members:* promote the dialogue concerning risk identification, strategies for risk management and the use of financial instruments made available by the IDB for investments related to Natural Disasters.
3. *Risk Reduction in the Project Cycle:* include risk analysis and reduction in the programming process and in the identification, formulation, execution and evaluation of projects.

4. *Bank Focal Points for Disaster Risk Management:* support preparation of risk reduction programmes in the countries and coordinate activities of prevention and response among sector divisions and Bank representations.
5. *Alliances:* Create an integrated network with information and response which includes the preparation of pre-investment studies, financing of investments for prevention and reconstruction and to establish inter-institutional protocols for disaster response.

Strategic Actions Executed with Relation to Natural Disasters since 2001

The Bank has made a new mechanism for with fast disbursement, the Disaster Prevention Sector Facility, available to its borrowing members and revised its Immediate Response Facility instrument.

In its country dialogues the Bank has increasingly emphasized natural disaster prevention and mitigation and the development of capacity for effective risk management. This includes various initiatives to incorporate risk reduction in the investment planning processes. The Bank collaborates with other institutions, among other issues to promote the interchange of information concerning best practices for responding to emergencies and to develop effective emergency reconstruction plans.

3

Earthquake Disaster Management and Role of NGOs

INTRODUCTION

Asia has been the region of different disasters in recent and historic past. Disaster data of last 25 years shows that around 38% of the world's disaster events occurred in Asia (Data Book, 2000). While the number of people died in these disaster mounted up to 51% for Asia (compared to 37% in Africa and 9% in Americas), the affected people was 88%.

Also, the amount of damages in Asia was 47%, compared to 27% in Americas, and 23% in Europe. It shows that disasters affected both life and properties in Asia the most in last 25 years, when compared to the rest of the world. Needless to say that Asia contributes to 60% of the world population. South and South-east Asia has a population growth rate of 1.4 to 17.7 % (UN 2001a).

Therefore, continued disaster risk in Asia is perceptible. Among different disasters, it is found that earthquakes killed the maximum number of people in terms of percentage. While the number of people affected is the most for flood, followed by draught, the property loss in terms of total damages is highest for earthquakes (44% compared to 31% for flood, 16% for draught).

The increasing population growth, increasing complexities of urban, rural and livelihood problems, and constrained resources has restricted the activities of the government sectors in both developing and developed countries. It has been understood that for single machinery, it is almost impossible to secure safety and sustainability of human lives. The importance of non-government organizations (NGOs) has been visualized, realized and emphasized in different aspects, with special focus on the humanitarian activities, in recent years. Most common field of NGO interventions includes the human right issues, health, poverty reduction, education, and environment. The need of NGO activities in the field of disaster reduction has been discussed for several years, however the United Nations International Decade for Natural Disaster Reduction (IDNDR: 1990-1999) has given a big boost to these activities. During the mid-term meeting of IDNDR in Yokohama, Japan (1994), NGOs from different continents met and decided to form the Global Forum of NGOs for Disaster Reduction (GFNDR) to work more closely towards safer 21st century (GFNDR 1994). Asian NGOs took a leadership role in the formation of this global forum, and as a result the presidency of this forum is held by the NGO from Philippines, and the secretariat is located in India. This initiative has been acknowledged and appreciated by the UN Secretary General Kofi Annan in his report to the 52nd General Assembly of the United Nations (UN, 2001b). It has been stated that 'Non-government organizations will play an increasingly important role in the continuation of disaster reduction activities in the twenty-first century'. The roles of NGOs in the field of community participation, formulation of social development interests and integrated approaches have been stressed.

In contrast to the many good things about the NGO operations, it has often been criticized for its rather anti-government move. Sustainability and resources are other problems, faced by the NGOs. In this short paper, the characterization of the NGOs has been done and a few successful case studies of NGO involvement have been provided, with specific focus on the earthquake disaster management. Finally, a framework of effective NGO cooperation has been described.

CLASSIFICATION OF NON-GOVERNMENT ORGANIZATIONS

A non-government organization has been defined as any non-profit, voluntary citizen's group, which is organized on a local, national or international level (UN, 2000). However the diversity in task, goal and activities, strains any simple definition of NGO. It can be stated that the NGO include a wide range of groups, which act independent of government, and characterized by preliminary humanitarian activities, with focus on the citizen's need and demand.

The term of NGO varies from county to country, e.g., while in the USA, it is often called as a 'private voluntary organization', in the African countries, it is often termed as 'voluntary development organization'. Although the universities and research organizations may be non-governmental, this directive refers principally to the private organizations, that pursue activities to relieve suffering, promote the interest of poor, protect the environment, provide basic social services, or undertake community development (World Bank, 1991). Following are the criteria of NGO, defined by the development banks (Causins 1991):

1. Non-profit making, voluntary service oriented organizations,
2. Organization of private individuals who believe in certain basic social principles,
3. Social development organization, assessing in empowerment of the people,
4. Independent of any external control with specific objectives or aims,
5. Independent, democratic and non-sectarian people's organization working for the empowerment of economic and/or socially marginalized group,
6. An organization not affiliated to political parties, generally engaged in aid and development and welfare of the community,
7. An organization committed to the root-cause of problems, trying to better the quality of life specifically to the needy people,
8. An organization established by and for the community without or with little interventions from the government,
9. An organization that is flexible and democratic in its organization and attempts to serve people without profit for itself.

There are different classifications of NGOs, based on their missions or levels of operations. The World Bank has classified them as per mission: Charitable NGOs, Service-oriented NGOs, Participatory NGOs, and Empowering NGOs. Whereas as per the operation, they can be classified as: Community based organizations, Citywide/district-wide organizations, National organization and international organizations (Sakya, 2000). Besides, there is a classification of national and international NGOs, based on the field/area of activities. Also, there is another classification of NGOs from developed countries (having primary work area in the developing countries with specific expertise and knowledge), and NGOs from developing countries. In some countries like Philippine, NGOs are classified as internationally-based resource NGO, internationally-affiliated NGO, national NGO, corporate-based NGO, province-based NGO, and community-based organizations (Luna, 2000). Thus, it can be stated that the definition, and classification of NGO depends on the types of activities, mission, and geographic area of work.

We propose here a different classification, which is specifically relevant to the disaster related issues. This classification has a major connotation to the South Asian countries, where the NGO activities have been relatively strong, and continued for last several years. The current NGO activities can be grouped into two major types: 1) Professional NGOs, which has specific professional expertise and knowledge and consists of people from different professional background; and 2) Social NGOs, which is more related to the social and humanitarian activities. The social NGOs can also consist of professional people, but for the Professional NGOs, their work is defined by the professional expertise of the people in their group. Both these NGO can be divided into two further groups, national and international, based on their activities. It is to be noted that well-known international NGOs like Oxfam, Care, Red Cross, Save the Children comes to the Social type NGOs in this current classification.

CURRENT STATE OF NGO ACTIVITIES IN ASIA

The role and status of NGOs has been different in different countries, depending on the culture, and context of the political activities. Countries having its specific laws and rules for the civic activities, the role and effectiveness of the NGOs are different. In some countries, NGO activities are regarded essential, and has rather well established status in the society. However, in some other countries, the NGO activities are generally considered as the anti-government movement.

In East Asia, Japan has been the lead country to promote NGO activities with special focus on disaster reduction. The civic and community based organizations have shown their potentiality and effectiveness in different disaster related activities, in both pre and post disaster scenario. A new system has currently established, known as Japan Platform, which aims at the cooperation of NGOs, business communities and government.

This is a unique system to provide emergency relief after major disasters worldwide effectively and quickly. The platform is characterized by an equal partnership of NGOs, business and government, with each constituent making full use of its resource and characteristics. The business world, led by the Federation of Economic Organizations has committed to support this platform in terms of resources like funding, technology, equipment, human resources and infrastructures. This is interesting to note that the Ministry of Foreign Affairs of Japan also supports this activity by providing relevant information through the diplomatic channels. Also, MOFA is committed to a certain amount of regular funding for the activity. Thus, this scheme of cooperation helps to attain sustainability and stability of the activities, and helps to take prompt action. In contrast to the Japan, the NGO activities in China has been less prominent. In recent days, US-China environment, science and technology cooperation has promoted the NGO activities, which are more focused on the environment and human rights related activities (First NGO Forum, 1999). Regarding the disasters, the international NGOs like IFRC, World Vision, OXFAM have worked together with the international organizations during the relief and rescue work.

In the South-east Asia, Philippines have been the leading country having well-established institutional and legal framework for disaster management and NGO involvement (Luna 2000). The post-Marcos governments have made the mainstreaming of concept and opportunities of NGOs through different community based activities. Disaster management has become a specialization among the NGOs, and different organizations have started showing their interest in this field. The main activities of these NGOs include community based disaster management, undertaking socioeconomic projects, capacity building through training, small scale structural measures, institutionalization of the disaster management work with local government units, and advocacy for preparedness and awareness raising. One significant aspect is the dependence of the NGOs on external funding, and thus making the organizations rather vulnerable to the sustainability. Some of these NGOs work very closely with the local government units to increase the capabilities in terms of disaster management and mitigation.

South Asia has been the focus and centre of NGO activities for last several decades. Increasing problems regarding poverty, health, population and environment have urged the people to form many community-based organizations. In India, there have been different NGOs, which are involved in the disaster related activities. Some of them work in close cooperation with governments, both at the national and local level, some work with the international NGOs, and some work independently. The ranges vary from the professional to the social NGOs, and the major funding sources are the individual donations, help from the business community and consulting work for government and international organizations. Recent disasters have shown the positive and negative side of the NGO activities. While government was able to handle the policy and institutional subjects, the NGOs are better placed to deal with field level and community issues, and act as the most effective means of achieving an efficient communication link between the disaster management agencies and affected communities (Sharma 1997). In several cases, it has been observed that the effective pre-event collaboration can increase the potential strength and capacity of during and post-disaster relief and rehabilitation activities. Sharma (2000) stressed the NGO-government collaboration with specific focus on the training of the NGOs, making partnership through joint project initiatives, and sharing appropriate information.

Central Asia, earlier being a part of the Soviet Russia, the NGO activities are not pronounced. A few sporadic events have taken place with special emphasis on Turkmenistan, where the international NGO called FOCUS has been active in creating disaster awareness in the community level. The west Asia is also relatively lack of NGO activities. The Aga Khan Foundation group has been doing voluntary humanitarian work in different parts of the Central and West Asia. One interesting activity is the promotion of disaster education through school earthquake safety initiative. This has led to the construction of earthquake resistant schools through self-help program (Shaban 2001).

In summary, country's economic, political and social status has caused the variation of the NGO activities in different parts of Asia. In certain countries, NGO activities has been very successful, where in some other places, it is not no prominent. A few success stories have been described below with specific focus on the disaster cycle.

ROLES OF NGOS IN EARTHQUAKE DISASTER MANAGEMENT

The disaster management framework can be defined as different elements of the disaster cycle, which is composed of actions before disaster, actions immediately after disaster and long-term recovery process after disaster. Although it is more or less similar to different types of disasters, in the current discussion, specific emphasis will be given to the earthquake disasters.

Prevention and preparedness are pre-event elements, response (rescue and relief) occurs immediately after the event, and reconstruction and rehabilitation occur in the long-term recovery process after the event. Here, we will describe the successful activities of several NGO groups, with related to different elements of the earthquake disaster.

Pre-disaster: Mitigation, Preparedness and Awareness

A unique effort of collaboration between the national and international NGO has been demonstrated by the NSET (National Society for Earthquake Technology)-Nepal and GeoHazards International (GHI) of USA. Nepal has been an earthquake prone country, with several major earthquake events in the last decade (KVERMP, 1999). However, there was no focus on the pre-disaster mitigation and prepared ness aspects so far. GHI and NSET jointly launched an initiative for the mitigation program called Kathmandu Valley Earthquake Risk Management Program (KVERMP), with administrative support from Asian Disaster Preparedness Centre (ADPC) and financial assistance from USAID-OFDA (Office of Foreign Disaster Assistance). The goal and objective of the project was to create an easily understood earthquake damage scenario, targeting the common people and other stakeholders; and to prepare a risk management plan based on this scenario. The scenario was made by combining the results of different building, infrastructure and lifelines agencies, and was written by a journalist. This process of scenario and action planning was later used in the United Nations IDNDR RADIUS project in nine cities worldwide. The project not only was able to achieve a substantial level of awareness, but it also created a National Earthquake Safety Day, which was observed every year, and was linked to several awareness-raising activities. The project also included a school earthquake safety component, where there were focus on the mason training, school retrofitting, disaster education or children, parent and teachers. The project officially ended in early 2000, however the initiative was ongoing. The salient feature of the project can be highlighted as follow:

1. Development and institutionalize the earthquake risk management efforts by establishing the earthquake safety society,
2. Establish a strong linkage between the community and the high level political leaders and government bureaucrats for effective mitigation of risk,
3. Catalyzing the efforts of earthquake risk management and to start the chain reaction, which has been taking place spontaneously onwards,
4. Disseminating the information in a wide areas, both locally, nationally and regionally, and
5. Establishing a model of successful operation and cooperation of NGO activities.

Beside this cooperation, as an international professional NGO, GHI has been able to successfully promote the risk mitigation concept through its network, and activities. It has been working with the UN organizations for the RADIUS project, which used a similar methodology of that of KVERMP. Besides, to assess the city's risk in global level, it has selected several cities under the Global Earthquake Safety Initiative (GESI), which has been again a joint initiative with the UN. All these activities were aimed to alarm the local policy makers and decision makers for the risk of their respective cities, and to provide a few options for effective risk mitigation. The most significant thing in all these efforts was to transfer the ownership of the problem and the solution to the local people, which were regarded as the basic tool for sustainable disaster mitigation.

During Disasters: Rescue and Relief Operations

The activities of national and international NGOs during the disasters have been exemplified in the Hanshin-Awaji earthquake of Kobe, 1995, Marmara Earthquake of Turkey 1999, and the Bhuj earthquake of India 2001.

The Rescue phase commences immediately following the earthquake where the primary focus is on pulling out victims from the debris of structures and providing medical assistance as required. Rescue from debris generally requires a high degree of skill and knowledge of behaviour of damaged buildings.

Rescue phase usually lasts for the first 48 hours after a disaster when the rate of survival of trapped victims is high. Although different groups gather after the disaster, very few NGOs are well equipped with knowledge and expertise for the search and rescue operation, which is generally regarded as the duty of the government or that of army.

AKUT (Arama-Kurtarma Derneoi, in English, the Search and rescue Society) of Turkey is one of its rare kinds, which is involved only in search and rescue operation in different types of disasters, including the Marmara Earthquake of 1999. It is well equipped with manpower, equipments and experiences. Motivation, skilled human resources and organizational set-up were the main tools for their success story. After the Marmara Earthquake, it has been observed that the tent of AKUT has become the official coordination point for relief materials. Being encouraged with its successful operation in the Marmara Earthquake, AKUT has sent his teams to Greece. AKUT is also engaged in the effective education and training program for the search and rescue operation, with the financial help from the international development bank. The aim of this program is to disseminate the latest technology and knowledge to the people and organizations, and thereby increase their capabilities for effective operations. The training program has received remarkable support from the public, government and local and international NGOs.

In contrast to the rescue operation, the relief has been a rather commonly observed phenomenon where NGOs take a leading role. In the current Bhuj earthquake, it has been found that the NGOs have been able to reach the remote villages, where the aid and relief materials could not reach through the government mechanism (Shaw et al. 2001). The most outstanding thing to note here is that there has been a daily coordination meting among the NGOs, lead by a group called Abhiyan, which was attended by all different NGO groups, international organizations and the government relief coordinator. The purpose of this meeting was to share information on the daily activities of different groups, and to ensure that the relief is well distributed, and the efforts are not duplicated. This has been a remarkable achievement of the successful NGO coordination (Coming Together, 2001).

Post-disaster: Rehabilitation and Recovery

This field gives a mixed impression from the past history of different disasters. There have been some very successful interventions, while in some cases it is found not be effective due to lack of sustainability. The Hanshin-Awaji earthquake of 1995 is related to a successful intervention a NGO group, called NGO-Kobe. The group started its voluntary activities after the earthquake of 1995, and initially focused on the temporary shelter issues. Immediately after the earthquake, the victims who lost their houses were mobilized to the elementary schools, where there was a shared life-style for almost two months. Government prepared temporary shelters with the cooperation of different voluntary organization. This NGO group was involved in different counseling activities, including the problems of the aged and disable people till 1998. In 1998, they formed this NGOs Kobe as an organization and coordination centre for the NGO groups in Kobe and adjoining areas. Although there has been improved coordination between government and NGO, it is found that the NGOs, being independent organizations, rarely coordinate and share information. Thus, it is a significant achievement in the sense of cooperation and networking (Kobe Action Plan 2003). To disseminate its experiences of the rehabilitation and reconstruction, the group has done work in different countries, in different disasters, including the major earthquakes of Turkey, Taiwan and India. After each major earthquake, the group makes fundraising efforts through its member organizations, and put that fund into the rehabilitation activity in the affected areas. After the Gujarat earthquake of 2001, the NGO Kobe has been actively involved in coordination with the local Indian NGO for the rehabilitation of a model village in the worst affected area. In this activity, the framework of cooperation has been established among different organizations and stakeholders, including government, research, and international organizations. A long-term rehabilitation process should be community-driven, and needs to incorporate the livelihood issues. The model rehabilitation program thus not only focus on the reconstruction of earthquake-resistant houses, but also includes sustainable livelihood options for people, improvement of the quality of life including education, health and environment (Shaw et al. 2003). A special emphasis has been given to empower communities so that it is aware of its own needs and is actively able to strive to achieve them, and to establish suitable standards for disaster resistant communities by assisting the community demonstrate its achievements in the post earthquake scenario.

However, it is to be noted that the NGO activity is not always successful for the long-term recovery process. After the Latur earthquake of India (1993), it has been observed that while a group of 350 non-government voluntary organizations gathered at the initial stage, only 35 organizations remained till the end of the recovery process (Vatsa 2001). This sustainability issue is discussed in the next section.

FRAMEWORK OF COORDINATION MECHANISM FOR SUCCESSFUL NGO OPERATION

Immediately after the disaster, the role of people is the most important, since neighbors and community becomes the first respondent after the event. The key word of rescue operation is the technical skill and training and cooperation with the local residents. In the relief field, it is very important to have a proper coordination among different stakeholders: government, international organizations, people and international NGOs.

A well-coordinated relief operation makes a difference in reaching the needy people, and reduces the duplication of efforts. Rehabilitation and reconstruction process needs commitments of efforts. As stated earlier, after the major earthquakes, there are a concentration of different NGOs in the relief and rescue phase. However, the continuation of the efforts in the reconstruction and rehabilitation phase needs long-term commitments. In this phase, NGO can play an important role as the interface between the people and the government, by communicating community's needs and priorities to the government. The most challenging part is the preparedness aspect, where the lessons learned from the post-disaster reconstruction is transmitted to future generation to cope with the next event. This is especially important for earthquake, which is a low frequency but high consequence event in most cases. Cooperation is the key word in this phase.

The issue of NGO participation, especially in earthquake disaster management incorporates training, preparedness, awareness, housing and reconstruction, social issues like food, environment micro finance but NGO can also play constructive role in research and advocacy. However, there are some cross cutting issues like vulnerability, risk assessment, gender, monitoring and evaluation, which need to be addressed appropriately. Sustainability of efforts, flexibility in approaches, and motivation and dedication in endeavors are the key elements for the successful involvement of NGOs in earthquake disaster management.

CONCLUSION

Involvement of NGOs in earthquake disaster management is the most critical, where the event is not so frequent, unlike other disasters. NGOs play a very vital, responsible and important role in every stages of disaster cycle. Search and rescue needs technical skills, relief needs coordination, rehabilitation needs commitment and preparedness needs cooperation. But the most important is that it should be a multi-disciplinary action, involving different stakeholders. Addressing the needs of people, cooperation with government sectors, linking the efforts to the development practices, and professionalism and motivation are the key issues for sustainability of efforts of NGO involvement.

RUSSIAN FAR EAST ENVIRONMENTAL PROBLEMS

The Far East Region includes ten eastern entities of the Russian Republic: the Republic of Sakha; Primorye and Khabarovsk Territories; Amur, Kamchatka, Magadan, and Sakhalin Oblasts; the Jewish Autonomous Region; and Koryak and Chukot Autonomous Districts. It occupies a sizable territory of 6.215 million square kilometers or 36.4 percent of Russia. As of January 1, 1997, the region was inhabited by 7.421 million people or only 5.03 percent of the nation's population. The average density of the population is 1.19 persons per square kilometers or one-seventh the national average. A recent downward trend in the population has developed as migration to other regions increases. Strangely enough, development of the region began from the north. Russian expeditions initially explored Chukotka and Kamchatka in the first half of the eighteenth century. Exploration of the southern part of the region began only in the second half of the nineteenth century.

Slow development of the region was related to its remoteness and unfavorable climatic conditions. Yet the region enjoys an important geopolitical location, for it provides access to the Pacific Ocean and to the frontiers with Japan, Korea, China, and the United States. Industrial, economic, and cultural development of the region was carried out by military forces, by newly arrived workers, and by prisoners-all perceived as temporary residents. Historically, genealogically, and culturally, most of the region has been linked to Central Russia and Siberia.

The region is rich in natural resources-fish, timber, oil, gas, and minerals such as gold, diamonds, coal, and non-ferrous metals. With 5.03 percent of the population, the region produces 9.0 percent of the nation's timber and 67.1 percent of the fish catch.

Industrial output reached 4.7 percent in 1990 and 4.6 percent in 1996, while farming was 3.2 percent and 2.9 percent, respectively. During the period of reforms, the share of these industries was on the rise, although the share declined considerably in other sectors. Consequently, recent trends are toward increased resource-extraction industries with growing pressure on the environment. The main environmental problems in the region relate to preservation of biodiversity, use of marine resources, pollution of rivers and lakes, preservation of forests, and urban development.

PRESERVATION OF BIODIVERSITY

The huge region spreads over several climatic zones from the polar area in the north to the subtropical areas of Primorye Territory, including continental, coastal, and island areas. It has unique biological diversity-vegetation, animal, and marine. The southern areas of the region were not exposed to ice formation during the glacial period, which resulted in preservation of ancient biospecies. The southern area of Primorye and Khabarovsk Territories exemplifies a unique coexistence of both northern (e.g., larch, stone birch) and southern (e.g. liana, lotus) plants. Such a unique mix is also typical for the animal world.

There are more than 5,000 vascular plant species and more than 1,500 types of mushrooms. In the south of Primorye territory there are more than 1,200 types of plants, 120 mammal species, 50,000 insects, and 550 birds. There are 104 types of fish in the Amur River alone. Diversity was preserved to a great extent due to the low level of development of the region as compared with other regions of Central Russia.

There are many ancient plants in the area. For example, in the Sikhot Alin mountains, among the 800 plants 200 fall into the class of ancient relics.

Three groups stand out among the relics of vegetative and possibly animal origin: relics well adapted to current conditions and renewable by nature, mobile relics, and relics that are being reduced by natural and anthropogenic forces. A distinguishing feature of the region is the availability of unique endemic plants and animals. Many of the over 250 endemic plants are on the verge of disappearance and are now in the Rare Species Book. The principal challenges to biodiversity are:

- o Natural and anthropogenic disasters.
- o Reduction of growth areas due to impacts such as deforestation and industrial development.
- o Predatory and poaching extermination of tigers, musk deer, ginseng, lemon trees, and the Amur sturgeon.
- o Lack of proper resource management.

Reduction of biodiversity in the Far East is inevitable due to a weakening of governmental control over resource-related activities, curtailment of funds for nature protection, poaching, and a sharp growth of smuggled exports. Different measures could counter biodiversity reduction. Among such steps are an increase in the size and number of protected areas, environmental education-particularly for school children-control of poaching and smuggling, and better resource management.

PROBLEMS IN THE USE OF THE PACIFIC SEAS

Problems arising from man's marine activities include loss of biodiversity, impacts of shipping, pollution from the Navy's activities, wastes from off-shore oil and gas production, and industrial and household dump sites. Ocean problems are often of an international character. Loss of biodiversity is often associated with fishing on the high seas as well as in coastal waters. Problems arise with international quotas and harvesting methods. It is not easy to implement an agreement when on frequent occasions each party tries to attain an excessive share of the resources and to hide its catch. Even though there is recognition of the importance of observing the agreement by the government, it is hard to persuade businessmen, sailors, and fishermen to comply.

In recent years, poaching for illegal export has reach an industrial scale. The process from fishing to payment involves many activities on the sea. Government control is complicated, although the state is trying to use fishing inspectors and Coast Guard capabilities.

The poaching of mollusks and trepangs (sea cucumbers) is taking on a massive scale in coastal waters. Trepangs are widely used in Chinese medicine and are therefore bought and smuggled out of the country in volumes that threaten the disappearance of the species. Artificial cultivation of seafood could be an alternative to reduce poaching. But this activity has not been developed due to a lack of investment funds and the mentality of the population, which prefers to rely on nature rather than cultivation. The negative environmental impact of marine industries is associated with the fact that the Russian fleet is aging.

In the past 15 years there have been practically no new ships. Privatization and creation of joint-stock companies have resulted in small shipping companies that violate all the rules and regulations concerning marine ecology and navigation safety. The sinking of the Russian tanker Nadezhda with a resulting oil spill not far from Japanese islands is an example of the problems.

Many ships are even banned from entering foreign ports. The Navy's activities, including cruises of nuclear-powered vessels, also damage the marine ecology. Apart from technical problems connected with the Navy's operations that impact the coastal areas, the military mentality is in principle unfriendly toward the environment. This is true in any country, not only Russia. Graveyards of decommissioned warships are a threat to coastal waters, although recently some problems were solved by the dismantling of vessels.

Off-shore oil and gas production has begun near Sakhalin Island under a Russian-American-Japanese project. But due to the novel character of the program, there is a serious risk of negative environmental consequences. There is a problem associated with industrial and domestic waste disposal in the seas. Vladivostok provides a typical negative example. Poorly processed wastes have been discharged for over one hundred years into Amur Bay. As a result, the bay is polluted and swimming is unsafe. To solve this problem there is a need to build wastewater treatment facilities and to control their operations. Unfortunately, economic and political chaos has slowed down such activity. The environmentally oriented world community is greatly concerned about the dumping of liquid radioactive waste from nuclear power plants into the seas. A new facility should be built to clean up such waste. One inadequate facility exists in Bolshoi Kamen.

AMUR RIVER CHARACTERISTICS AND CHALLENGES

The Amur River is among the ten largest in the world, with the following characteristics: length of 4,444 kilometers, annual runoff of 350 cubic kilometers, delta runoff of 10,900 cubic meters per second, and a runoff area of 10,900 square kilometers. A 10,000-kilometer stretch serves as the border between China and Russia, with the source of the Amur River lying in Mongolia. A main characteristic of the Amur River is biodiversity. In the northern hemisphere it is second to only the Mississippi River in this respect. The Amur has over 100 fish species, with two-thirds of them being food fish. There are relic species in the river, since its watershed was formed in ancient times. The watershed was not affected by ice during the glacial period, which led to the preservation of species.

With respect to the ichthyological diversity in Russia, the Amur is comparable to Lake Baikal. The Amur sturgeon is well known for its large size and weight of over one ton. It is similar to white sturgeon in the Volga River and American white sturgeon in the Columbia River. There are specific features of the Amur River, particularly the international aspects involving a number of disputes over the border despite treaties that date back one and one-half centuries. Problems also arise concerning engineering structures, fish catches, environmental monitoring, and industrial and municipal waste discharges.

In the judgment of specialists, poaching has been the main problem with regard to disappearing fish resources. Poaching now exceeds legal fishing, with 1,500 tons of Siberian fall salmon taken legally in 1997 but 10,000 tons taken illegally. In Khabarovsk, endangered species are sold openly while enforcement measures are ineffective. Poaching is growing due to unemployment, and the situation cannot be returned to normal without solving the social problems. Legislation seems incomplete and even ridiculous. For example, selling of all types of fish nets is authorized despite a ban on the use of certain types of nets. In practice the poachers are allowed to sell their catch. At the same time sport fishing is growing, and it too is not controlled. The public needs to take a more active stand on poaching. In the United States an organization in Oregon, the Wild Salmon Centre, provides an example of effective activity to protect rare fish species. They are involved not only in the United States, but also in the Russian Far East. The Amur River also faces the "phenol" smell problem. This permeates the fish and prevents the sale of fish. It is similar to the smell of the chemical phenol. The first response of the public was that it was linked to industrial spills. However, tests and investigations showed that the problem was more complex. Most of the course of the river is fed by marsh runoff saturated with organic substances of vegetative origin. As a result of the biochemical interactions with the flora and fauna of the river, xenobiotics are released and penetrate the fish through respiratory and trophic channels.

Although the origin of this problem is mainly nature, anthropogenic discharges, particularly waste dumps, can trigger the process. Also, man-caused discharges into the river may create additional toxic xenobiotics, and efforts to reduce discharges should not slacken. At present the problem cannot be immediately solved, but investigations can provide information about the timing and places of the problem. Specialists of the Khabarovsk Research Centre have been of considerable assistance in addressing this problem. As for public environmental organizations, they have not been helpful. Initially they simply cast blame on those directly involved in industrial production and on the authorities. Then they relied on scientists who were not competent to investigate the problem.

FOREST FIRES

The Far East region has considerable timber resources. They are of great importance in the formation of the planet's atmosphere. Woods are concentrated primarily in the southern areas, i.e., in Khabarovsk and Primorye Territories and in Amur and Sakhalin Oblasts. Severe fires occur there on the average of once every 22 years, with the last spate of large fires in 1998. The periodicity is apparently related to cyclic arid conditions and to the build-up of combustible material during the periods between fires. Also, in the eastern areas of the region there are frequent fires. Overall, probably 85 percent of the fires of the region are triggered by human activities. The 1998 fires occurred in the spring and lasted six months. Over 2.5 million hectares burned completely, although the fire area was much larger. Each burned hectare released 100 tons of particulate containing 55 percent tar and water, 25 percent soot, and 20 percent ash. These particles are harmful when inhaled by humans or animals. In addition, 10 to 12 tons of nitrogen, sulfur, and carbon oxides were discharged, including oxides with toxic effects. In sum, the fires resulted in the discharge of 250 million tons of particulates and 25 million tons of harmful gases with widespread impacts. For example, in Khabarovsk, located 200 kilometers from the fires, cars used headlights during the day. Pollution lasted for a few months and increased death rates. The impact on newborn children was particularly harmful. The UN Council on Humanitarian Issues reported that the fires had caused a large-scale problem of international concern. Fires have many negative impacts. They destroy animal habitats. They change the flora composition of the forests. They change the insect population and may cause sudden outbreaks of some species. Runoff may pollute reservoir. And of course fires hamper reforestation efforts.

Prevention and elimination of forest fires should be of a comprehensive character including legislative, administrative, environmental protection, educational, and social programs. One factor responsible for the extent of the fires is the lack of agreement between the federal government and entities in the territories with regard to forests. Forests are federal property with regard to timber exploitation areas and timber sales. However, forest protection, fire fighting, and reduction of the consequences of fires are under the authority of the region. Unfortunately, lengthy discussions on these topics between the federal and Khabarovsk authorities in 1998 were largely a waste of time as the fires ignited.

RADIATION SITUATION

In the region there are a few sources of possible radioactive contamination-natural, household, industrial, military, energy supply facilities, and radioactive waste storage facilities. Natural sources are associated with specific geological structures that give off radon that results in the background levels. In Khabarovsk, the background from radon is 20 percent higher than the average for Russia. Particularly high background is associated with rocks containing uranium and thorium, with the levels dependent on porosity. Surveys indicate that 15 percent of city apartments using local building materials are moderately hazardous, 10 percent are hazardous, and 2 percent are particularly hazardous. Other sources include radioisotopes used for research, production, and medical purposes and for standard measurements. Fifteen years ago, such sources in the Far East were in the tens of thousands, with 13,000 in Khabarovsk alone. The number has declined greatly due to curtailment of production and related activities. For example, in Khabarovsk the number has decreased by a factor of 22. Therefore, associated risks of contamination have also declined. In the meantime, however, there has been an increase in problems associated with waste disposal of radioactive sources. Quite often the sources are simply thrown out with ordinary waste rather than being delivered to appropriate waste storage sites.

Industrial sources include manufacturing and maintenance activities for nuclear submarines at Komsomolsk-on-Amur and Bolshoi Kamen. At present, production facilities at the former are closed, and decommissioned submarines are being dismantled at the latter. Also, at Bolshoi Kamen a plant for liquid radioactive waste processing is under construction. The state enterprise Radon has a storage facility for solid radioactive waste not far from Khabarovsk. It stores mainly household radiation sources from the entire Far East region. Neither the authorities nor environmentalists are concerned with the condition at the facility. The Bilibino nuclear power plant in Chukotka operates normally, according to the press. Additional military sources of radiation relate both to nuclear weapons and to the nuclear power units of submarines, but little information is available on relevant activities.

ENVIRONMENTALLY ORIENTED NGOS

There are many environmentally oriented NGOs, totaling a few hundred in the Far East region and over 50 in Khabarovsk alone. However, it is difficult to describe their activities as effective, meaningful, or discernible. NGOs may be divided into four groups: (1) opponents of the policies of the government, (2) "prisoners of conscience," (3) educational organizations, and (4) promoters of new technologies. The first group uses existing environmental problems as a basis for opposing the government. They appeared in large numbers in the mid-1980s, when environment was considered an area in which citizens could openly disagree with the state authorities. Many opponents intent on resolving political problems became involved in environmental activities. The opposition was of a radical character.

Subsequently, when they had other opportunities to become involved openly in political activities, they left the environmental movement. Also, as soon as some of them gained power, they changed their stand toward environmental problems. Thus, in the early 1990s deputies of the Primorye Territory Duma, who were members of NGOs, and other environmentalists opposed even conducting a feasibility study for the proposed construction of a nuclear power plant in the region, yet today they support such a project in view of the power crisis. Those who continue to join NGOs rely on the NGOs primarily as a channel for obtaining grants and fluids from other sources. The second group of NGOs, the "prisoners of conscience," represent organizations that unite people who are concerned over a safe environment and work for its improvement. The public Committee on the Protection of the Amur in Khabarovsk is such an NGO. However, despite their noble objectives and motivations, they lack the persistence and assertiveness characteristic of the first group. Often their activities are simply complaints in the press or emotional statements to limited audiences. These organizations need assistance from the local authorities and from the community. The third group includes organizations oriented to educational activities and advocacy of environmental protection and preservation, particularly among high school students and other young people. This is the most important trend, since it involves the education of a new generation of people and the future communities. The activities of these NGOs should be linked to work in youth and children's organizations including both the universities and the schools. But they also need the support of the authorities at all levels. The fourth group of NGOs unites efforts of workers involved in production activities who try to promote the integration of "soft" or environmentally friendly technologies into existing production processes. Though the first three groups actually exist, the fourth group is still largely a dream that is urgently needed in reality. The solution of environmental problems should be considered within the framework of sustainable development of entire communities and the whole nation. Sustainable development implies the integration of social and environmental problems. Indeed, over the past ten years social conditions of the population, particularly indigenous populations, have become worse. It is difficult to convince people not to set fires in the taiga area or to stop poaching rare fish.

In a society there should be moral and psychological relationships between individuals and the environment. Unfortunately in Russia, during the period of economic reform-a period of wild capitalism-different approaches were in vogue aimed at generating material goods for individuals. Those shifty and energetic people who made a great deal of money felt indifferent to the needs of society and the environment. A substantial disparity in property status has made Russian society very unstable. Over the past decade, a young generation has grown up focused on solving their own financial problems with no glances at the surrounding world. To improve the situation the scientific community, first of all the Academy of Sciences and environmental NGOs, should be actively involved.

4

'Participatory Management' for NGOs

The NGO management debate has attempted to address the question: what style of management is appropriate for NGOs? In so doing, the debate is valuable. However, given that participation in decision-making is a feature of governmental and commercial organisations, the association of a participatory style of management with a distinctive approach to NGO management is unhelpful. It is more useful to examine the advantages of participation to organisations generally, and to NGOs in particular, and then identify those factors in the NGO context which make a participatory approach more appropriate for them.

There are a number of perspectives on the increasing interest in participation in the commercial sector. Guest and Knight (1979) argue that it represents part of the search for... a new means of overcoming industrial and economic problems, changing market conditions internationally, rising expectations of the workforce, and interest in the concept of industrial democracy. The emphasis on changing environmental conditions is taken up by Lawler (1986: 19) who insists that 'the societal, business, product, and work force changes that have occurred argue strongly for a change in management style', and who believes that 'in most situations some form of participative management is the best answer' (Lawler, 1986: 11). At the same time, Wall and Lischeron (1977: 1) point out that in contemporary society 'participation, in one form or another, is seen as one means of improving the quality of working life'.

However, the increased interest in participation cannot simply be seen as stemming from changed contextual factors and a desire for greater work humanisation. An instrumental view of participation-that greater participation will lead to greater efficiency, and consequently greater profits-is fundamental in the commercial sector (Beardwell and Holden, 1994), and is particularly reflected in the 'hard', rather than the 'soft' approach to Human Resource Management (Storey, 1987).

That participation is linked to improved performance is evident from Ouchi (1981) who states: Decision-making by consensus has been the subject of a great deal of research in Europe and the United States over the past twenty years, and the evidence strongly suggests that a consensus approach yields more creative decisions and more effective implementation than does individual decision-making. Moreover, the participation of staff is inextricably linked with the concept of 'learning organisations'.

Senge (1990: 3), for example, argues that 'the organisations that will truly excel in the future will be the organisations that discover how to tap people's commitment and capacity to learn at all levels of an organisation'. 'Participatory management' and 'participatory development' As noted earlier, several authors argue that a participatory approach to management is particularly suitable for NGOs whose work involves the promotion of participation and the empowerment of beneficiaries. Chambers (1983: 210), for example, insists that such a management style is more in keeping with 'bottom-up development' or a participatory development approach. NGOs require a 'new professionalism' based on fundamental 'reversals' in the values, attitudes and behaviour of NGO staff, so that the people whom the NGO aims to support are truly empowered. Carroll's (1992: 205) study of NGOs in Latin America demonstrates that an open, collegial management style builds confidence and trust among beneficiaries and support organisations, and is, therefore, a key organisational quality for promoting popular participation. Similarly, the British Overseas Development Administration points out that 'culture, management structure, goals and sources of funding, all influence the manner and extent to which an aid agency can enhance the participation of other stakeholders' (Eyben, 1994: 4.3). Indeed, Roche (1992: 188) argues:

Experience suggests that a decentralised structure with semiautonomous, self-managed federated units, coupled with information and cooperative learning, is perhaps the most appropriate organisational design for supporting micro-development. A second theme that emerges in the literature is that NGOs need to develop decentralised and participatory decision-making structures, and adopt a problemsolving rather than a predictive blue-print approach to management, to ensure flexibility and maintain the ability to adapt to constantly changing realities.

In particular, participatory planning processes are important as it is the field staff who normally have closest contact with beneficiaries (Sahley, 1995).

This 'effectiveness' argument is also taken up, for example, by Brodhead and Herbert-Copley (1988), who suggest that NGOs must adopt a participatory approach in order to have wider impact.

A third theme which emerges is the expectations of NGO staff. Clark (1991: 61), for example, states that: NGO staff are generally highly committed to their work because of widely shared values and a belief in the social change mission inherent in their work. This generates a sense of ownership which, when combined with the widespread expectation that organisations promoting democracy and participation should themselves be democratic, means that 'an autocratic style simply wouldn't work: the staff require participation'.

Moreover, Hodson (1992: 135) argues that as NGOs grow 'decentralised and consensual forms of decision-making' are of particular importance 'if decisions are to be seen by staff as legitimate'. In addition, there is an assumption that respect for workers leads to improved organisational functioning. Clark, (1991: 62), for example, suggests: Naturally an organisation of principled and committed workers will function best if staff feel respected, and listened to.

The 'NGO management debate' cannot be easily resolved. In particular, a number of questions about the appropriateness of a participatory style of management for NGOs remain unanswered. Moreover, the debate about the appropriateness of 'participatory management' is constrained by a degree of definitional ambiguity which needs to be addressed.

A Case Study of Concern Mozambique

The aim of the case study is to explore the reasons why CONCERN Mozambique is seeking to adopt a more participatory style of management and to outline the proposals which emerged about the direction such change might take. The process of change in CONCERN Mozambique is underpinned by a number of assumptions made by management staff about the importance of participation, and its role in the management of an organisation committed to promoting participatory development. These are as follows:

A 'Natural' Approach for Participatory Development?

In the first place, the consensus among interviewees is that CONCERN's commitment to participatory development necessitates a participatory style of management. Such a management style is considered, for example, to be 'a natural approach', given that the organisation is committed to promoting participation in its development programmes. As one Programme Manager stated: You cannot do participatory development without participatory management.

In particular, it was noted that an organisation must practise what it preaches, and that since CONCERN Worldwide is promoting participation of the beneficiaries, the participation of staff is therefore essential. As another Programme Manager remarked: One can't expect staff to mobilise, animate and facilitate interest groups to analyse their own problems and set their own objectives if the organisation does not have a similar empowering approach with staff.

Programme Responsiveness

Secondly, there is among programme management a widespread belief that greater participation of staff, and particularly field-workers, in the management of the organisation will result in improved programme responsiveness.

This view is reflected in the 'CONCERN Mozambique Policy Framework' (1995) which states: As an agency that targets the poorest we need a management style that is flexible and responsive to the needs of the poor. A participatory management style enables those staff who are closest to the poor, those at project operational level, to guide the organisation in its programme design and implementation to allow the needs of the poor to be identified and met.

Furthermore, the interviews with the Country Director reveal a fundamental belief that staff at project level are in the best position to make decisions for that project. This view is echoed by one interviewee who remarked: We get reality in decisions... if people further down the line are involved in the decision-making.

Staff Empowerment

At the same time, the general view is that 'participatory management' is not just about involving staff, but about 'empowering' them, and creating 'voice'. As the Country Director remarked: CONCERN is here to deliver a service. The most important people in that service delivery are the field workers (they are the most important people in the organisation in many ways). Space has to be made for those people to have a voice in the organisation. While most programme management staff spoke about 'participatory management' resulting in improved decision-making and ownership of decisions, a number of Programme Managers also suggested that 'participatory management' is an appropriate management style given that CONCERN Mozambique is committed to building up local staff capacity, and in particular, to creating the conditions necessary for sustainable development.

Better 'Downward' Accountability

'Participatory management' is also seen as enhancing 'downward accountability'. This is evident from the 'CONCERN Mozambique Policy Framework' (1995) which incorporates the idea, originally suggested by CONCERN Worldwide's Southern Africa Division (correspondence, September 1995), that teams and teamwork at management and project level will 'avoid the emergence of a tall hierarchical structure between the target group and field management' and, more especially, will 'ensure that field resources are not diverted away from the poorest'.

Promoting Democracy

Finally, while Programme Managers, in general, see 'participatory management' in terms of its having a crucial role in improving organisational effectiveness, the wider implications of adopting a participatory style of management were noted by one Programme Manager who commented on the importance, in a fledgling democracy, as Mozambique is, of promoting democracy within the workplace. In summary, the case study suggests that while a number of different reasons may be identified, they are all related to the ultimate aim of improved development practice, and in particular, are inspired by a fundamental commitment to participatory development.

Improved Development Practice

Participatory management is seen therefore not as an end in itself, but as means of reaching organisational goals more effectively. As one senior staff member commented: The only reason we have participatory management is to facilitate our development approach. It is not for its own sake. The study revealed the crucial role of leadership. It is clear that, on a practical level, CONCERN Mozambique has initiated this process of institutional change because the Country Director strongly believes in the importance of such an approach, and more significantly, has acted on that belief by taking advantage of a number of opportunities which have enabled the process to take place.

The most important of these has been the support for the initiative from CONCERN Southern Africa Division, including its willingness to allow the budget flexibility necessary for the development of the new systems. At the same time, according to the Country Director, that this belief is shared by the Programme Managers and key national staff has also been crucial, as has their willingness to accept the new responsibilities that a participatory style of management involves.

The case study indicates, in the first place, that management staff in CONCERN Mozambique clearly see 'participatory management' not as a collection of tools and techniques, but as a fundamental approach to management.

At the same time, it is understood as something which must be created, or allowed to evolve, over time: as one Programme Manager pointed out, it is essentially a process of 'introducing things bit by bit'. Secondly, though the possibility of including other stakeholders had been briefly discussed, the general understanding among CONCERN programme management staff is that 'participatory management' is, for the time being at least, only about the greater involvement of staff members, and in particular field staff, in decision-making.

It is therefore perceived as overlapping with, but distinct from, CONCERN Mozambique's commitment to 'participatory development', which pledges it to securing 'the participation of interested parties in all stages of the programming process-government, team, target groups, informal structures etc.' At the same time, 'participatory management' is not seen as representing in any way a rejection, or diminution, of standards of professionalism and accountability. There have been no changes to the financial or administrative systems, nor are any intended, and auditing and input control remain crucial. Indeed, at a meeting of senior programme staff with the Southern Africa Regional Director in March 1995 it was agreed that 'by ensuring that tasks are better defined, such control mechanisms can be enhanced by participatory objective-led planning'.

These changes also require a firm hand. 'Participatory management' is not about the adoption of an unstructured, 'laissez-faire' style of management. On the contrary, it is seen (though not always positively) as quite procedural, and very structured. As the Country Director remarked:

Participatory management is not less structured; it is more structured if anything. It's quite prescribed, but people are involved in the prescription. Finally, 'participatory management' is linked to a 'reversal' in the way in which the organisation is conceptualised and represented. In the first place, it is informed by an understanding of the organisation as directly related to, and in service of, the beneficiaries (who are conceived of as 'clients'). In addition, it is underpinned by a view of the NGO as a 'bottom-up' organisation in which the most important members are those closest to the clients. The present CONCERN Mozambique organogram, which is based on the concept of an 'inverted triangle', reflects these views.

The study also reveals that there is a crucial link between the adoption of a more participatory style of management and institutional change. Indeed, as one Programme Manager remarked: A participatory approach to development requires changes at all levels of the organisation.

The resulting programme proposals CONCERN Mozambique's commitment to such change is evident in the five programme proposals, each of which states: CONCERN Mozambique is going through a process of institutional change aimed at creating a management style that is conducive to the type of community development programme being proposed here. These changes commenced in 1994 and are still ongoing, are structural and cultural in nature, and have taken several forms.

A 'Flatter' Organisation

'Participatory management' is clearly identified with the creation of a 'flatter' or more 'horizontal' form of management, and the reduction in the layers of authority between senior management and field-workers. This facilitates speedier and more participatory decision-making, and is assumed to increase programme responsiveness. Additionally, it narrows the gap between the organisation's target group and senior management.

Team Structures

Secondly, the study reveals that the adoption of a team approach, both at project and country levels, is central to the style of management adopted by CONCERN Mozambique. A project team (referred to as a 'General Assembly') has been formed in each of the five programme areas, and is the most important aspect of the new structure at project level. Comprising all staff directly involved in project activities, it meets every three months.

Its responsibilities include the design of work plans using the ZOPP methodology, the evaluation and re-design of existing methodologies, and the evaluation of the management team. Furthermore, two new fora have been established at country level, and meet annually: a 'Wider Group', which is concerned with national policy and strategy, and a 'Steering Committee', which is responsible for ensuring that policy is implemented.

Other Changes

The study also reveals that adoption of a more participatory style of management is not just about changing organisational structures. It is also clearly seen to involve the creation of an environment in which dialogue, communication, and particularly organisational learning, are facilitated and encouraged. The establishment of the staff magazine, in June 1995, is an important development in this regard. Furthermore, the conducting of an evaluation, by the staff in early 1996, of CONCERN Mozambique's strengths and weaknesses during the previous year, and the publication of the results in the staff magazine, reflect the link between 'participatory management' and a commitment to the development of a culture of openness.

Levels of Participation

The study confirms that, in CONCERN Mozambique, staff are now more involved in both project and country management. This parallels 'participative management' practices at 'shop-floor' and 'plant' levels (Guest and Knight, 1979). Moreover, the involvement of employees at country management level, in decisions that relate to the entire country programme rather than just projects, illustrates that the participation of staff in CONCERN Mozambique is, to use Strauss and Rosenstein's (1970) framework, both 'immediate' and 'distant'. At the same time, however, the adoption of a participatory style of management does not, for the time being at least, imply the participation of non-management staff in decision-making at levels higher than the Mozambique country programme.

Secondly, the study reveals that the participation of staff in the design of work is perceived by senior staff as central to 'participatory management'. In this regard, the ZOPP methodology, introduced in 1995, is crucial. As the Country Director remarked:

ZOPP is at the core of participatory management: it gives staff a language, puts people on an equal footing, and gives people the confidence and the skills to sit with their boss and argue.

At the same time, 'participatory management' is understood to involve more that just the design of work. Four of the eleven field-workers surveyed, for instance, mentioned their involvement in deciding the responsibilities, tasks and procedures of the project team as an example of the way in which they are now more involved in decisionmaking. Indeed, staff are increasingly invited to participate in decisions about work conditions (for example, staff salaries and benefits) as well as in decisions about administrative issues (such as staff appraisal, staff selection, and transport policy).

The study also reveals that there are different degrees or 'intensities' of participation within CONCERN Mozambique, and suggests that 'participatory management' is more than just improved information-sharing and greater consultation of staff. More authority has been delegated than previously, and indeed, there has been, and continues to be, a transfer of power. However, the degree to which this takes place varies according to situational factors, and more particularly, occurs within carefully defined parameters. The study also suggests that the intensity of participation depends not only on the level of the decision-making, but on the nature of the decision. The decision-making power of the Steering Committee is a good example: Moreover, when looking at areas of decision-making not related to the design of work, there has, to date, been more in terms of consultation than delegation. This is indicated by the results of the focus group discussion with the national staff of the Maputo office, during which staff were asked to identify recent decisions made and staff participation in them.

NGO PERSPECTIVES ON THEIR PARTICIPATION

The cleavages observed previously in the opening section of this chapter regarding the claimed roles for NGOs in the political process are also present in this section. A first element has to do with the origin and political meaning of the participation of NGOs in PLANAFLORO. Excluding the respondents for FETAGRO and KANINDÉ, all remaining interviewees believed that the official participation of NGOs in the internal decision-making bodies of PLANAFLORO represented an unequivocal victory for the NGO movement in Rondônia. In addition, there was also generalized belief that such inclusion was a result of the organized efforts of local and transnational NGOs, and not simply a concession by either the World Bank nor the State government. A different perspective was offered by members of FETAGRO's Board of Directors. According to both Walmir de Jesus and Vandeir Pereira, the participation of MSOs and GSOs should be characterized more accurately as a maneuver by the World Bank to enhance the legitimacy of its economic programs rather than as a real willingness to democratize the implementation of PLANAFLORO. This evaluation was accompanied by a belief that PLANAFLORO had little to offer their grassroots within the scope of the program.

Nonetheless, despite these distinct interpretations concerning the origins and efficacy of NGO participation, respondents were unanimous in their view that their organization involvement represented a hedge against the repetition of the key problems faced by POLONOROESTE.

Among those concerns to be avoided in their involvement in PLANAFLORO respondents listed: the top-down technocratic approach utilized to implement the program, the waste of funds through either corruption or poor planning, and the disregard for the social and environmental impacts created by the program's implementation.

This concern to avoid repeating the mistakes of POLONOROESTE in PLANAFLORO was clearly evidenced in the list of roles claimed by MSOs and GSOs in the process. The objectives displayed by NGO respondents can be split into political (i.e., increased accountability, to "watch-dog" against corruption, and defend the interests of specific social groups) and technical (i.e., influence the technical aspects of the program, and participate in the direct implementation of components) categories. The combination of these claims reflects a FORUM-wide desire to dispel popular perception of the possible hegemony of governmental agencies in the implementation of PLANAFLORO. In most cases, respondents indicated that State hegemony in PLANAFLORO could be kept in check through a combination of internal (e.g., participation in the CD and CNPs, meetings with the World Bank missions) and external pressures (e.g., press releases to the local and national media, networking with national and transnational NGOs) on both the State and on the World Bank's management.

Among the MSOs, respondents for FETAGRO and OSR shared similar overall goals towards their participation in PLANAFLORO. Respondents for both organizations suggested that they had entered the process to conduct a strong that their basic objective had been to defend the interests of Indian communities.

The answers provided by the GSO respondents indicated that these organizations defined more narrowly their roles in PLANAFLORO. In most cases, these interviewees of their role was restricted to trying to influence the implementation of specific components of the program and to increase its social accountability; especially the need to preclude the occurrence of corruption.

A clear source of tension among the GSOs participating in PLANAFLORO was related to their participation in the direct implementation of PLANAFLORO projects. The majority of respondents (i.e., CIMI, CPT, ECOPORÉ, KANINDÉ) shunned any direct involvement, fearing the potential loss of political autonomy that could undermine their political legitimacy.

However, respondents for INDIA, IPHAE and PACA indicated that their direct involvement in the execution of the program was not only ethically correct, but that it would also reinforce the political legitimacy of other NGOs participating in PLANAFLORO. As a concrete development of the view that the participation of NGOs in the direct execution of PLANAFLORO was legitimate, members of INDIA, IPHAE and PACA were already providing services to different State agencies, implementing specific components of PLANAFLORO.

NGO PARTICIPATION STRATEGIES

The Terms of Understanding for PLANAFLORO established that the composition of Deliberative Council (CD) and Technical Commissions (CNPs) bodies would be based on equal levels of representation for both governmental and non-governmental organizations. The operation of all PLANAFLORO's governing organs begun to operate in June, 1992.

The Local Approach and its Perceived Limited Efficacy

Most NGO representatives were dissatisfied with the results of their participation in the CD and CNPs. A first line of criticism was directed to former governor Oswaldo Piana and his administration whom NGOs representatives unanimously believed was not sincerely interested in allowing a real functioning of the bodies created jointly to run PLANAFLORO. In addition to what was perceived as a lack of political willingness by the Piana administration to implement the agreement, the respondents observed that functioning of the CD and the CNPs also had been plagued by repeated occurrence of administrative problems and that they lacked real decision-making power in the program's implementation.

Among other facts cited was that the allocation of program funds usually did not follow the decisions taken by either the Deliberative Council or the CNPs, and that decisions were instead taken based on the Piana administration's political priorities.

This perception was further enhanced by the decision of governor Raupp to remove the financial management of PLANAFLORO from the "*Secretaria do PLANAFLORO*" (SEPLANAFLORO) — the Secretary of PLANAFLORO— to the "*Secretaria de Planejamento*" (SEPLAN) — the Planning Secretary. Because of this institutional arrangement, SEPLAN had the final decision on the allocation of funds, despite not having direct participation in the program's technical preparation. Moreover, clear animosity was displayed by most governmental technicians towards the NGO representatives who tended to respond in the same fashion. According to Iremar Ferreira (representative of CIMI) this dysfunctional environment caused most meetings held in 1992 and 1993 to become very polarized and, as a result, agreements between the two different sides were rare.

The NGOs' Internal Weaknesses

A second line of criticisms, however, is directed towards the FORUM's NGOs themselves. A first factor addressed by most respondents was that NGOs were not institutionally prepared to participate in the process (i.e., NGOs lacked infrastructure, personnel and technical expertise). Most respondents repeatedly pointed out that, because of their faulty institutional capacity, NGOs failed fully to utilize spaces which had been created for them in the program and that their technical contribution often was of a poor quality when it occurred.

My content analysis of the minutes prepared by the CNPs of Agrarian and Indian Issues regarding the participation of representatives of governmental agencies and NGOs tend to corroborate these evaluations. In the CNP of Agriculture the participation of NGOs was only effective in 1992 and 1993, and they faced even greater difficulties to participate effectively in the Indian CNP.

Moreover, the minutes for both CNPs indicate that discussions were centered on the approval of POAs. Several NGO leaders suggested that predominance of POAs in CNPs' activities had two major drawbacks. First, NGOs did not have any control of the POAs' design which was entirely done by the governmental agencies. Second, according to Iremar Ferreira (representative of CIMI in the Indian CNP), the technical preparation of POAs by governmental agencies was always behind schedule. As a result, there was very little time for a critical analysis of its contents by NGO representatives. According to Iremar Ferreira of CIMI, NGO representatives often felt compelled to approve the closed packet presented by the governmental agencies because otherwise they would risk blame for the lack of implementation.

Meanwhile, Mara Carneiro indicated that NGOs also made tactical mistakes, especially in the selection of the CNPs in which they should participate more intensively. For example, while most NGOs had selected representatives for the CNPs of Environment and Agriculture, the CNP of Infrastructure was left with a robust majority of governmental agencies in which IPHAE was basically the sole participating NGO.

According to Carneiro, it was a clear mistake given that the bulk of the funds spent during the initial three years of PLANAFLORO were heavily concentrated in POAs prepared by the CNP of Infrastructure. Finally, Iremar Ferreira (CIMI's representative) suggested that the intensive workload imposed by participation in the program's governing organs had caused negative impacts on his organization's ability to continue its work at the grassroots level. Similar concerns were expressed by respondents linked to the three MSOs (i.e., FETAGRO, 0SR, and CUNPIR).

NGOS: ADVANTAGES AND DISADVANTAGES

Advantages

- They have the ability to experiment freely with innovative approaches and, if necessary, to take risks.
- They are flexible in adapting to local situations and responding to local needs and therefore able to develop integrated projects, as well as sectoral projects.
- They enjoy good rapport with people and can render micro-assistance to very poor people as they can identify those who are most in need and tailor assistance to their needs.
- They have the ability to communicate at all levels, from the neighbourhood to the top levels of government.
- They are able to recruit both experts and highly motivated staff with fewer restrictions than the government.

Disadvantages

- Paternalistic attitudes restrict the degree of participation in programme/ project design. Restricted/constrained ways of approach to a problem or area.
- Reduced replicability of an idea, due to non-representativeness of the project or selected area, relatively small project coverage, dependence on outside financial resources, etc.
- "Territorial possessiveness" of an area or project reduces cooperation between agencies, seen as threatening or competitive.

Components that Change as an Organization Gets Stronger

Capacity building includes empowerment and strengthening in various dimensions. Here are sixteen elements of an organization that change as it gets stronger.

Altruism

The proportion of, and degree to which, individuals are ready to sacrifice benefits to themselves for the benefit of the organization as a whole—reflected in degrees of generosity, individual humility, communal pride, mutual supportiveness, loyalty, concern, camaraderie, sister/brotherhood. As an organization develops more altruism. It develops more capacity—where individuals, families or factions are allowed to be greedy and selfish at the expense of the organization, this weakens the organization.

Values

The degree to which members of the organization share values, especially the idea that they belong to a common entity that supersedes the interest of members within it. The more that an organizations members share, or at least understand and tolerate, each others values and attitudes, the stronger their organization will be. Racism, prejudice and bigotry weaken a community or organization.

Services

An organizations facilities and services: office space, equipment, washrooms, tools, supplies, access to toilets and other personal staff facilities, working facilities, physical plant, potable water; their upkeep: dependable maintenance and repair; sustainability, and the degree to which all the organizations members have access to them. The more that members have access to needed communal or group facilities, the greater their capacity, the greater the capacity of the organization.

Communications

Within an organization, and between itself and outside, communication includes speaking, electronic methods—for e.g. telephone, radio, TV, Internet, printed media such as newspapers, magazines, books, networks, mutually understandable languages, literacy and the willingness and ability to communicate—which implies tact, diplomacy, willingness to listen as well as to talk in general. As a organization gets better communication, it gets stronger-with communication equipment, methods and practices available to staff. Poor communication means a weak organization.

Confidence

While expressed in individuals, how much confidence is shared among the organization as a whole? For example, an understanding that the organization can achieve what ever it wishes to do. Positive attitudes, willingness, self motivation, enthusiasm, optimism, self-reliant rather than dependency attitudes, willingness to fight for its rights, avoidance of apathy and fatalism, a vision of what is possible. Increased strength includes increased confidence.

Context

An organization will be stronger, more able to get stronger and sustain its strength more, the more it exists in an environment that supports that strengthening. This environment includes political, including the values and attitudes of the leaders, laws and legislation and administrative, including attitudes of civil servants and technicians, as well as Governmental regulations and procedures elements. When politicians, leaders, technocrats and civil servants, as well as their laws and regulations, take a patronizing approach, the organization is weak, while if they take an enabling approach to the organization acting on a self-managed basis, the organization will be stronger.

Information

More than just having or receiving unprocessed information, the strength of the organization depends upon the ability to process and analyse that information, the level of awareness, knowledge and wisdom found among key individuals and within the group as a whole. When information is more effective and more useful, not just more in volume, the organization will have more strength. Note that this is related to, but differs from the communication element listed above.

Intervention

Leadership: Leaders have power, influence, and the ability to move the organization. The more effective its leadership, the more stronger is an organization. The most effective and sustainable leadership—for strengthening the organization, not just strengthening the leaders—is one that operates so as to follow the decisions and desires of the organization as a whole, to take an enabling and facilitating role. Leaders must possess skills, willingness, and some charisma. The more effective the leadership, the more capacity has the organization. Lack of good leadership weakens it.

Networking

It is not just *what you know* but also *who you know* that can be a source of strength. As is often joked not only *know-how * but also *know-who* gets jobs. What is the extent to which the organizations members, especially leaders, know persons—and their agencies or organizations-who call provide useful resources that will strengthen the organization as a whole? The useful linkages, potential and realized, that exist within the organization and with others outside it. The more effective the network, the stronger the community. Isolation produces weakness.

Organization

The degree to which different members of the organization see themselves as each having a role in supporting the whole—in contrast to being a mere collection of separate individuals, including in the sociological sense—organizational integrity, structure, procedures, decision making processes, effectiveness, division of labour and complimentarity of roles and functions. The more organized, or the more effectively organized, an organization is the more capacity or strength it has.

Power

The degree to which the organization can participate in national and district decision making. Just as individuals have varying power within an organization, so organizations have varying power and influence within the district and nation. The more political power and influence that an organization can exercise, the higher level of capacity it has.

Skills

The ability, manifested in individuals, that will contribute to the organization and the ability of it to get things done that it wants to get done, technical skills, management skills, organizational skills, mobilization skills. The more skills—group or individual—that an organization can obtain and use, the more empowered is that organization.

Trust

The degree to which members of the organization trust each other, especially their leaders, which in turn is a reflection of the degree of integrity—honesty, dependability, openness, transparency, trust-worthiness-within the organization.

More trust and dependability within an organization reflects its increased capacity. Dishonesty, corruption, embezzlement and diversion of organizational resources all contribute to organizational weakness.

Unity

Unity means a shared sense of belonging to a known entity i.e. the group composing the organization. Although every organization has divisions or schisms—religious, class, status, income, age, gender, ethnicity, clans—the degree to which its members are willing to tolerate the differences and variations among each other and are willing to cooperate and work together, a sense of a common purpose or vision, shared values.

When an organization is more unified, it is stronger. Unity does not mean that everyone is the same, but that everyone tolerates, even celebrates, each others differences, and works for the common good.

Wealth

The degree to which the organization as a whole, in contrast to individuals within it, has control over actual and potential resources, and the production and distribution of scarce and useful goods and services, monetary and non monetary, including labour, land, equipment, supplies, knowledge, skills.

The more wealthy an organization, the stronger it is. When greedy individuals, families or factions accrue wealth at the expense of the organization as a whole, that weakens the organization.

5

Role of NGOs in the Chemical Disarmament Process

INTRODUCTION

Russian Green Cross is a part of an international association, organized in accordance with a decision of the UN Conference on Environment and Development which took place in Rio de Janeiro, Brazil, in 1992. Participants of the Conference representing governments and parliaments of 156 countries from all over the world decided to organize a global world organization as an ecological analogue of the Red Cross.

The organization, named "Green Cross," was to be concerned about the problems of global ecological catastrophes. The former President of the Soviet Union, Mikhail Gorbachev, was invited to be a founder and the first president. Inauguration of the International Green Cross took place in Kyoto in 1993. National organizations participated. At first, three national organizations were founded in Japan and then in Russia and the United States. The U.S. organization is not named Green Cross as are the others, but Global Green. In America somebody else already used the name Green Cross. Together with Academician Nikita Nikolaevich Moiseev, the most noted ecologist of the country, we established the Russian Green Cross (RGC).

RGC is registered with the Ministry of Justice. Its principal activity is protection of the environment. "Collaboration, not confrontation" is the main motto of both the International Green Cross and our organization. It is a basic principle. We try to solve all ecological problems using this principle. As a rule, all problems cause contradictions. Disputes between authorities and inhabitants come either from an ecological problem or from one with ecological roots affecting the environment and public health.

The general program of RGC is "Ecological Education." It deals with ecological training and organization of different ecological studies beginning in the first years of childhood. The program includes international exchanges among pupils, students, professors; workshops and training for teachers; and an annual international conference "Ecological Education." Public hearings on ecological problems of disarmament and elimination of arms also take place. "The Cold War Heritage" is another program. RGC deals with ecological problems of nuclear weapons, chemical weapons, and conventional armaments. It studies the impact of mass production of armaments, their storage and testing on the environment, and public health. All armaments produced during the arms race to some extent have influenced and still influence the environment. Unfortunately, they will influence it further. They cause many ecological problems that need resolution. Our authorities are not ready to resolve them now. Only nongovernmental organizations try to resolve the issues.

More than one thousand nongovernmental ecological organizations are registered in Russia. RGC is not alone in the NGO world. However, in contrast to the Wildlife Fund, for example, which is busy with conservation of biodiversity and environment protection in the most beautiful parts of the country, we have to work in the territories with difficult ecological problems, such as nuclear contamination, storage or destruction of chemical weapons, polluted aerodromes, and missile depots. They are the territories where the military-industrial complex left behind a difficult heritage in the earth, water, and atmosphere.

PUBLIC HEARINGS ON ECOLOGICAL PROBLEMS OF DISARMAMENT

Public hearings are an effective way to resolve conflicts between residents and officials-conflicts due to the reluctance of the authorities to listen to citizens who live in these godforsaken regions of the country. In the case of civil society, it is the responsibility of the State to sponsor dialogs and reach conclusions from conversation with the people. But while Russia is just searching for its path to civil society, a difficult role belongs to public (nongovernmental) organizations, and RGC in particular.

The concept of hearings has a history. In post-Soviet society, RGC carried out open public hearings in 1995 in Saratov. They were devoted to the problem of future destruction of chemical weapons in the settlement of Gorny in the Krasnopartizan region of Saratov Oblast. At this time, society has come to understand that difficult political, social, ecological, and other types of problems need new ways of solution. Many people know the case of Chapaevsk. When the Soviet leaders made the decision on elimination of chemical weapons stored in the Soviet Union, it was done in secret.

They began to build a plant for destruction of chemical weapons in Chapaevsk, Samara Oblast. Neither the population of Samara Oblast, nor people living near the factory, knew about the decision. Moreover, they were told it would be a semiconductor plant. While the plant was under construction, the political system changed in the country, and Russia became "democratic." The secret was disclosed when Minister of Foreign Affairs Shevardnadze declared somewhere abroad that Russia had built a plant for destruction of chemical weapons in Chapaevsk. The people of Chapaevsk and adjacent regions were shocked. A protest movement began. People went into the street. The plant did not open as a result of their struggle. Large funds were wasted. The process of chemical weapon destruction stopped for a long period. This result of social confrontation is an example of the wrong approach to such problems involving our authorities and our state.

A similar situation took place in Saratov Oblast in 1994-1995, when Prime Minister Chernomyrdin issued a secret Resolution about building a plant for chemical weapon destruction in the settlement of Gorny. There were the same processes as in Chapaevsk. At that time RGC came into the political arena with the idea of public hearings. Three parties always exist. The first one is people living alongside the plant, who are interested in the purpose of the building. The second one is the local authorities, who understand the people's expectations and are also interested in the situation. Then there are the federal authorities, who are interested only in resolving the problem such as elimination of weapons, as in this case. Hearings bring together all three components. Decision-making ought to be foregone until after a careful discussion. All the parties must obtain all information. Unfortunately, in our country decisions are made without adequate data or even in secret. We spent a year until the hearing was realized. We had to appeal to President Yeltsin to gather the three parties of the society. Representatives of the federal authorities that deal with the problem (including the Ministry of Defense, which was responsible for elimination of chemical weapons, the Ministries of Ecology, Health, the Armaments Industry, and others) agreed to take part in the hearing only after President Yeltsin wrote "I support the hearings" on the letter of RGC and after his instructions to Grachev, the Minister of Defense, to Danilov-Danilyan, the Minister of Ecology, and to Baturin, the Secretary of the Security Council. Only then, the Governor of Saratov Oblast also decided that his party would take part in the public hearings carried out by a nongovernmental organization. The hearings were held in October 1995.

They helped the people of Krasnopartizan region surrounding the settlement of Gorny obtain information directly from decision-makers. Local residents had a lot of questions. A Resulting Document was published after the hearings. It was delivered to the President, to the Federal Assembly, to the Assembly of Saratov Oblast, and to all departments and nongovernmental organizations. A lot of people, the mass media, and even foreign observers attended the hearings. Since that time RGC holds annual hearings in the regions of chemical weapon storage. Federal representatives of interested departments go there with pleasure to meet with residents and answer their questions. Hearings help them find a decision which is suitable for federal authorities, residents, and local authorities. The hearings conclude with a Resulting Document. It is important that the document is adopted by consensus instead of by voting.

It is also important that the decisions in the document are executed even though they are only recommendations to different branches of government, residents, and public organizations. For example, the Resulting Document of the first hearing contained an idea of a public commission of experts. All the participants in the hearing approved it. So, the advice to organize a public expert examination of the plant identified for destruction of chemical weapons was adopted. This part of the decisions of the hearing was fulfilled. A public expert examination of the plant in the settlement of Gorny was carried out. Such nongovernmental organizations as Saratov's Health to Children, RGC, and Union for Chemical Security were involved. It was the first step towards a civil society.

One of the items of the Resulting Document of the second hearing (Izhevsk-Kambarka, 1996) requested the State Duma to speed up development of the Law "On Elimination of Chemical Weapons" as a starting point for a legislative base for the chemical weapon elimination process. It should be noted that it was an appeal not of RGC but of all the participants of the hearing, which resulted from open disputes and discussions. A consensus was reached concerning approaches to the problem of elimination of chemical weapons. The communities of the Republic of Udmurtia-especially representatives and officials of the settlements of Kizner and Kambarki where chemical weapons are stored- supported adopting the Law on Chemical Disarmament. After difficult disputes in the State Duma and the Federal Assembly, the Law was adopted and signed finally by the President. Surely, everybody knows that like any law this Law is not ideal. It is the first one among a series of laws that will form the legislative base for chemical weapon elimination. It is the beginning. But it is a step forward, and it is a result of the activity of public organizations.

International experience is also important. We did not invent the idea of hearings. This practice exists in other countries. It is not a secret that the United States, our former main adversary in the arms race, produced many different weapons too. So they have the same problems. They have mountains of armaments: chemical, nuclear, and conventional. They have to eliminate weapons according to international agreements. This causes just the same problems. Nobody is happy to know that somebody is going to destroy chemical weapons or solid rockets in his backyard. But a culture of interaction between people and power is better developed in the United States and Europe, so such hearings are always carried out when there are health and environment problems. We have adopted this positive experience.

ESTABLISHING PUBLIC COMMISSIONS

Establishing public commissions is another useful idea of our American colleagues. We try to realize this in our country. The population ought to take a direct part in decisions concerning chemical weapon elimination. How can people participate? In the United States public commissions called "Citizen Advisory Committees" have been working for several years in every state where chemical weapon storage facilities or plants were built and elimination has started. They unite representatives of different public organizations, reflecting interests of local residents. A Citizen Advisory Committee is organized pursuant to a Governor's order and consists of community representatives. They have a legislative mandate and take an active part both in decision-making and in monitoring implementation.

These Committees connect people and officials of a state or country (republic or oblast in our case) and help develop decisions, taking into account the interests of the people. RGC suggested this initiative at the second public hearing in Udmurtia (in Kambarka and Izhevsk) where the problem of building a plant for destruction of chemical weapons was discussed. A decision was proposed at the hearing, and it was written in the Resulting Document. But we could realize it only this year. Such a project was accomplished due to the efforts of Russian experts including ones from Udmurtia (Vadim Petrov, the president of the Union for Chemical Security of Udmurtia, participated in work) and our American colleagues who prepared a synthesized book of the rules for U.S. committee activities. Now it is published only in one region, Kurgan Oblast. Discussion of the project is underway in Udmurtia in Penza Oblast. Many Federal departments (Ministry of Defense) and some governors (Kurgan Oblast) still do not understand the necessity of Citizen Advisory Committees.

PROJECTS TO SUPPORT RESIDENTS OF REGIONS OF CHEMICAL WEAPON STORAGE

Public Information Network for the Population It is necessary to inform people about the processes touching their essential interests. Local residents have the moral right to express their views on chemical weapons storage. First of all, it is necessary to obtain data from the authorities and the numerous departments and bring it to the attention of the people. Then we should inform the authorities about the people's opinion and will. For such an informational exchange, RGC organized a number of public information centers in the regions of storage of chemical weapons.

The main goal of the centers is to inform people as much as possible about chemical weapons, their storage and future destruction, about the people's rights and state guarantees, about the role of western states in chemical disarmament, and so on. For this purpose, RGC issues popular booklets and information leaflets, distributes on-line data about activities in regional and federal centers, and distributes information about international organizations (particularly, the Organization for the Prohibition of Chemical Weapons) by means of the local mass media.

Representatives of the centers visit schools, offices, and colleges where they both inform people and carry on direct dialogues with them. If representatives of the centers cannot answer questions immediately, they send the questions with the help of the Moscow Center to federal departments and specialists in destruction technologies for chemical weapons.

This complex process of communication between the people and the authorities leads both to a decrease in the level of conflict and to an overcoming of mutual suspicion, chemophobia, and other concerns caused by the atmosphere of secrecy that has surrounded chemical disarmament for many years. It is necessary to stress that the U.S. Congress finances American informational centers within the framework of chemical disarmament expenses. In Russia, the Duma never assigns such funds, so nongovernmental organizations such as RGC have to carry out this difficult and expensive activity.

Independent Expert Examinations and Projects

In order to overcome the people's distrust of government activity in chemical disarmament, RGC has played a role of independent arbitrator in the continuing dispute between officials and residents. For this purpose, a number of independent public expert examinations were carried out along with the state ecological expert examination. First of all, these were examinations of projects for future destruction facilities of chemical weapons in Kurgan Oblast (the settlement of Shchuchye) and Saratov Oblast (Gorny). The public examination is at a higher level than the state one. This is due to the higher professional skill of the experts and the wider range of opinions of different public organizations taking part in the examinations.

Nowadays the implementation of a disarmament project is impossible without a public expert examination. It is one more achievement of the "green" community. Other interesting initiatives of RGC were an independent examination of the people's health in different regions of the country connected with chemical weapons (Saratov Oblast, Penza Oblast, Kurgan Oblast, Bryansk Oblast, and Udmurtia) and an independent hazard assessment for residents of regions of storage of chemical weapons (Udmurtia-Kizner and Kambarka, Kurgan Oblast-Shchuchye, Kirov Oblast-Maradykovo).

The results of this independent research were reported at all public hearings organized by RGC. Reports, monographs, and popular booklets were written. Visitors to the RGC information center have access to them. Ecological Health Centers Taking into account the difficult social and ecological life conditions in the regions of chemical weapon storage, RGC decided to organize summer recovery camps and health centers for children from poor families living near chemical weapon storage sites. The main goal is social support of residents and invigoration and ecological education of children. The first ecological health center of RGC in Vladimir Oblast in the summer of 1997 was visited by 300 children from all regions of chemical weapon storage. Since 1998, recovery camps and health centers have been located closer to the storage regions in Udmurtia (children from Maradykovo, Kizner, and Kambarka), in Penza Oblast (children from Leonidovka, Pochepa, Gorny), and in Kurgan Oblast (children from Shchuchansk and Shumikha regions) and Chelyabinsk Oblast. In 2000, the first winter center was organized near Izhevsk for children from Udmurtia. Plans for 2001 include two winter and five summer health centers and camps for children from ecologically unfavorable regions of Russia.

This extensive program raised new problems for RGC, such as leader training and development of guidelines for organizers of ecological education.

These problems are solved now. Swiss Green Cross carried out in Kiev a workshop for organizers of ecological recovery camps from Russia, Belarus, and Ukraine. In spring 2001, RGC is going to carry out the second leader training (the first one was in Moscow in March 2000). The Chief of the RGC National Committee of the "Ecological Education" program, Professor V.Nazarenko, prepared guidelines for teachers and organizers of ecological education of children during their rest in RGC ecological recovery camps. RGC also realizes other projects in the regions of chemical weapon storage. For example, sociological interviewing on the chemical weapon destruction problem was held in Kurgan Oblast and Udmurtia. Another example is a number of educational workshops for doctors of civilian and military hospitals in the storage regions, carried out together with Swiss Green Cross in 1999-2000. And RGC made inspections of sites of former chemical weapon destruction near Penza and studied the possible impact of the destruction "products" on the main regional water body, the Sura reservoir.

The results of this investigation were published both in the local and central mass media. The Governor of the Oblast and the Ministry of Defense have received advice for taking measures. Unfortunately, the only measure that was accepted was to ask RGC to find the funds for implementing the solution of the problem somewhere abroad.

This fact proves that our authorities, on one hand, either cannot or do not want to solve conflict problems, and on the other hand, they prefer to get rid of their work by giving it to a public organization.

These results of activity in chemical disarmament of one of Russia's public organizations show the influence of the community on one of the most difficult and contentious problems of our society, elimination of weapons of mass destruction. On the other hand, one can see that both the authorities and nongovernmental organizations have a long way to go towards a civil society.

ORGANIZING IN DIRECTLY IMPACTED COMMUNITIES: THE SOCM STORY

This presentation is a case study of a particular kind of NGO in the United States that is different from others presented at this conference. First, let me paint you a picture of the situation that existed in rural coalfield communities of Tennessee at the time SOCM was organized.

In 1971 in five rural mountain counties of Tennessee where at that time 90 percent of the coal in the state was mined, conditions were very difficult for the retired underground miners, subsistence farmers, and other low-income and working class people who lived there. o Ten large land companies, most of them from out of state and one from London, England, owned 80 percent of the mineral land and paid no taxes on their mineral holdings.

- o Unregulated strip mining on steep mountain slopes brought earth, rock, and trees down the mountains and onto roads, into streams, and onto people's land. Blasting through rock also blasted and cracked homes and wells, the only available water supply. Filled up streams flooded land of residents.
- o In some places land companies or coal companies legally owned the mineral rights under the surface and the mineral owners' rights were ruled by courts as superior to those of surface owners.
- o The underground mines, which historically had provided many jobs, were largely closed because there was more money to be made by strip mining; unemployment was very high.
- o These were some of the poorest counties in the state with few basic county services, partly because little revenue was generated for the county from the land and coal companies.

In 1972, after seeing research by some university students about land ownership and taxes paid in the five counties and the fact that the state constitution requires taxes be paid on minerals, 13 citizens filed a legal petition to make the local tax assessors appraise minerals as part of the value of land. They won the petition and, having obtained several hundred supporting signatures, decided to form an organization they called Save Our Cumberland Mountains (SOCM, pronounced "sock-em"). Unregulated strip mining of coal was one of the first issues they decided to take on.

From the beginning, SOCM was organized to be membership-based and member-run. People would speak for themselves, not have staff speak for them. SOCM would work on projects members chose to work on. Through the method of community organizing, members in a local community came together to form a group. They listened to each other, told stories about how they were affected by problems in the community, and received strength from being together. As a local group they decided what to work on, who were decision-makers who could do something about their problem and how to influence them. They found scientists who were allies, and they learned science themselves. They always knew, however, that in order to win, they needed to build a strong grassroots base of political power to influence decision-makers and public opinion.

They incorporated culture into their meetings, singing old union struggle songs and writing their own songs. Staff did lots of training and leadership development. Members learned how to research issues and how to think through a comprehensive strategy. They developed stronger skills in running their own meetings, talking with the media, recruiting new members, and conducting grassroots fund raising. Members practiced and role-played before taking action, had lots of encouragement, and evaluated activities later for lessons learned.

SOCM's organizing is based on the belief that regular citizens, both those with little formal education and those with more, have great potential to learn, to speak, and to act for themselves, and that participating in public life is what democracy means. For the first several years as SOCM members took action, there was a backlash from the coal companies. Many people received threatening phone calls. Some homes were burned by arsonists, but no one was ever prosecuted. Some members were physically attacked. Because of the principle of multiple leadership, however, coal companies couldn't destroy SOCM by intimidating any one or several leaders. From the beginning SOCM was multi-issue and multi-county. In local communities members worked to have roads improved and streams cleaned up.

They worked together for a severance tax on coal which was passed by the state legislature to bring in revenue to the coal counties for roads and schools. They worked with others in the state to have a state strip mine law passed and then worked even harder to have it enforced.

Over the years (SOCM is now 28 years old) the organization expanded in a number of ways. Geographically it expanded first to Cumberland Plateau counties, called the "southern coalfields of Tennessee," and then both east and west beyond the mountains. More recently, SOCM has formed new multi-racial chapters in middle Tennessee. It expanded from several hundred to nearly 3,000 members. Currently, there are SOCM members in about two-thirds of Tennessee's counties. From working primarily on coal-related issues, SOCM members have gone on to address both locally in their communities and state-wide a range of other issues that impact them, including problems related to toxic and hazardous waste, solid waste, oil and gas, other extractive minerals, forestry practices, state tax reform, and abuse of temporary workers. SOCM has helped form and provided leadership for many coalitions and alliances at the state, regional, and national levels.

STRUCTURE

In a county, members form a local chapter to work on local issues, to build a stronger grassroots base in that area, and to support SOCM's organization-wide work. Governance at the organization-wide level is provided by a Board made up of representatives elected from each chapter and officers and three at-large delegates elected by the membership as a whole. Issue committees are organized to focus on strategies for broader campaigns to address roots of problems being faced by many local communities. Internal committees, also made up of members, oversee the internal functioning of the organization's finances, personnel, and long-range planning.

HIGHLIGHTS OF SOME STRATEGIES USED

Highlighted here are some strategies that may be of interest to Russian colleagues. Research We've always known in SOCM that we need accurate information and sound research for campaigns. We need access to research that others have done, and in some cases we must do our own. Here are two examples of SOCM research studies to address situations of concern to members.

- o To show that reclamation seldom works when mining in very toxic coal seams (in Tennessee the most toxic is the Sewanee coal seam), SOCM interns field tested water quality coming off areas that enforcement agencies called "reclaimed mine sites" (where the bond had already been released). They found that over 80 percent of these sites were still leaching acid mine drainage with an average pH equivalent to that of vinegar. That research was used as SOCM pressed for and won precedent-setting rulings about the need for special kinds of toxic material handling plans when mining the Sewanee seam.
- o To show that the state regulatory agency was not enforcing the state strip mine law, SOCM researched hundreds of files of enforcement actions in state agency offices and prepared an "Enforcement Study," a documented expose of poor enforcement.

Partly based on that study, the federal government took over the regulation of strip mining in Tennessee. Help from the Scientific Community SOCM has had wonderful help from volunteer scientists who have given significant amounts of time to review documents and to testify at public hearings along with regular SOCM members. Included in this group are geologists, hydro-geologists, ecologists, soil scientists, biologists, and others. These scientific allies come from universities in Tennessee, from the Oak Ridge National Laboratory, and from private firms. SOCM is grateful for the important contribution of their thousands of hours of time. Emphasis on Economic as Well as Environmental Aspects of Issues SOCM stresses the economic as well as environmental and human health aspects of issues it works on. Here are two recent examples: o In an almost ten-year campaign to force the Department of Interior to declare the watershed of Fall Creek Falls State Park unsuitable for mining (members of a SOCM chapter live in the watershed), an economics professor from the University of Tennessee compiled a study of the impact of the park on the economy of surrounding counties. The study concluded that pollution of the spectacular waterfalls and other water features of the park could result in loss of over 700 jobs and millions of dollars in revenue to nearby counties. SOCM was also able to obtain resolutions of support for our petition from local county governments in those surrounding counties. Last June after years of SOCM's work, the Department of Interior designated 61,000 acres of the watershed off-limits to mining.

o A current effort involves obtaining some regulation of giant chip mills that are increasingly locating in the south. In an eight-hour shift a chip mill can grind up 60 acres of forest land. Besides the impact on land and water and the threat of over-harvesting SOCM members stress the loss of value-added jobs that rely on the availability and affordability of hardwoods.

A group of hardwood-using businesses are supporting our current effort for state legislation. Use of the Media SOCM uses the media in campaigns both to help mold public opinion around particular issues and to establish SOCM as a player in the public arena. Here are two examples:

o In an eight-year successful effort to win the strongest surface owners' rights law in the country, SOCM members met with editorial boards and received editorial endorsements from every major newspaper in the state.

o On several occasions SOCM has used a major media campaign strategy which involves an intensive several-month effort to place as many stories in as many media outlets as possible (newspapers, radio, magazines, talk shows, etc.).

The campaign culminates in a major event and press conference. In the Fall Creek Falls campaign, a 150-foot banner was lowered next to the park's spectacular 256-foot waterfall with the message, "Bruce Babbitt, Don't Let the Falls Down!" In a campaign to highlight the need for forestry legislation, volunteer pilots flew reporters from all over the state over a 1,600-acre clear-cut site, showing filled up streams from erosion on the site, in conjunction with a press conference. Lawsuits as a Strategy of Last Resort When other strategies fail, SOCM has used lawsuits as a strategy. Here are two instances:

- o SOCM forced the state of Tennessee to implement its own water quality law and to set up a division of surface mining
- o Along with another organization, SOCM forced the federal government to collect fines and set up a system to track down violators of the federal surface mining law

Grassroots Fundraising From its earliest history when SOCM members "passed the hat" at meetings for money to help pay for expenses of the organization, SOCM has emphasized member involvement (as well as staff) in raising money for the organization's budget. Money from foundations has been and still is a critically important source of operating funds. However, currently, over 40 percent of the organization's budget is raised by membership dues, mail appeals, chapter fundraisers, organization-wide fundraisers like walkathons and concerts, house parties, major donor contributions (defined in SOCM as donations of $50 or more), phonathons, and other activities.

CONCLUSION

Over its 28-year history of organizing, SOCM has learned that it sometimes takes a long time to win and that the wonderful victories are often accompanied by what seem like heart-breaking setbacks along the way. For SOCM members, losing becomes just another way to learn. SOCM has been determined to stay in the struggle for the long haul. While it's great to win, it's just as good to see what happens when ordinary people become more skilled and more confident and their world becomes larger as they learn about the struggles of others in different communities in the state, in the country, and even internationally. Their analysis of the roots of problems sharpens. Care is taken to develop sensitivities and understanding about the race and class barriers that so often divide people who really have much in common. It was vitally important to win the Fall Creek Falls issue. Just as important, however, was seeing Landon Medley, a factory worker from Doyle, Tennessee, and chair of SOCM's strip mine issue committee, speak eloquently about the power of citizen efforts in bringing about the victory.

There are many community organizations like SOCM in the United States in virtually every state and working with virtually every ethnic group and race in the country. My experience is that community organizing, where people themselves are transformed in the process, is both a method to bring about the changes needed for a better environment and a more just society, and a way to truly build a working democracy in our country. Thank you so much for the opportunity to share SOCM's experiences with you and to learn from you at this workshop.

GLOBAL FOREST WATCH: AN EXAMPLE OF INTERNATIONAL PARTNERSHIP WITH RUSSIAN NGOS AND SCIENTISTS

The World Resources Institute (WRI) was founded in 1982, in Washington, DC, as a nongovernmental, not-for-profit organization. The John D. and Catherine T.MacArthur Foundation supplied a large initial grant. Today, funding comes from many sources, including private foundations, corporations, agencies and cooperating organizations (such as a number of United Nations agencies, the World Bank, agencies for development aid, and many others), and individuals. WRI currently has 125 employees from about 20 countries.

WRI is active in many policy areas. These include biological resources, climate, institutions and governance, economics, business management, and information (see Box 1). A well-known product is the World Resources Report, a semi-annual book of world statistics and topical assessments prepared together with the United Nations Development Programme (UNDP), the United Nations Environment Programme (UNEP), and the World Bank. The latest edition, the Millennial Edition, presents a comprehensive assessment of five of the world's major ecosystems.

From the very beginning, WRI's goal has been to propose practical policy solutions to environmental and resource problems. Attention to facts and analytical excellence has always been emphasized. In the beginning and for many years, the typical WRI product was a report, rich in text, written for official policy makers and their advisors. And this is still the case, sometimes.

But the world has changed, and so has the way that WRI works. Public participation in policy-making has become more important, and so has the positive role of industry. Our experience shows that reports, no matter how well written, sometimes end up rather quickly on the bookshelf, where they lose much of their intended power.

THE WORLD RESOURCES INSTITUTE

- o Provides information, ideas, and solutions to global environmental problems.
- o Our mission is to move human society to live in ways that protect Earth's environment for current and future generations.
- o Our program meets global challenges by using knowledge to catalyze public and private action. o Our goals are:
- o - To reverse damage to ecosystems.
- o - To expand participation in environmental decisions.

o - To avert dangerous climate change.

o - To increase prosperity while improving the environment.

CONNECTIVITY

In order to maintain its influence on the policy agenda, WRI is increasingly emphasizing something we call connectivity: additional contacts and cooperation with individuals and organizations outside government, including both industry and the community of nongovernmental organizations (NGOs). When adding connectivity to analytical excellence, WRI is trying to make the most of the new information technology. An increasing number of people worldwide meet WRI through its website (www.wri.org). WRI is increasingly turning its website into a connectivity tool: not only a place to get information (although this is significant), but also a place for real dialogue. Global Forest Watch (GFW) is a recent initiative of WRI that emphasizes connectivity and the use of new technology.

GLOBAL FOREST WATCH

Created in 1998, GFW is an international data and mapping network that combines on-the-ground knowledge with digital technology to provide accurate information about the world's forests and threats to them. The overall objective of GFW is to infuse transparency and accountability into the decision-making processes that determine how forests are managed, and for whom. The GFW network includes NGOs, universities, and other institutions that are monitoring logging, mining, and conducting other development activities within major forested regions of the world. GFW is governed by an international Steering Committee consisting of representatives of national GFW Chapters, while the secretariat (GFW International) is housed within WRI. GFW is currently active in Indonesia, Canada, Gabon, Cameroon, Venezuela, Chile, and Russia. Activities are planned for the United States, the Baltic countries, Romania, and the Amazon basin.

THE GFW CONCEPT

The GFW concept is built on the power of accuracy, transparency, and connectivity.

- o Accuracy is achieved by a scientific approach. The systematic use of modern technology is coupled with a rigorous review of all maps and data products: an expert review to build accuracy and a stakeholder review to build credibility.

- o Transparency is achieved by sharing GFW products as widely as possible, typically at no cost to the user, again using modern technology and media approaches. Through an interactive website (www.globalforestwatch.org), and through printed reports, media coverage, and op-ed articles, GFW information reaches different stakeholders and interested citizens worldwide.
- o Connectivity is inherent in the GFW bottom-up approach, relying as far as possible on local and national groups and capacities, creating and catalyzing new national networks, creating new international collaboration. GFW should not be seen as a limited-life project. Rather, GFW is a continuous, systematic, and rigorous civil-society based auditing process of forest conditions and utilization.

FOREST WATCH RUSSIA

The Russian Chapter of GFW, called Forest Watch Russia (FWR), was born in November 1999 at a meeting in Krasnoyarsk in Siberia. FWR is a unique national coalition of Russian NGOs with the interest and capacity to map and monitor forests.

Member organizations represent all corners of Russia as well as outstanding technical expertise. The goal of FWR is to improve the conservation and utilization of Russia's forests by means of high-accuracy forest mapping and monitoring.

RUSSIAN INTEGRITY AND WRI'S ROLE

FWR is a thoroughly Russian network, despite its close links with WRI and GFW. Priorities and plans reflect Russian concerns, and FWR relies entirely on technical capacity inside Russia. WRI's role is limited to fundraising, facilitation, and light overall coordination.

The work is currently financed through a donation from the company IKEA.

Fwr Steering Committee

- o Lars Laestadius, WRI (Chairman)
- o Academician Alexander Isaev, International Forest Institute, Moscow (methods and data review)
- o Dmitry Aksenov, Socio-Ecological Union, Moscow (national GIS function, data issues)
- o Mikhail Karpachevskiy, Biodiversity Conservation Centre, Moscow (national GIS function, editor)

- o Andrei Laletin, Friends of the Siberian Forests, Krasnoyarsk (coordinator Eastern Siberia)
- o Anatoly Lebedev, Office for Regional Public Campaigns, Vladivostok (coordinator, Russian Far East)
- o Olga Tarakanova, Transparent World, Moscow (remote sensing, administrative coordination)
- o Alexey Yaroshenko, Greenpeace, Moscow (coordinator European Russia, map verification)
- o Alexander Yumakaev, The Fund for 21st Century Altai, Barnaul (coordinator Western Siberia).

NGO LINKS

FWR is cooperating with environmental NGOs from all over Russia. A prominent member organization is the International Forest Institute, led by Academician Alexander Isaev, former chairman of the USSR State Committee for Forests. This informal link with the Russian Academy of Sciences is very useful for FWR. The Forest Service of Russia has been participating as an observer.

INTERNATIONAL LINKS

Being a member of the GFW family connects FWR to the world. Maps and information on Russia can reach the world quickly and effectively through the network and communications capacity of GFW International. Approaches, methods, experiences, and people can be exchanged with other GFW countries Canada is an interesting parallel for Russia.

The international connection also allows Russian know-how to be available outside of Russia. The members of FWR have significant experience and advanced competence in forest mapping using satellite images and geographical information systems. Russia is without doubt a world leader in this kind of mapping.

STRUCTURE AND CAPACITY BUILDING

Russia is a large country where regional balance and reach are crucial. FWR has adopted a structure with four macro-regions (Far East, Eastern Siberia, Western Siberia, and European Russia), each with a Regional Data Center based in existing organizations and networks in Vladivostok, Krasnoyarsk, Barnaul, and Moscow. In Moscow the Center doubles as the FWR National Data Center.

The plan is for these centers to serve as coordination points, providing organizational and technical know- how, equipment and software, training, and outreach, and also as data management centers, (such as regional libraries for satellite images and GIS data).

FWR OBJECTIVES AND ACHIEVEMENTS

The initial task of FWR is to map all remaining frontier forests, and particularly large blocks of intact forest in Russia. An FWR partner, Transparent World, has prepared a draft map at the scale of 1:1 million, which would be more than 8 meters wide if printed to scale, using recent medium resolution images from the Russian satellite Resurs and high resolution images from the American LandSat. This is the first map of Russian forest cover that has been made from such detailed images. FWR partners conducted field verification of the map during 2000. The map will be published at the end of 2001, following revision and review by experts and different stakeholders.

Transparent World has also supplied the Regional Data Centers with images and interpretation software and conducted training courses for their staffs. The Regional Data Centers, in turn, have trained and organized local groups to conduct field verification (ground truthing) of the map. FWR plans to continue to build technical capacity among Russian NGOs as it expands and refines its mapping activities.

ROLE OF INTERNATIONAL RELATIONS IN THE DEVELOPMENT OF ECOLOGICAL NONGOVERNMENTAL ORGANIZATIONS IN RUSSIA

"The Russian power will increase with the help of Siberia..." These prophetic words of the great scientist M.V.Lomonosov have become historical reality. Siberia makes a large contribution to ensure Russia a significant place among the great world powers.

About 90 percent of Russia's natural resources are within Siberia. They make up 45 percent of the world's gas resources, 13 percent of oil, 23 percent of coal, and 20 percent of fresh water. In recent decades, powerful intellectual and industrial potentials have been created in Siberia, including branches of three Russian academies and dozens of scientific research institutes and educational institutions. An interregional association of economic interaction among the administrative units of the Russian Federation-Siberian Accord (hereinafter IASA)-has been created. IASA is a public non-commercial organization, uniting on a voluntary basis 19 subdivisions of the Russian

Federation. IASA helps ensure the most effective use of unique Siberian resources, improving new methods of management in the conditions of economic decentralization and market relations on the regional and interregional levels, as well as achievement of sustainable development under new conditions.

More than 24 million people live in an area of 10 million square kilometers (38 percent of Russian territory). In October 2000, IASA celebrated its tenth anniversary. Priority directions of IASA activities are: maintenance of power, food, and ecological security of Siberia, health protection of its multinational population, and unification of its socio-cultural and educational activities.

The highest body of IASA is the Association Council, uniting the chiefs of the executive and legislative branches of the 19 territorial authorities. Twenty-five coordinating councils work in various directions: legislation and law-making, scientific and technological policy, conversion and industrial policy, power, transport and communications, waste disposal, agricultural processing, engineering industry, ecology, investment and foreign trade, and social and cultural programs.

The Executive Committee directs the operations of IASA. During the current decade, the Association has demonstrated an open policy, various forms of constructive partnership, and efficient interactions with organizations on the international, federal, and interregional levels. It has cooperation agreements with the Federal Council and with the government of Russia, Ministry of Fuel and Energy, Ministry of Science and Technology Policy, Ministry of Transport, and Ministry of General and Professional Education; Siberian Branch of the Russian Academy of Sciences (RAS); Russian Aerospace Agency; Trade-Industrial Chamber; and a number of foreign organizations.

The ecological strategy of Siberia, developed in IASA together with the RAS, provides for the rational use of nature and maintenance of environmental quality. This development should ensure renewal of natural resources, a favorable quality of the environment, and the health of the people; protection of the genetic potential and landscape variety; and the opportunity of further sustainable development of the Siberian region. The main evaluation criteria of the work in these directions are the environmental conditions and the population's health.

The development of resources and the manufacturing and processing branches in Siberia have caused pollution and degradation of the environment. This in turn has resulted in negative tendencies in the demographic situation, quality of life, and health of the present and future populations of Siberia.

A decrease in the population and its reproduction potential has caused a decrease of the able-bodied population. This threatens ecological and economic security and also has geopolitical aspects.

The chiefs of all departments are responsible for radical measures to reverse this developing situation.

A Coordinating Ecological Council (hereinafter-CCE) plays a key role in decisions on ecological problems and solutions of such problems as ecological health, ecological reconstruction of food production processes, drinking water supply, and waste treatment; environmental monitoring and managing the population's health and natural resources; formation of the ecological way of thinking and solving the problems of rational use of nature; and ecological education.

CCE uses the report "UN Conference on Environment and Development," prepared by Academician V. A. Koptyug, who participated in the work of the conference as a representative of Russia. CCE joins forces with other coordinating councils to solve ecological problems, taking into account their interrelations with all spheres of life in the region.

THE PROBLEM OF WATER SUPPLY AND USE

While water is one of the main life-forming natural factors, the problems of the drinking water supply of the Siberian population and Russia as a whole have become very sharp. According to data of the State Sanitary-Epidemiological Inspection, 30 percent of the urban and 70 percent of the rural population of Russia use substandard drinking water. Because of the unsatisfactory condition of the drinking water supply in the region, CCE recommends priority in the territorial budgets to water treatment. According to a decision of the IASA Council (June 1995, Tyumen, with participation of Prime Minister V.S.Chernomyrdin), an Instruction of the Russian Government about the development of the Federal Special Purpose Program "Use, Restoration, and Protection of Water Resources of the Ob River Basin" was adopted in 1996. The regional experts developed the program concept. As a result of a Federal Law "On Taxes for the Use of Bodies of Water," the regions received financing in 1998.

Also CCE has paid attention to problems of water resources of world importance. The problems of land protection in the case of the Bolshoye Vasyuganskoye Swamp, the largest swamp in the world, were considered. The international scientific community discussed its inclusion on the list of water-swamp lands of world importance (the Ramsar List) and the formation of an inter-regional preserve of federal importance on its territory. The richest natural resources of drinking water are concentrated in several territories (Altai Region, Khakass Republic, and Altai Republic). The International Conferences "Pure Water of Altai" (August 1998 and August 2000, Lake Teletskoye) were devoted to ecological problems of the Altai Republic water fund.

This republic has a special role with significant resources of fresh ground water that supply the surface runoff of the upper Ob River basin. Taking into account the role of the territory, the development of ecological control and water resources monitoring is recommended as a strategic direction. Glaciers and snow packs of the Altai are considered. The Executive Committee of IASA included the problem of Altai water monitoring into the CCE schedule on space monitoring. But, the support of international organizations and funds is also necessary. Significant methodological and scientific organizational work on the solution of urgent problems of water use in the Siberian region has been performed by the international faculty of UNESCO's "Ecological Education in Siberia" (Altai, 1996). International schools on water management are carried out every year. Under the aegis of UNESCO, the world community carries out complex work on the protection of the "pearl" of world importance-Lake Baikal.

PROBLEMS OF TREATMENT AND UTILIZATION OF MANUFACTURING AND CONSUMER WASTES

According to the data of the State Sanitary-Epidemiological Inspection, 80 billion tons of waste have been accumulated in Russia. In this context, the sanitary- epidemiological situation in some territorial units has a crisis character, including on the IASA territory. The Federal Special Purpose Program "Wastes" is not functioning, and therefore CCE's recommendations for the priority solution of the problems were accepted at the regional level. Following on to the discussion "About the Sanitary-Epidemiological Conditions in Siberia" at a meeting of the IASA Council (Kemerovo, January 15, 1999, with the participation of Prime Minister Ye. M. Primakov), it was decided to develop a special purpose program "The Management System for Dangerous Wastes." It takes into account the problems of ecological safety and economic expediency both for destruction and for treatment and utilization of manufacturing and consumer wastes.

The Coordinating Councils of Ecology, Energy Saving, and Housing and Communal services joined efforts to solve the problem "On Use of Combustible Wastes of Manufacturing and Consumers as a Source of Heat." The plasma combustion method of destruction of domestic, medical, and other harmful wastes was accepted as a method of world importance. The experimental installation in Siberia (Novosibirsk) for the combustion of used syringes and other medical wastes uses this technology. The Siberian project "CRTS" (complex regional thermal stations) was developed by the Institute of Thermal Physics and is supported by IASA. It uses domestic wastes as additional sources of thermal energy. Within the framework of a decision of the IASA Council (December 1999, Omsk), the CCE held a meeting on "Treatment of Toxic Wastes: Business Conditions, Problems, and Ways of their Solution." This meeting analyzed the experience in Omsk and Sverdlovsk Oblasts and in foreign states (Denmark, Germany, and Austria). The participants visited the open waste dumping ground, which is unique in Siberia and up to world standards. The meeting recommended that administrative heads provide financing for realization of a program for this special purpose. It was also recommended that normative materials, prepared with financial support of the International Bank for Reconstruction and Development, be applied in different territories of the Siberian region.

The "Regional Monitoring System of the Environment and the Population's Health" should play a leading role in the development of the program. Space monitoring (the only possible way of monitoring for certain territories) became an important tool for the protection of the environmental conditions and the population's health in the Siberian region. In order to supply organizations with satellite data, the Natural Resources and Ecological Monitoring Center of Siberia was organized in Novosibirsk (The Siberian Center of Space Monitoring, SCSM) in May 1997. Remote sensing data help address the following problems: inventory of natural resources, yield forecasts, forest fires, floods, burning of industrial dumps, oil overflow, gas pipeline leaks, power lines, and artificial reservoirs.

With the participation of interested federal territorial bodies (Ministry of Natural Resources, Ministry of Emergency Situations, State Ecological Committee) SCSM generated "The Siberian Block" and submitted it in December 1998 to the Ministry of Natural Resources and the State Ecological Committee as the subprogram "Space Monitoring of Siberia." This formed the basis for the Federal Special Purpose Program of the General State System of Ecological Monitoring. An important tool for realization of "The Siberian Block" is the Agreement on Technological Cooperation between the Russian Aerospace Agency and IASA signed in December 1998. Its goal is use of the newest informational space technologies for socio-economic development of the Siberian region. The IASA Council (January 1999, Kemerovo) created the Coordinating Council of Space Monitoring of Siberia (CC SMS). A working expert group of CC SMS prepared program measures for realization of the "The Siberian Block" of the Russian General State System of Ecological Monitoring in 2000-2001.

A large role in the ideological and practical development of the Space Monitoring of Siberia was played by IASA together with interested departments, RAS, Ministry of Natural Resources, Ministry of Emergency, Ministry of Science and Technology, State Ecological Committee, Russian Aerospace Agency, Russian Hydrometeorological Committee, and the Siberian Branch of the RAS. A wide discussion of this problem was held on the regional, federal and international levels.

For example:

1. A system for monitoring from space was discussed at the international seminar "Space Monitoring of Siberia" (February 1998, Novosibirsk). More than 30 organizations took part in the seminar, including the firm SPOT Image (France), the European Space Agency, federal ministries and departments, and representatives of the territories of IASA. The discussion resulted in a Program of Activities for Space Monitoring of Siberia. This program provides an inter-regional center in Novosibirsk for the reception of remote sensing data from foreign satellites (SPOT, ERS, IRS) and distribution of the data within the Siberian territory. Also, there is now an array of informational-space services based on remote sensing and thematic processing.
2. A working meeting of representatives of the territorial centers (Novosibirsk, Kemerovo, Tomsk, Barnaul, Khanty-Mansiysk) on space monitoring (April 1998, Tomsk) developed the Federal Special Purpose Program of the General State System of Ecological Monitoring for the Siberian region. The integration of the "Space Monitoring of Siberia" system into the All-Russian and international systems of space monitoring was supported. The proposed Subprogram of Space Monitoring of Siberian resources will promote solution of problems of the region.
3. Representatives of 48 Russian and foreign organizations (France, Norway) participated in an international meeting on application of satellite data to the solution of problems of remote sensing (December 1998, Novosibirsk). The meeting participants learned about modern technologies of radar tracking and discussed scientific research and practical applications in the field of space monitoring of the Siberian territories. They decided:

   - On the basis of Article 3 of the Agreement between the Russian Aerospace Agency and IASA, to ask the Aerospace Agency to support efforts of SCSM and the Siberian region in the organization of data reception and processing using Russian and foreign all-weather satellites.

- o To propose to the European Space Agency an agreement on cooperation in the field of remote sensing of Siberia.
- o To consider an International Space Monitoring Center of Siberia. Its main task would be the coordination of cooperation among regional and foreign space monitoring centers and GIS-centers for reception, storage, processing, and distribution of satellite data.
- o To draw attention of the Russian Aerospace Agency, the Ministry of Science and Technology, and the Russian Hydrometeorological Committee to the main characteristics of space vehicles and to parameters for receiving signals.

Since 1998, SCSM has carried out monitoring on the base of contract relations with the territories. Considering the key role of space monitoring in the rational use of resources, CCE for the first time put before the departments of Russia the problem, "Regional ecological problems resulting from separated parts of rockets." A working meeting (Abakan, March 1999), with participation of representatives from the Russian Ecological Committee, Russian Aerospace Agency, and Strategic Rocket Forces of the Russian Defense Ministry, identified 10 territories as the regions where separated parts of rockets and missiles fall with a complex of legal, ecological, economic, and social problems for the inhabitants and administrations. A solution was worked out: free insurance for persons and their property as well as social responsibilities of the government for protection of human health. The solution accepted at this meeting and the subprogram "Space Monitoring of Siberia" developed by the Siberian Space Monitoring Center were handed to the Temporary Commission of the Russian Federation Council on the Protection of Administrative Units Interests, Legal Persons, and Citizens from Unfavorable Consequences of Space-Rocket Activity. The Commission was created according to a Decree of the Federal Assembly (485-RF, November 12, 1998, Moscow). It includes 11 governors and chairmen of legislative assemblies.

The purpose of regional measures to protect the environment is to protect the population's health and longevity. A major role in life-support in the Siberian region is played by ecologically balanced food as an element of survival. For the first time in Siberia, the exhibitions of the international trade organization Siberian Fair were devoted to food problems. The definition "ecological pure production" sounded as a refrain during all exhibitions. Now there is not a uniform system for monitoring food products in the region, but monitoring is a tool in the solution of ecological and demographic problems. Adequate food is not mentioned in presenting environmental conditions and their influence on the population. The International Siberian Fair became a powerful means of information exchange among food institutions. The conference recommended an increase in multi-science knowledge of manufacture and consumption of food products, including special-purpose food.

Ecological problems are caused of course by socio-economic factors. Consequently, it is impossible to solve them only with technical means. Modern approaches to life-support and radical changes of value scales are necessary. The formation of a new social consciousness that defines a favorable environment as a whole is a priority. It is high time to do away with the arrogance of "creators and nature conquerors" and to transform consciousness to rational use of nature based on personal harmony with the environment and knowledge of the laws of nature. As continuous ecological education, training, and population knowledge increase, the development of environmental sciences, including ecology, must play a key role.

Mankind's future depends on general ecological education. Ecological education and training has been raised to the level of State policy (Governmental Decree "On the Improvement of Ecological Education," 1994). The Program "Ecological Education of the Russian Population" was accepted in 1996. An Interdepartmental Commission on Ecological Education was formed. The development of a continuous ecological education and training system at the regional level is based on general principles and approaches ("the biosphere is uniform and indivisible," "knowledge is international and has no boundaries"). They take into account the specific character of the Siberian region: its geopolitical situation; natural resource richness; recognition of some regional territories as the preserves of the planet's natural ecosystems; high scientific and industrial potential; and vulnerability of Siberian nature.

The formation of a regional system of continuous ecological education started in 1995 under the aegis of ECC. Scientific-methodological management was provided by the Department for the Problems of Sustainable Development of Mendeleev University of Chemical Technology (headed by N. P. Tarasova). Today we can say with satisfaction that IASA is an experimental platform for Mendeleev University and the UNESCO Center of Chemical Science and Education. This experimental platform deals with the continuous ecological education and training for sustainable development of the Siberian region.

Dozens of regional schools with special courses on ecology and environmental protection use the books and training material received from

Mendeleev University free of charge-for example: Chemistry and Society from the American Chemical Society, Chemistry and Life (Salters Chemistry) by a collective of British scientists and teachers, and From Competition to Cooperation, a practical handbook on active methods for ecological education prepared by a group of authors headed by the American scientist D. L. Meadows. Pedagogical collectives that use these books highly evaluate the efficiency of such training and its role in the development of contemporary ecological education.

It was the beginning of 1990s when a series of regional training seminars was led by Professor Tarasova in Krasnoyarsk Territory with regional teachers and experts and with the support of the regional administration. Hundreds of teachers and experts from IASA territories completed the course of training on innovative methods of teaching.

Krasnoyarsk Territory plays the leading role among the IASA territories in the development of innovative methods of education to deal with the problems of ecological safety and sustainable development of Siberia, as well as in the interactions with international ecological organizations and funds.

The head of the Ecological Laboratory of Krasnoyarsk State University, N. E. Gapanovich, was rewarded with national recognition for a contribution to the development of the regional system of continuous ecological education.

PRINCIPLES OF THE REGIONAL SYSTEM OF CONTINUOUS ECOLOGICAL EDUCATION

The purpose of an educational ecological program is the creation of the necessary conditions for organization, functioning, and development of a system of continuous general ecological education and training for the administrative units of IASA.

Program Principles:

- o Variety of forms and methods of ecological education and training
- o Continuity of the programs at different levels (vertical integration)
- o Integration with other educational programs
- o Integration among programs at each level
- o Capability of adaptation
- o Recognition of local characteristics
- o Unification of general, professional, and ecological education
- o Connection with practical activity

Problems:

- o Coordination of activities in the field of ecological education and training
- o Creation of a general methodological base
- o Achievement of normative-legal standards
- o Creation of a general informational base
- o Creation of organizations for generalization of work experience and adaptation of educational methods to local conditions

Realization Conditions:

- o Coordination
- o Annual financing
- o Creation of a general database
- o Regular data exchange

A system of regional ecological education has a multi-level structure: from kindergarten to school to college to retraining of personnel for the national economy. The study of ecology is organized both as an independent discipline and as ecological parts of special courses. Special attention is paid to the practical forms of education-expeditions, competitions, reviews, conferences, exhibitions, and working with the people. Ecological solutions are possible only with the participation of interested citizens.

Let us consider some cases from continuous ecological education in the region. On the base of the State Ecological Committee of Tomsk Oblast, the Department of Natural Resources and Environmental Protection was founded. There students directly participate in the solution of nature protection problems. The Regional Youth Center works with a discussion club of pupils "Way To the Twenty-First Century," with the motto "Who, if not We." "Ecological Theatre Poez" has been formed within the regional public organization of the Novosibirsk State Pedagogical University, Ecoclub Avies. The club organizes ecological seminars for the teachers from Novosibirsk Oblast. The magazine Oikis is issued. The natural museum of the Berdsk Station of Young Naturalists is a methodological base for teachers and regional population.

For children of different ages there is a "dialogue" with the world of plants and animals-Small Motherland. Here children learn to understand the necessity of careful attention to nature and readiness to save every species of life on Earth. Kindergarten children together with their parents plant their own trees. Thus, the museum makes a real contribution to ecological education. The development of a number of educational ecological structures became possible with the support of Russian and international non-budgetary funds (office equipment, computers, and expeditions). Several approaches for postgraduate education and retraining are used. For example, the Omsk Governor approved the decree "On Professional Ecological Education of Directors, Specialists, and Citizens." The program involves three higher schools and the UNESCO section at the Altai State Technical University.

In Novosibirsk, Siberian Ecofund promotes education, with participation of scientists and industrial specialists in training programs. According to the multilevel system of continuous ecological education in the region, conferences and seminars devoted to modern approaches to sustainable development are carried out (Omsk, Krasnoyarsk, Kemerovo, Tomsk, and Novosibirsk). The main purposes of the conferences and seminars are exchange of experience, unification of efforts, and further development of the regional system of continuous ecological education.

A regional seminar "The Development of Ecological Education" took place at the Tomsk Municipal Lyceum of Tomsk Polytechnic University (April 1997). Certificates were given to the seminar participants. The Scientific-Practical Conference "Ecological Education for Sustainable Development of Siberia" (November 1998, Krasnoyarsk) concluded that education based on scientific and engineering achievements plays a leading role in deep understanding of contemporary problems. It should promote positive steps in the people's activities and development of critical thinking habits and solution of problems.

Dozens of seminars under the Soros project "Environment and World Society, Ecology and Culture of Health" have been carried out in various territories of IASA. Representatives from 40 State and public organizations of Novosibirsk, Novosibirsk Oblast, and other territories of Siberia participated in the International Conference "The Role of Siberia in Global Climate Change" (November 15-16, 1997, Novosibirsk). "The Ecological Train from Europe to Kyoto" involved representatives from England, Germany, Herzegovina, Georgia, Poland, Romania, Ukraine, Finland, and the United States with a total of about 150 persons. It involved 30 reports of leading Russian scientists. The guests learned about Siberia, its potential, and its activities in sustainable development.

This conference produced a resolution devoted to stabilization of greenhouse gas emissions (December 1997, Japan). During the public forum, which was held in Japan at the same time as the UN conference in Kyoto, six representatives from Siberia participated. The International Seminar for State

Committees of Environmental Protection of Russian Administrative Units considered foreign experience in environmental protection (Tomsk, December 1999). It was devoted to "The Development of the Monitoring System in Tomsk Oblast." Experts from the Ecological Agency of Great Britain took part. The seminar included the following: introduction of new methods for use of natural resources, development of ecological management systems and ecological audits, and role of public organizations. The territorial representatives received useful information from a two-year team effort between the State Ecological Comittee of Tomsk Oblast and the British Agency.

Participants of the Conference "The Siberian Standard of Life: Ecology, Education, and Health" (Novosibirsk, December 1997) developed a network of demonstration projects for multi-level ecological education in the region. Also they noted the contribution of CCE to special program courses (ecology of food, ecological medicine, culture of health).

The ecological-economic forum "Extremes of Siberia-98" (October 1998) considered the problems of economic reform, the worsening of ecological conditions, and the unfavorable consequences for the population.

The participants of a roundtable devoted to the system of continuous ecological education noted the necessity of a complex program of the national survival. They recommended development of a complex program for fundamental understanding of person-environment interactions and multi-level continuous ecological education: pre-school-school-senior-higher-postgraduate.

Due to its work on ecological education in 1998, IASA became an associate member of the UNESCO Center of Chemical Science and Education. Among the main directions of the Center's work is education and retraining of teachers in the field of sustainable development. Some examples of IASA's Work in the Center Program are: o CCE of IASA together with the Problem Commission of Novosibirsk State Medical Academy addressed educational levels in food sciences, from pre- school education to staff education to retraining.

- o Qualification courses in hygiene, sanitation, ecological safety, and health science were organized in the production and consumption areas.
- o The innovation project "The Siberian Standard of Life" was prepared. The project is awaiting financial support from the British Council.
- o Experts of the Center organized the conference "Ecological Education of Children of Pre-school and School Age in the Context of Ecological Safety and Sustainable Development in the Siberian Region" (April 1999, Novosibirsk).

- o IASA experts helped revise educational programs in the technical high schools. The first group of engineers-ecologists graduated from Novosibirsk State Academy of Water Transport this year. Twenty-three students devoted their diploma work to water use and water transport problems in the context of ecological safety and sustainable development.
- o IASA authors prepared the monograph "Basics of Ecological Medicine" (Novosibirsk, 1999), which can be used in educational programs for addressing problems of life-support in the Siberian region.

The activities of CCE within the IASA territory are regularly reported in the regional press and mass media. This informs the population about IASA measures directed to ecological normalization of the environment and easing of social tension in the region. The Territorial State Committees of Environmental Protection are full partners in the formation of regional components of educational programs. They frequently render organizational and financial support for trainees. Databases established by the State Committees (using advanced GIS- technology) and processed data (airborne and space monitoring and computer modeling) in the form of different ecological atlases and maps are available to interested educational institutions in the framework of IASA. A number of higher schools of the region (Tomsk Polytechnical University, Novosibirsk State Technical University, Novosibirsk State Medical Academy) have displayed initiative in helping school pupils select their professional careers. They created the opportunity for realization of innovative educational methods through special ecological courses. The professors from these higher schools-experts of high qualification in different spheres-are teachers. Effective training in ecology is possible only by recognizing the power and culture of the Motherland. We have reason to be proud: rich natural resources, educated and talented people, rich spiritual and cultural treasures. "How light-blue and small is our planet!" exclaimed Yury Gagarin, who opened the way to Space. But we should remember that only with full knowledge about the world and with the participation of the world's society in sustainable development can we preserve our Earth with favorable living conditions.

PUBLIC DISSEMINATION OF INFORMATION TO SUPPORT SAFE MANAGEMENT OF CHEMICALS

- o First, because the Hampshire Research Institute (HRI) is a somewhat unusual nongovernmental organization, I would like to describe who we are, what we do, and how we support this work.

- o The second part is concerned with the history of direct public dissemination of environmental information in the United States. I will briefly note the origins of these efforts, describe some of the progress that we have made, and note some of the continuing challenges.
- o The third and most extensive part will focus on international initiatives dealing with the dissemination of environmental information to the public and the use of that information by the public. My belief is that the experiences of a variety of nations are more likely to provide cases that are useful in Russia than would an exclusive focus on the U.S. experience.

Equally important, there are a number of international initiatives that will likely influence Russian environmental initiatives, as part of the larger issue of Russian participation in the global economy. HRI is a different kind of NGO in several ways. Perhaps the most basic is that it began as a for-profit business (government consulting). Many U.S. NGOs started as small groups of citizens concerned about particular local issues working on a volunteer basis, and they have grown into nationwide organizations with hundreds of thousands of members and professional staffs. Hampshire Research Associates was founded by Warren Muir, formerly the Director of the Office of Toxic Substances in the Environmental Protection Agency, with a focus on the analysis of information systems and methods for assessing the risks posed by exposure to toxic chemicals.

After nearly a decade of operation, a related non-profit institute was created, with the focus of providing information directly to the public (including other NGOs), rather than via reports to the government. In the past decade, the non-profit institution has grown to eclipse the government consulting work, and the consulting firm now operates as a subsidiary of the NGO. Another difference between HRI and other NGOs is the way we work. If many U.S. NGOs can be viewed as "warriors" defending the environment, HRI is instead an "armorer," providing the public with the information and analytical tools they need to participate in public debate and decision-making concerning the environment. As might be expected for an organization founded by a chemist, and which hired two toxicologists as its first staff, our focus is quite specific. We are concerned with the potential adverse effects of chemicals, whether via intentional use in commerce and industry or as by-products of modern industrial society. Our main role has been to take data that are available to the public at least in a hypothetical sense, and to provide data formats, analyses, and tools that ensure that those data are really available to support public participation in environmental deliberations.

Two key issues have been the dissemination of data on the releases of industrial and commercial chemicals to the environment (PRTRs) and the development of user-friendly tools for risk assessment. In the latter area, we have long enjoyed the collaboration of Dr. Tarasova and the Mendeleev University. While most of our work is no longer on behalf of government agencies, it has received substantial financial support from the government, in the form of grants and cooperative agreements. We have also had significant support from private foundations. Increasingly, our work has been supported by multilateral institutions, including UN agencies (UNEP, UNIDO, UNITAR), OECD, and the North American Commission on Environmental Cooperation (CEC). In the United States, there is a wealth of environmental data available to the public. The key problem that we have encountered is that government agencies vary widely in the extent to which they provide the data in a form that is usable to any but a small group of experts and the level of effort that they require a citizen to expend to get the data.

Probably our best known data source is the Toxics Release Inventory (TRI). It reports annual data on releases and transfers of some 600 chemicals and chemical classes from a range of U.S. industries. This success story had its beginnings, however, in failure. Most sources credit the passage of the enabling legislation with the environmental disaster at Bhopal, which was closely followed by a similar, if far better controlled, incident at Institute, West Virginia. Without this disaster and potential disaster, the law (which addresses both ongoing releases and disaster preparedness) might never have been passed. At the time, the Environmental Protection Agency held that it was unnecessary, and unlikely to provide information not obtainable elsewhere. TRI only requires reporting of data to the public, and yet it is associated with major improvements in environmental performance. Over the ten years for which consistently reported TRI data have been available (1988-1997), there has been a substantial decline in releases of listed chemicals from reporting facilities: Substantial declines have been seen in on-site releases from 1988 to 1997 (49.2 percent overall): to air, down 55 percent; to surface water, 64.7 percent; to underground injection, 21.9 percent; to land, 26.2 percent. These decreases were not offset by an increase in transfers, but reflect real advances in environmental protection.

Academics still argue over exactly how reporting alone has led to improved performance, but most agree that the annual reporting of data linked to the specific facilities responsible for emissions is a key element. There are many other databases that are less well used (likely because they lack a comparable mandate for public reporting).

They are likely targets for further efforts at effective public dissemination. We are beginning to explore the use of new tools, including Geographic Information Systems, to increase the utility and availability of these data. Despite the benefits of public reporting, there are still challenges to making sure the public obtains the data it needs to participate in environmental protection. Over the past decade, the range of chemicals and industries covered by TRI reporting has expanded significantly. At each turn, there is major resistance from affected industries. More recently, there has been a major challenge to the fundamental concept of public access to data, under the guise of concern about terrorism and security.

A recent law imposed a new "balancing" test on risks and benefits of information dissemination, despite a complete absence of any evidence that these data have been used in terrorism. In consequence, new regulations have severely restricted public access to data on the potential impacts of industrial disasters. These restrictions, among other effects, have precluded any analysis at a national or regional level of the safety of our industrial facilities.

Sadly, some evidence also suggests that government agencies are becoming less willing to work with the NGO community to provide effective access to information for the public. At this point, I hope that this is an accidental consequence of government restructuring efforts. As I noted in my introduction, it may be that activities in a variety of international forums are of greater relevance to Russia that are the specific experiences that we have had in the United States.

In this regard, I want to briefly describe the recent progress of the international community with regard to PRTRs and discuss some potential political implications for reporting in Russia. The latter will rely on observations regarding possible parallels that have been observed elsewhere. You will have to judge for yourselves whether they have any relevance to the situation in Russia.

Finally, I will provide a brief discussion of technical resources relative to establishing a PRTR. While this has been a massive effort in the United States, the experiences of other countries suggest that effective implementation can be done far less expensively. While perhaps not directly relevant to a vast industrial nation such as Russia, the experiences of small European countries may be particularly relevant in addressing the problem of disseminating information in the face of budgetary constraints.

The TRI and other early PRTRs began as independent national efforts, but over the past decade there has been an accelerating pace of work in the international community. Available evidence suggests that there will be significant harmonization of PRTR reporting on a global scale among the industrialized nations.

This harmonization is occurring within a context of the globalization of trade, and significantly involves international economic organizations. It may well be that there will be an economic impetus to instituting such reporting. While I am not aware of any concrete evidence, it is not hard to imagine that public reporting of facility environmental data could become an important part of marketing products globally.

Many multinational corporations have adopted a "triple bottom line" (profits, environment, social accountability) approach to evaluating business success, and they are imposing corresponding conditions on firms that wish to serve as their suppliers.

There are several documented cases where multinational companies have discontinued relationships with suppliers on the basis of their environmental performance.

PRTRs first came to general attention on the international scene at the Rio Conference in 1992, albeit in rather general language, as was true of much of the conference resolutions. Chapter 19 directs governments to implement and improve data bases about chemicals including inventories of emissions, with the co-operation of industry and the public, and cites PRTRs as an example.

There has, however, been significant action in multilateral organizations since then, with increasing specificity about an international consensus on public availability of environmental data.

Perhaps the most significant event is the signing of the Convention on Access to Information, Public Participation in Decision-Making and Access to Justice in Environmental Matters in June 1998 under the auspices of the United Nations Economic Commission for Europe.

The European Union is moving to harmonize its member requirements with this convention. The striking contrast of the Aarhus Convention to Chapter 19 of Agenda 21 is that the language is far more specific with regard to what is required of signatories. The "pillars" of this convention are directly related to the focus of our present meeting, and so the relevance of this convention to Russia is a topic that bears serious examination.

It is anticipated that a sufficient number of ratifications will occur to bring the Convention into force in 2001. The signatories have had two subsequent meetings, as well as several meetings of implementation/working groups.

Moreover, PRTRs are one of three explicit centers of attention for working groups under the Convention. The PRTR group is being led by the Czech Republic.

The Czech Republic has independently been active in this area for several years. It has developed considerable expertise with regard to PRTR implementation in a transition economy faced with severe budget constraints. In North America, cross-border comparisons have become a major element in PRTR reporting, both with regard to its public visibility (they are very popular with the mainstream press) and in terms of whether and how PRTRs are implemented.

Significant differences in comparable facilities across the U.S.-Canadian border have drawn interest in the popular press, resulting in the widespread dissemination of data and of information on how to access the data.

The greater range of chemical coverage in the United States and the wider range of facilities in Canada have driven continuing evaluation of the adequacy and relevance of each nation's reporting. Ongoing reporting of U.S. and Canadian data, in the context of a free-trade zone, have created considerable pressure on Mexico to implement a comparable set of reporting.

In the context of these effects, it is instructive to note that the earliest ratifiers of the Aarhus Convention are, with a single exception, immediate neighbors of Russia to the south and west. Only the Russian NGO community can determine its interest in pursuing PRTRs or comparable reporting systems, in light of its knowledge of the legal, political, and technical conditions that prevail here.

Such an effort may or may not be a priority for any Russian NGO.

To the extent that there is interest, however, there are technical resources that can dramatically reduce the effort involved in instituting such a reporting system. For example, there are several national and international sets of guidance on how to estimate emissions from various industrial processes. Given the range of industrial infrastructure that these diverse sources represent, at least some should be relevant or adaptable to conditions in Russia.

Many of these technical documents are directly available on the Internet. In addition to the resources listed below, which deal primarily with the problem of generating data to report, there is a wealth of available information (with more under development) on how to implement the reporting and dissemination of these data. The international institutions listed below represent a good starting place for any NGO interested in PRTR implementation.

6

Radiation Hazard Awareness

Experience from radiation accidents, and especially the accident at the Chernobyl plant, has shown the impact of information on the population, both for individuals and for society, in comparison with the impact of radiation. On the one hand, the impact comes from perception of radiation hazard; and on the other, it is a result of a mechanism of social aggravation. Let us consider in brief the reasons and peculiarities of perceptions of radiation hazard. The starting point of radiation awareness as danger was the creation of nuclear weapons, the bombing of Japan, and large-scale nuclear weapons testing. One of the main reasons for formation and strengthening of extremely tense and unequal perceptions of radiation hazards has been the arms race, which for one-half a century has involved all nuclear countries (from the United States, Great Britain, and the USSR in the late forties to India and Pakistan at the end of the nineties). Still, opposition to nuclear activities in general is a reason too. Ionizing radiation is considered to be not only dangerous for health, but also an inevitable hazard for future generations.

Many factors have affected the perception of ionizing radiation. They are: secrecy, which has surrounded nuclear weapons production everywhere; international campaign drives for elimination of nuclear weapon testing; new types of production (H-bomb, N-bomb) in certain countries; international alarm over the danger of expansion of nuclear weapons; intensive attention to radiation effects on human health and the environment. Thus, a strong base exists for a special perception of radiation hazards in everyday life. It is seriously aggravated due to peculiarities of man-made accidents and catastrophes. Society more easily withstands natural disasters even if they have huge effects. This has been proven with quick revival of regions suffering from earthquakes, floods, hurricanes, and tornadoes, even if the danger of repeated disasters remains very high. In case of a man-made disaster, the first social reaction is to search for a reason and for culprits. The higher the level of responsibility, the harsher the social perception of the catastrophe. Thus, accidents and disasters at state-controlled factories appear to be the most serious for their social effects. Also, radiation accidents are certainly characterized with harsher social effects because it is the State which controls the use of radiation activities and especially nuclear energy activities.

We can see great differences in social attitudes to accidents and disasters. One is characterized by an adequate response including the following stages: defining the scope of a catastrophe and precise classification of victims; searching for reasons and culprits; paying compensatory damage, mainly, by insurance systems; punishing the responsible bodies (a producer, an operating organization); and identifying reasons (construction, organization, human factors) in order to prevent repetition of the accident. Such accidents include fires and traffic incidents. Society has adapted to traffic accidents in spite of the number of victims. Loss of life of dozens, hundreds, and thousands of people in train wrecks, car crashes, and shipwrecks does not cast doubt on their necessity. It means the society regards such hazards as socially acceptable.

The other extreme is rare man-made accidents. Social attitudes toward them are much more intricate and sharp. These include radiation and chemical accidents. The initial reaction of populations to information about such accidents, and first of all, those involving radiation, is concern about their own health and the health of their progeny. The circle of victims is uncertain. Soon the State is blamed for giving permission for the activity that caused the catastrophe. A mechanism of social aggravation starts to work. With the help of the mass media and organizations interested in public attention or recognition, the situation is dramatized. In its turn, the mass-media dramatization intensifies concern of the community and extends the circle of "victims." It can cause different social effects up to radical changes of public attitudes toward science and certain activities.

Let us briefly outline those people and organizations that can take an active part in this aggravation scheme. First are local authorities and political figures. They seem to be quite sincere and have different reasons (from a desire to increase state compensation to an interest in receiving public attention). Nevertheless, a lack of comprehension, a reluctance in obtaining official data from specialists, and a logic of opposition inevitably make them dramatize the post-accident situation. In conditions of high information capabilities of local authorities and greater public confidence in them in comparison with the State as a whole, their influence on the population is very profound. For example, in 1991 after adoption of both republic (Ukraine, Belarus, and Russia) and all-union laws, areas eligible for benefits and compensation increased. Authorities asked for their regions to be added to the list of radiation pollution areas. The only exception was Krasnodar Territory, where some resorts were polluted. The local authorities preferred to decontaminate polluted areas on their own rather than lose the image of the resorts.

The second group that is able and ready to take part in the social aggravation process includes ecological and anti-war organizations. The orientation of their reaction inevitably results from their usual stance because dramatization of accidents proves the correctness and significance of their previous activity. The movements of victims of radiation accidents play a certain role too. The members are inclined, on the one hand, to preserve their victim status and collect corresponding compensation and benefits and on the other hand, to mythologize about their participation in radiation accidents.

The third group of people that can play a very dramatic role in the aggravation of consequences includes cultural workers, artists, and intellectuals. A custom of identifying oneself as the nation's conscience together with the stereotype of the radiation impact can often increase the psychological after-effects. For example, after the Chernobyl accident cultural workers offered to discuss not only the danger of the burial of Chernobyl victims, but also the impossibility of burying them in "contaminated" land. Both problems (except in a few unique cases) had no sense at all, but they strongly influenced the community. The same problems with burial of radioactive accident victims took place in Goiania (Brazil, 1988) as the local population sharply protested. Cultural workers also try to change professional terms. For example, radiation pollution, which means appearance of harmful (in this case radioactive) substances in the soil, is changed to radioactive contamination (saturation with pathogens) or even more dramatically to health damage of the area.

In the case when a radiation accident takes place under conditions of economically successful activity, organizations and groups using alternative technologies can also participate in dramatizing the situation. It would be mistake to exaggerate the role of these factors after atomic plant accidents, but a number of cogent arguments are raised in arguing against atomic and for thermal power. The role and activity of the above mentioned groups can change at different stages after a radiation accident. Thus, cultural workers always deal with the problem for a short period. Ecological organizations usually act for a longer time, independent of any positive results of their activity. For example, campaigns conducted to collect money to send children for rest from the moderate climate conditions of central Russia to the south in the Crimea or Cuba give doubtful results. The reason for money collection is to support children who were exposed to radiation, but often healthy children benefit. So, information after the Chernobyl accident resulted in the following characteristics of radiation hazard awareness:

- o Radiation hazard is associated only with industrial business (power plant, defense industry), with all other sources of radiation hazard (natural sources, medicine) posing little hazard.
- o Radiation hazard is excessively high in comparison with other hazards.
- o Only the State is responsible for measures to decrease risk.
- o The current policy of risk reduction is insufficient.

None of these statements is true. Natural sources and medicine are the main part of radiation hazard (see Table 1). The share of radiation accidents and man- made sources in overall radioactivity is negligibly small even on territories with nuclear plants. But in dealing with problems of radiation hazard, the mass media say nothing or little about the facts. Proven ways to reduce risks, such as staying out of the sun or avoiding radon impacts, do not receive attention. As a result, the greater part of the population is not only ignorant of radiation hazard, but they also do not want to take even simple prevention measures. One can even state that the present Russian community is like a "zombie" on the whole problem of radiation hazard and the Chernobyl consequences. Most people repeat the mass media stereotype and equate radiation hazard to Chernobyl.

SCIENTIFIC VALIDITY OF DECISION-MAKING

Every large ecological problem, especially a radiation accident, is a unique event with a number of particular features. Therefore, scientific research and necessary scientific support take on special significance in the decision-making process that concerns safety measures and elimination of after-effects. Nevertheless, as shown later, many decisions have been made without scientific support or contrary to scientific recommendations.

Let us consider a number of examples showing the role of science in reduction of the Chernobyl consequences. Table 2 deals with dates of decisions (by the government or authorized ministry) on safety measures for the first five years after the accident and some characteristics of these measures, including their scientific validity.

They are divided into five groups according to the type of decision:

1. Sanitary code and regulations (S) approved by the Chief Sanitary Doctor of the Soviet Union or a republic

2. Executive decrees concerning certain settlements (ED), usually decrees of supreme public authorities
3. Government decrees and orders concerning recommendations and instructions on working procedures, departmental guides, and instructions (DG), usually dealing with regulations and instructions according to the characteristics of the radiation environment
4. Conceptual (C) decisions of Soviet National Committee on Radiation Protection (NCRP), later Russian NCRP, for the main intervention levels and their need in corresponding legislation and administrative decrees
5. Legislative decrees (L) on execution of certain measures by executive organs or determination of intervention levels.

The scientific and technical validity of the decisions is based on conclusions made by radiation safety specialists, which engender society's confidence. A number of actions inconsistent with the real danger made by political groups, the mass media, and others proved that a biased distrust of specialists appeared during the first month after the accident. The situation improved a little by the middle of summer 1986. Then the crucial decision-making process was completed, based on scientific and technical validity, while a number of incorrect decisions were revised. By the end of 1988, a large amount of data was collected for long-term radiation prognosis of polluted areas. Moreover, real opportunities for all safety measures were realized, as well as limiting negative consequences for the population that resulted in restrictions. The environment became better in some polluted areas. In these circumstances the Soviet NCRP suggested its 35-rem concept of total lifetime extra dose limit equal to 350 mSv (hereinafter, the concept of safe habitation). Practical realization of the concept provided for very limited resettlement of the most polluted settlements and significant lessening of restrictions in other areas.

Nevertheless it did not work due to a number of social reasons. Beginning in 1988, a great number of articles on the Chernobyl problem were published simultaneously with the development of "glasnost" policies. The mass media adopted strictures on the concept of safe habitation. In 1989, taking into account the complex political situation in the country and in fact impeaching the credibility of its own specialists, the Government of the Soviet Union made an official request to the International Atomic Energy Agency (IAEA) for coordination of an "international examination of the concept of safe habitation in the areas contaminated with radioactivity after the Chernobyl accident developed in the USSR and an assessment of effectiveness of measures for public health protection within these areas."

As a result, the International Chernobyl Project (ICP) started in the spring of 1990. An independent international advisory commission of 19 members was organized under the chairmanship of the outstanding scientist Dr. I.Shigematsu, Director of the Radiation Effects Research Foundation in Hiroshima. Two hundred independent experts from 23 countries and seven international organizations took part in the project. Fifty scientific groups visited the USSR. Laboratories from several countries including Austria, France, and the USA helped to analyze and assess the data.

Initial information on the ICP was favorably reported. However, after the news that ICP members considered the measures in progress as quite adequate, the mass media changed their opinion on the project. Dozens of publications blamed the ICP members for trying to hide the radiological consequences of the accident for the sake of the international "nuclear Mafia." The resulting documents of ICP contained sharp criticism of both implemented and planned safety measures.

They were formulated as follows: "The International Advisory Commission noted that the adopted and planned long-term measures, though guided by good intentions, exceeded the strict requirements of radiation protection. Resettlement and foodstuff restriction measures are unsuitable from the standpoint of radiation safety. Nevertheless, any relaxation of the current policy almost certainly would give a negative effect due to the high level of stress and alarm of residents in contaminated areas and their current expectations. It is agreed, however, that social and political factors should be taken into account, so responsible and competent authorities should make the final decisions. In any case, future changes should not lead to stricter restriction criteria. "More specific criteria reducing foodstuff restrictions would be preferable to resettlement, taking into account all the social and economic factors connected with public health. Further application of the restrictions for use of local foodstuff products in the polluted areas means a significant worsening of quality of life for some people. The only way to avoid it is to resettle them to such regions where they could live in their previous manner if it is possible. Comparatively high criteria for foodstuff restrictions might have aggravated these problems..."

One could think the ICP results might close a debate concerning the possibility of habitation of polluted areas. In fact, the USSR Government planned a number of actions in June-August 1991, including meetings of socially active citizens with executive and legislative authorities. Large sections of the public should have been acquainted with the ICP results. However, the situation in the country became worse; events of August 1991 resulted in the USSR's collapse and prevented both practical realization and the acquaintance of the general public with the ICP advice. As a result, the governments of Belarus, Russia, and Ukraine in fact rejected both points: the NCRP suggestion of limited resettlement and the ICP view that rejected any resettlement.

Thus, neither the opinions of national specialists nor the views of leading international experts were taken into account. On the contrary, populist decisions resulted in significant economic and social waste.

ROLE OF POLITICAL FACTORS AND THEIR EFFECTS

Public discontent was stirred up by some persons who made a political, administrative, and public career based on the Chernobyl accident and incited the authorities to change their previous decisions. Since specialists did not support this revision, they were just excluded from the decision-making process. Subsequent measures were realized according to soil pollution criteria instead of dose criteria, which are the only correct criteria for radiation safety. Just after the accident, soil pollution might be justified by lack of radiation data. Further, "territory pollution density" criteria should be used only for agriculture purposes. However, the adoption of dose principles is an important component of radiation accident reduction. This component was lost in the Chernobyl accident reduction effort.

By 1990 more than 500,000 people received different benefits because of the Chernobyl accident. By 1991 it turned out that many people were interested in further expanding the so-called radioactive contaminated zones. These circumstances caused problems in realizing rational ideas of developing a Unified Program of radiation accident reduction (as well as adopting the law on social protection of victims). The following persons insisted on using radiological principles in determination of radioactive contaminated zones:

- A few specialists in the radiation protection sphere, including those who had encountered public opposition.
- A number of outstanding scientists recognizing the role of radiation and other hazards in life.
- Some economists versed in the necessary costs.

Active supporters of maximum expansion of the radioactive contaminated zones were:

- Republic authorities of Ukraine and Belarus and Russian regional administrative elites interested in financial and material support from government funds.

- o Numerous mistaken public figures who did not anticipate negative results of their activity, though they connected their political fortunes with the consequences of the accident.

Due to unclear positions of the politically weak Moscow Government, almost all demands of the Republics were completely fulfilled. They resulted in the broadest interpretation of radioactive contaminated zones. The so-called zone with privileged social-economic status with lower pollution density border at 1 Ci per sq. km. was of fundamental importance. This zone with its numerous benefits did not correspond to any radiological criteria. It should be mentioned that the authors of the decision concerning this zone did not know that more than 30 percent of the territory where the pollution density exceeded 1 Ci per sq. km. was situated outside the USSR. It is necessary to stress that there were no claims for damage nor indemnities for health injuries in the majority of foreign countries impacted by the Chernobyl accident.

Unfortunately, the price of incorrect decisions included more than money for benefits and compensations. The psychological health of many people was damaged because they were officially considered as accident victims. Strange as it may seem, health control based on the law played a significant role here.

Humane but abstract ideas gave negative results in specific circumstances during the last phase of the Chernobyl accident. Large resources were spent on health control using a list of possible health effects. First of all, it included thyroid gland cancers that were discovered during total screening. The law, in fact, required searches for any evidence of public health decline.

This surely was found in situations of decreasing living standards and unfavorable demographic trends. But inhabitants of polluted regions linked in their mind health problems due to many reasons with radioactive effects. Some of the health workers who dealt with increased death rates and other effects as the living standard declined were especially sure of this relationship. It is necessary in this regard to stress that the polluted areas and regions did not differ from other regions of Russia according to the main demographic criteria. Standards for participating in programs for eliminating accident after-effects were established in too simplified a manner. They caused an unjustified increase in the number of participants. By spring 1989, when the most extensive work was fulfilled, the number of participants was estimated as 250,000 people. It was a large but realistic number; but several years later it increased more than three times to 800,000 people.

A fundamental change of the basic structure of the Chernobyl law might be the only rational way out. But a serious change of public opinion toward radiation hazard and an increased ecological culture of the whole society is needed. It is possible only when there is societal confidence in scientists and specialists. One should stress the role of ecology organizations, which should base their activity on scientific arguments instead of propaganda stereotypes.

ROLE OF GREENPEACE OF RUSSIA AND OTHER PUBLIC ORGANIZATIONS IN THE CONSERVATION OF RUSSIAN FORESTS EVOLUTION OF ECOLOGICAL PROBLEMS

An extensive pattern of forest use exists in Russia dating back to the 1930s. It is characterized by exploiting more and more ancient forests instead of intensive forestry in developed regions. The best wood according to quality, supply, and accessibility is taken in the first cutting, with an absence of efficient reforestation. As a result, timber resources are disappearing quickly. Deforestation of the remaining ancient forestlands is inevitable. For example, only 6 percent of the taiga zone in European Russia has natural forests. Greenpeace of Russia made a map, "Last Remaining Forestlands of the European Taiga," based on space imagery and special nature studies..

Most of the forestlands may be destroyed in five to ten years. Gas and oil producing industries, gold mining, and other extractive industries are also responsible for deforestation. Enterprises and exploration activities of these industries are the main causes of fires. Forestland destroyed by fire is comparable with that destroyed as a result of felling.

The present pattern leads to the total destruction of natural forest ecological systems in a great part of the forest zone of Russia as well as to depletion of timber resources. It causes an avalanche of social problems. In the 1970s, the timber industry decline began in most taiga regions. It became especially evident in the end of the 1980s and in the 1990s. The main reason for the decrease is the depletion of woods in the vicinity of enterprises founded in the 1940s, 1950s, and earlier. Since the beginning of the 1990s, about one million employees here lost their jobs in the timber industry or will soon be unemployed.

Several thousand "wood settlements" mainly in remote districts of the European North, Siberia, and Far East with four million residents are left without a livelihood. The pattern of depletion is stimulated by extremely low payments for forest exploration rights (forest tax). For example, standing wood has a token price of not more than one dollar for one cubic meter. That is about 2 to 5 percent of the commercial value of round lumber. As a result, the State has a lack of money for an efficient forest service. In 1999 the payment for forest exploration rights was about 15 percent of the total costs of the Federal Service of Forestry. The present pattern of forestry leads both to the total destruction of the last remaining ancient forests and to ecological disturbance of the forest zone (water balance, swamping, soil decay, biodiversity decrease). The whole state timber industry is unprofitable. Also, life in timber settlements is socially unstable due to a decrease of earnings and unemployment.

THE IMPACT OF GOVERNMENT DECREES

For the last decade, no government decrees for radical change of the situation and for stable forest exploitation have been adopted. The Forest Code of the Russian Federation requires timber owners to carry on multiple-purpose and sustainable forestry while promoting biological diversity. This requirement is not fulfilled because of the absence of appropriate laws. Even the existing nature protection legislation on forestry and forest exploration is not observed. For example, the Law "On Ecological Assessment" adopted in 1995 requires an ecological assessment of "schemes of protection and use of water, forest, land, and other nature resources," including organization and management projects for forestry and felling. Nevertheless, most projects are realized without any ecological assessment. Conservation of species under special protection is usually not addressed because these species are not identified within the scope of forest husbandry and planning. Forest husbandry, the base for forestry planning and management, is aimed entirely at accounting for timber resources.

"The Principles of Determination of Woodcutting Areas..." adopted in 1987 are still in force. They provide "a level of major harvest and regeneration felling for 20 to 30 years." Economically inaccessible woods are included into production reserves. As a result, forests located near roads in populated regions are subject to more intense cutting. The full use of woodcutting areas is impossible in the majority of regions due to a lack of economically accessible forest resources. Enterprises often try to solve this problem by disregarding ecological limits including those provided by legislation. "Criteria and Indicators of Sustainable Management of Russian Forests" adopted in 1998 does not have parameters of sustainable forest management and does not provide for any change in the present forest management system. Moreover, the majority of forestry employees know nothing about this document. The general type of felling is final harvesting on a large area (up to 50 hectares). This causes heavy soil erosion, swamping, and catastrophic changes of the forest environment, with an absence of reforestation and disappearance of many species of forest flora and fauna. The current Forest Legislation disregards international conventions for biodiversity conservation and does not include up-to-date scientific achievements for sustainable forest husbandry.

ROLE OF NONGOVERNMENTAL ORGANIZATIONS

A number of public organizations are involved in forest conservation. The most active ones have joined the Forest Club of Russian NGOs. It is an informal working group consisting of representatives of NGOs. Forest Club members are:

- o Greenpeace Russia
- o Socio-Ecological Union Forest Campaign
- o Conservation Center for Wild Resources
- o Druzhinas (Student Corps) for Nature Conservation Movement
- o Information Center of Taiga Rescue Network-Russia
- o Save Pechora Committee
- o Individual activists

The main task of the Forest Club is to coordinate NGOs for forest conservation.

The Club's major activities are:

- o Improvement of Russian forest legislation, forestry regulations, and technical standards
- o Inventory of natural old growth forests and other valuable forest areas
- o Monitoring of protected territories for illegal logging and poaching
- o Promotion of ecologically and socially responsible forestry and independent forest certification
- o Publication of the Forest Bulletin

The current state forest management system does not ensure participation of NGOs in forest management and development of forest policy. The overwhelming majority of Forest Service employees regard NGOs as hostile entities that should not interfere in forest affairs. Usually, the state bodies do not consider suggestions of residents and NGOs on changing felling practices, excluding some sites from exploitation, or changing the management system.

Consideration of public suggestions is not provided in the current forest legislation. Standard acts and forest legislation are usually developed in secret, excluding not only the general public, but also specialists outside the Forest Service.

The scientific and nature protection communities learn about a certain bill or project when it is introduced to the State Duma, registered at the Ministry of Justice, or confirmed with a department decree. As a rule, it is almost impossible to introduce any changes into the document at this stage. In those isolated instances when a project was open for discussion, specialist opinions outside the Forest Service were not taken into account. Since 1993, no representative from scientific or public organizations outside the Forest Service and other ministries and departments has managed to include any innovations in the documents. Efficient collaboration between the government and the public at the federal level is almost impossible. The only effective participation of the general public is open protest against certain state activities and projects.

RESULTS OF ACTIVITIES OF NONGOVERNMENT ORGANIZATIONS

NGO activities are diverse. The Forest Club has the following activities:

1. Improvement of Russian forest legislation; promotion of ecologically and socially responsible forestry; and independent forest certification. Detailed analysis of illegal felling shows the weakness of the current Forest Code, with 20 percent of timber being felled illegally. Greenpeace proposed a forest program of sustainable forest management that would provide timber settlements with regular work. In a clear manner, a reference book describes the current forestry structure, as well as felling standards and rules. It suggests possibilities of public participation in forest management in Russia.

   Greenpeace prepared standards for assessment of the less disturbed forest areas. These standards were published in a number of issues of the Forest Bulletin and were repeatedly discussed at conferences of environmental activists and forestry workers, including two conferences in 1998, devoted to problems of forest management and protection in Karelia and Sakhalin.

2. Inventory of natural old growth forests and other valuable forest areas. Since 1996, Greenpeace in cooperation with the Biodiversity Conservation Center, the Socio-Ecological Union, and other NGOs carried out an inventory of ancient taiga areas in the European and Ural areas of Russia. The work was based on 1999-2000 space images of middle and high resolution. The work included more than one hundred expeditions of NGOs; specialists of Moscow, Pushkin, Tambov, and other state universities; and reserve workers. The NGOs use

updated sources of information on the condition of forestlands and more up-to-date technologies in comparison with the state nature resource departments. The inventory of ancient taiga areas all over Russia is now carried out within the project "The Forest Watch of Russia." Russian research and production institutions, the technical center Skaneks, the International Institute of Forestry, and regional organizations, such as Altai-21 Century Foundation, Friends of Siberian Forests (Krasnoyarsk), and the Bureau of Regional Public Campaigns (Vladivostok) participate in the project. Undisturbed forest assessment criteria are used, research techniques are improved at model sites (usually they are reserves), and the basis for new reserves and national parks are developed. Identification Atlas of Taiga Plants of European Russia was published to assist field investigations.

3. Monitoring protected territories to detect illegal logging and poaching. Since 1997, Greenpeace workers have actively participated in revisions of forest management and forest husbandry in several regions, such as Moscow Oblast, Leningrad Oblast, Sakhalin Oblast, Republic of Buryatia, and Primorye Territory. In a few regions, the revisions were informal without participation of state bodies. In Moscow and Leningrad Oblasts the revisions resulted in improvement of forest management and observance of current legislation. In Primorye Territory, a protest was carried out against the export to Japan of illegally cut timber, bought and "legalized" by official wood exporters. As a result, the business activity of some companies was suspended for some time. Unfortunately, the situation has now returned to the original pattern. Demonstrations to attract public attention are important for NGOs. For example, in Moscow Oblast illegal felling took place in the immediate vicinity of a forestry office, but forest guards never reacted to these acts. This action was described in the press and shown on TV. As a result, the Board of the Moscow Forest Department organized the Public Council of Forest Management to solve such problems. As a result of protests of NGOs, Scandinavian companies and Russian wood importers declared a moratorium on purchase of timber from forestlands in Karelia in 1997. Due to this moratorium, the most valuable remaining timber stands were saved in Kalevala Forestland, which is as an official reserve. At present, an advisory panel is discussing the future of these forestlands.
4. Public participation in forest management. Opportunities for teamwork with local authorities in a few regions are wider than opportunities at the federal level. For example, for the last five years in Moscow

Oblast reviews of environmental legislation compliance were carried out with participation of NGOs (in fact, the reviews were completed thanks to the efforts of the NGOs themselves). One such example is the "Summary of the Results of the Interagency Commission on Assessing the Status of Forestry in Vyborg, Priozersk, and Vsevolozhsk Regions of Leningrad Oblast." According to the results of the revisions, rather strong sanctions were often applied to law violations. For example, commercial "clear cutting" in strictly protected nature reserves practically stopped in Moscow Oblast. State ecological examinations are now carried out for projects of forest management and felling plans. "Hot" problems may be discussed with forest department officials. Nevertheless some problems remain. In August 2000, the state reserve Atleka in Vologda Oblast was established as a result of a discussion among representatives of local authorities, forest industry companies, NGOs, and the scientific community. It is the first case of a strictly protected national reserve established by a logging enterprise. The Vostochny Reserve in Sakhalin Oblast is one more example of constructive collaboration between public and State structures. Unfortunately, examples of similar understanding by the authorities of the actions and demands of the "greens" are still very rare and in the majority of regions completely absent.

5. Educational activity, including education of members of environmental organizations and education of the general public. To improve professional qualifications of environmental organization members and forest officers, the Forest Club publishes the periodical Forest Bulletin as well as other materials, for example the book European Taiga on the Verge of the Millennium by A.Yu Yaroshenko. Booklets, calendars, and posters are published for the general public, such as the calendar for 1999 and a booklet devoted to Lake Baikal.
6. Lobbying of nature protection initiatives and attraction of public attention to regional and federal ecological problems. Organizing support for an environmental referendum was a main activity in 2000. The current legislation requires two million signatures. More than 2.5 million signatures were collected, so the referendum depends on the Russian Government. It may avoid the referendum by declaring signatures to be "faulty" or "inaccurate."

7

NGOs in Ecological Decision-making

It is necessary to develop a legislative mechanism providing for participation of NGOs in ecological decision-making. A way for information about government decrees and actions to reach NGOs and the general public is needed along with a way for ensuring responsiveness to suggestions from NGOs. Up to now, important decrees are usually prepared, unknown to the general public. Even if NGOs learn about a decree and put forward proposals, they are disregarded without discussion. To solve these problems it is necessary:

- o To distribute information for the general public about the substance of new draft laws and departmental and interdepartmental regulations if they are not connected with state secrets. The simplest way could be publishing the texts on the Internet and in the central mass media. The information should be published not less than a month before the date of their official consideration or, in the case of a federal law or interdepartmental standard, not less than three months before the date.
- o To develop a way to ensure responsiveness to suggestions from the public on the substance of new laws and standards, natural resource policies, and other problems concerning interests of different population groups. An obligation of a reasonable answer on such proposals from the state bodies within a limited time period is important. o To have a mechanism for monitoring ministries and departments that are active in environmental protection and natural resource use. In particular, regular restructuring of the departments in the regions with participation of public organizations in this restructuring is important. Public councils with participation of NGOs should be established and linked to federal ministries and departments and their regional

divisions. Participation of fictitious "public" organizations should be avoided.

- To make obligatory the participation of interested NGOs in commissions of experts conducting federal and regional ecological examinations. It is necessary to publish information on projects and territories that have already undergone ecological examinations.
- To require public monitoring of large investment projects, including those with foreign investments. The easiest means of doing this appears to be the establishment of a public council for every project with participation of NGOs. The council must have access to non-commercial data concerning the projects and all information about the current legislation.
- To provide free access for the general public and NGOs to data concerning implementation of projects for use of natural resources and for environmental protection. It is necessary to remove unreasonable obstacles for access to ecological data, including costs, particularly if they are already paid from budgetary funds.

PROBLEMS OF WASTE MANAGEMENT IN THE MOSCOW REGION

The scientific and technological revolution of the twentieth century has turned the world over, transformed it, and presented humankind with new knowledge and innovative technologies that previously seemed to be fantasies. Man, made in the Creator's own image, has indeed become in many respects similar to the Creator. Primitive thinking and consumerism as to nature and natural resources seem to be in contrast to this background. Drastic deterioration of the environment has become the other side of the coin that gave the possibility, so pleasant for the average person, to buy practically everything that is needed.

A vivid example of man's impact as "a geological force" (as Academician V. I. Vernadsky described contemporary mankind) is poisoning of the soil, surface and underground waters, and atmosphere with floods of waste that threaten to sweep over the Earth. Ecosystems of our planet are no longer capable of "digesting" everincreasing volumes of waste and new synthetic chemicals alien to nature. One of the most important principles in achieving sustainable development is to limit the appetite of public consumption. A logical corollary of this principle suggests that the notion "waste" or "refuse" should be excluded not only from professional terminology, but also from the minds of people, with "secondary material resources" as a substitute concept for them. In my presentation I would like to dwell on a number of aspects of waste disposal. It is an ecological, economic, and social problem for the Moscow megalopolis in present-day conditions.

PRESENT SITUATION WITH WASTE IN MOSCOW

Tens of thousand of enterprises and research organizations of practically all branches of the economy are amassed over the territory of 100,000 hectares: facilities of energy, chemistry and petrochemistry; metallurgical and machine-building works; and light industrial and food processing plants. Moscow is occupying one of the leading places in the Russian Federation for the level of industrial production. The city is the greatest traffic center and bears a heavy load in a broad spectrum of responsibilities as capital of the State. The burden of technogenesis on the environment of the city of Moscow and the Moscow region is very considerable, and it is caused by all those factors mentioned above. One of the most acute problems is the adverse effect of the huge volumes of industrial and consumer wastes. Industrial waste has a great variety of chemical components.

For the last ten years we witnessed mainly negative trends in industrial production in Moscow due to the economic crisis in the country. In Moscow the largest industrial works came practically to a standstill, and production of manufactured goods declined sharply. At the same time, a comparative analysis in 1998-99 of the indexes of goods and services output and of resource potential showed that the coefficient of the practical use of natural resources per unit of product, which had been by all means rather low in previous years, proceeded gradually to decrease further. At present we have only 25 percent of the industrial output that we had in 1990, but the volume of water intake remains at the same level. Fuel consumption has come down only by 18 percent, and the amassed production waste diminished by only 50 percent. These figures indicate the growing indexes of resource consumption and increases in wastes from industrial production.

Every year about 13 million tons of different kinds of waste are accumulated in Moscow: 42 percent from water preparation and sewage treatment, 25 percent from industry, 13 percent from the construction sector, and 20 percent from the municipal economy.

The main problem of waste management in Moscow city comes from the existing situation whereby a number of sites for recycling and disposal of certain types of industrial waste and facilities for storage of inert industrial and building wastes are situated outside the city in Moscow Region, which is subject to other laws of the Russian Federation. Management of inert industrial and building wastes, which make up the largest part of the general volume of wastes and of solid domestic wastes (SDW), simply means in everyday practice their disposal at 46 sites (polygons) in Moscow Region and at 200 disposal locations that are completely unsuitable from the ecological point of view.

The volume of recycled waste is less than 10-15 percent of the volume that is needed. Only 8 percent of solid domestic refuse is destroyed (by incineration). If we group industrial waste according to risk factor classes, refuse that is not dangerous makes up 80 percent of the total volume, 4th class low-hazard wastes 14 percent, and 1st-3rd classes of dangerous wastes amount to 3.5 percent.

The largest part of the waste is not dangerous-up to 32 percent. Construction refuse, iron and steel scrap, and non-ferrous metal scrap are 15 percent. Paper is 12 percent, and scrap lumber is 4 percent. Metal scrap under the 4th class of risk factor makes up 37 percent; wood, paper, and polymers more than 8 percent; and all-rubber scrap 15 percent. So, most refuse can be successfully recycled and brought back into manufacturing. This is related to SDW too. The morphological composition of SDW in Moscow is characterized by a high proportion of utilizable waste: 37.6 percent in paper refuse, 35.2 percent in food waste, 10 percent in polymeric materials, 7 percent in glass scrap, and about 5 percent in iron, steel, and non-ferrous metal scrap. The paper portion in commercial wastes amounts to 70 percent of the SDW volume.

A number of programs initiated by the Government of Moscow are underway for the collection and utilization of refuse and for neutralization of industrial and domestic waste. A waste-recycling industry is being developed in the city of Moscow, mostly for manufacturing recycled products and goods. One of the most important ecological problems is the establishment in the region of ecologically safe facilities for the disposal of dangerous wastes of 1st and 2nd class risk factors. Pre-planned industrial capacities for thermal neutralization of SDW will be able to take 30 percent of domestic waste and dangerous industrial waste. Construction of rubbish-burning works according to the old traditional approach is not worthwhile and should come to an end. Waste-handling stations have been under construction in the city for the last five years. In two years there will be six such stations which will make it possible to reduce the number of garbage trucks from 1,156 to 379 and to reduce the amount of atmospheric pollution they produce. In addition the switch to building stations with capacity of briquetting one ton of waste into a cubic meter will decrease the burden on waste disposal sites and prolong their life span by 4-5 fold. Trash hauling enterprises will also make profit because of lower transportation costs.

Putting into operation waste-segregation complexes (10-12 sites) would reduce volumes of refuse to disposal sites by 40 percent-that is 1,200,000 tons per year. The total volume of burned or recycled SDW would reach 2,770,000 tons a year. A total of 210,000 tons of waste per year would be buried. So, in the course of a five year period, full industrial recycling of SDW could be achieved in practice. Collection of segregated waste is one of the important elements in effective disposal and utilization of SDW. It facilitates recycling of waste and return of secondary material into the manufacturing process. Future trends in segregation and collection of SDW will demand wide popularization and improvement of the ecological culture and everyday behavior of people.

In recent years the high increase in the number of cars in Moscow has brought about not only higher pollution of the atmosphere, but also an avalanche-like accumulation of refuse from vehicles. Besides littering residential and recreation areas, cars represent a source for toxic pollution of land and reservoirs. At the same time, automobile wastes are a good source for recycled products. In the short-term outlook, Moscow has to resolve the problem of collection and utilization of decommissioned vehicles and automobile wastes with particular emphasis on activities of the private sector. Setting up a system for collection and utilization of bulky domestic waste and electronic equipment refuse is also on the priority list. In 1999 in Moscow the following volumes of secondary raw materials were produced or used in the city or were recycled: 300,000 tons of construction waste, 296,000 tons of metal scrap, 265 tons of car battery lead, 21,000 tons of glass, 62,500 tons of paper waste, 4,328 tons of oil-bearing waste, and 306 tons of refuse from galvanizing plants.

Such traditional secondary materials as metal scrap and paper waste are not recycled in Moscow but are shipped to other regions of Russia. The worldwide practice of sorting and recycling industrial and domestic wastes demands the establishment of an industry for secondary recycling. Otherwise segregation of waste becomes ineffective. There are restraining factors for the development of an effective system of assorted selection, segregation, and use of secondary raw resources, namely lack of sufficient manufacturing capacities and of suitable technologies for secondary recycling.

The problem of utilization of wastes is closely linked with the problem of modernization and sometimes even demands fundamental restructuring of industries. The practical use of equipment for less energy consumption and a smaller volume of wastes and a transition to the use of alternative raw materials are needed. Large enterprises-the main producers of dangerous wastes-are in a difficult financial situation now, which is an impediment for proceeding along these lines.

Private and medium-size enterprises are becoming gradually aware of the economic profitability in rational use of waste. For example, the firm Satory started as a transportation organization specialized in removal of scrap from demolished buildings and those undergoing reconstruction. It now benefits from recycling of waste, having developed an appropriate technology for the dismantling of buildings with segregation of building waste. So, as it has been already mentioned above, the first task for Moscow is to establish a basis for waste recycling.

HOW TO CHANGE THE SITUATION WITH WASTE

Transition to modern technologies in the utilization of wastes requires either sufficient investments or a considerable increase in repayment for waste on the part of the population. Obviously, these two approaches are not likely to be realized in the near future. The recovery of one ton of SDW with the use of ecologically acceptable technology requires not less than $70-100. Given the average per capita income in 1999 and the likely increase up to the year of 2005, in 2005 it will be possible to receive from a citizen not more than $14 per year. This means that the cost of technology should not exceed $40 per ton of recycled waste. Unfortunately, this requirement can fit only unsegregated waste disposal at the polygons (taking into account an increase in transportation costs by the year 2005).

Such being the case, it looks like there is only one acceptable solution for Russia to solve the problem of waste in an up-to-date manner: to introduce trade-in value on packaging and on some manufactured articles. In recent years domestic waste includes more and more beverage containers. Plastic and glass bottles, aluminium cans, and packs like Tetrapak stockpiled at disposal sites will soon reach the same volumes as in western countries. In Canada, for example, this kind of waste amounts to one-third of all domestic waste. A characteristic feature of this kind of waste is that the packaging for beverages is extremely durable and expensive. Manufactured from polyethylene terephthalate (PTA) and aluminum, it is sometimes more expensive than the beverage it contains. What are the ways for solving the problem?

Practically all of them are well- known, but most will not work in Russia in present conditions. The first problem relates to collection of segregated waste in the urban sector and in the services sector. A number of reasons make this system unrealistic, specifically in large cities. Sorting of waste at waste-briquetting sites and at polygons is possible. But if we take into account the present cost of secondary resources, this system turns out to be economically unprofitable and cannot be widely introduced. The introduction of deposits on containers for beverages is at present the most acceptable option for Russia. This system turned out to be most effective in a number of countries that have much in common with Russia. In fact this option is not at all new for us. Surely, all people remember the price of beer or kefir bottles. A system of deposit for glass bottles was in operation in the USSR, and waste sites were free from hundreds of millions of glass bottles and jars. We simply need to reinstate this system at present in the new economic conditions according to new types and modes of packaging. Deposits could be introduced also on glass bottles and jars, PTA and other plastic bottles, aluminium cans, and Tetrapak packing. Let us investigate several non-ecological aspects of this problem, because the ecological impact of secondary recycling of billions of bottles, cans, and packs is quite obvious.

Most of the population in Russia lives below the poverty line. When people buy bottles of vodka, beer, or soft drinks, they will have to pay a deposit value (10- 20 kopeks for a bottle). The poorest people will carry the bottles to receiving points. A system of collection of packaging will function by itself. Only receiving points are needed. Millions of rubles that are collected will be redistributed among the poorest people for their benefit, and a social problem of the poor will be solved to a certain extent not by charity, but with normal economic means.

A second point is also well-known. In a market economy one of the most important problems is that of employment. What happens when the trade-in value is introduced? Thousands of new jobs are created at receiving points and at enterprises that recycle glass, plastics, etc. And we don't need a single penny from the state budget. More than that, these enterprises will pay taxes and consume products of other branches of industry, thus yielding a return to the budget, not to mention income tax from new jobs.

There is another aspect of the matter. Considerable funding is needed from budgets of local governments, including communal repayments for waste collection and disposal at polygons and incinerators. Reduction of expenses for utilization of waste can be significant support for housing and communal reform in general. It is practically impossible to evaluate in general an ecological effect when thousands of tons of waste will cease to occupy plots of land near cities as long-term disposal sites. Operation costs of receiving points and transportation costs could be covered by funds obtained from manufacturers and from returned packaging. Besides, when a waste recycling industry develops and becomes profitable, recycling factories will be able to render partial support to receiving points. Trade-in value can be introduced on all types of packaging except milk products and products for children. It could amount to 15 or 30 kopecks per container, depending on its size. If all plastic bottles with water and beer are sold with trade-in value only in Moscow, the total sum will reach 450 million rubles a year. If we include glass bottles, aluminum cans, and packets, the sum will be one billion rubles. This sum will be redistributed at receiving points among people with scanty means when they receive the money for used packaging and jobs at receiving points and at recycling factories.

The bottleneck of the problem now is the absence in Russia of high technology industries for waste recycling. It can be resolved rather easily. At the first stage, used packaging can be sold as raw material for enterprises, including those overseas. There is unrestricted demand for PTA and aluminum on the part of foreign firms. When waste collection mechanisms are established, there will be limited investments in this branch of industry.

With regard to the inexhaustible source of free raw material, this recycling industry will become one of the most reliable from the point of view of recoupment of investments. The Government, regional authorities, the population, and of course ecologists should all be interested in having such a law. The same should be done with sales of cars, tires, and car batteries. Prices of every tire or battery should be higher by 30-50 rubles. These sums of money should be returned back to a buyer or credited when he buys a new tire or a new battery. For sure, such being the case we will not find used batteries thrown about the city dumps. In this case the task is even simpler because there are already a number of facilities for the recycling of tires and batteries. In fact, a law of trade-in value can change the situation with waste in Russia in a fundamental way. Russian legislation has already been prepared, and the concept of an ecological tax has been introduced in the new Internal Revenue Code. Now it needs to be competently introduced. The outlay for waste recycling has to become a type of ecological tax. To realize this task much work has to be done among the deputies and with the Government. Public ecological organizations, including international ones, should play a leading role.

ACTIVITY OF PUBLIC ORGANIZATIONS IN THE SPHERE OF WASTE MANAGEMENT IN THE MOSCOW REGION

We know examples of the ever increasing role of the general public in the solution of the problem of waste utilization, first of all in those countries that have well-developed democratic institutions. "Fight Against Waste" is one of the popular slogans of public organizations abroad. Public opinion has brought about measures of sanitary cleaning in cities, secured better work by municipal services, shut down hazardous industries, and restricted and prohibited incineration facilities. Nevertheless, the struggle against wastes in the economically developed countries, being a manifestation of an advanced attitude towards the environment, has in the long run brought about a paradoxical result. Transfer of hazardous industries to countries with lower environmental standards and inadequate public support- Russia, as an example-has made the world even more dangerous from the ecological point of view.

Russia has just embarked on the path of formation of environmental public movements by the establishment of nongovernmental organizations. Representatives of nongovernmental organizations from Russia took part in the international gathering in Bonn in March 2000 of nongovernmental organizations that are members of the International Persistent Organic Pollutants (POPs) Elimination Network. A declaration against incineration was adopted in Bonn by nongovernmental organizations, which called for elaboration of effective alternative technologies for utilization of waste and safe technologies for elimination of existing stockpiles of POP.

Quite a number of environmental organizations are operating now in Moscow. First to be mentioned is the All-Russia Society for the Conservation of Nature, which was established in Soviet times. There are other nongovernmental organizations: Ecosoglasiye, Ecolain, Ecological Union, and the Russian branches of Green Cross and Greenpeace. All these organizations collect and popularize environmental information and organize protest actions against policies of the Government or local administrations on ecological matters. A new political party- Russia's Movement of the Greens-is being formed. Laws currently in force in the Russian Federation ("On Protection of the Environment," "On State Ecological Examination by Experts," "On Production and Consumption of Waste") declare the right of the public to participate in environmental examination of projects that are to be implemented, including those on the establishment of facilities for elimination and disposition of waste. Public examinations can be organized by the initiative of citizens and public associations. For example, under the law of Moscow "On Protection of the Rights of Citizens while Implementing Decisions on Construction Projects in Moscow," public hearings are organized by the city's boards. Decisions taken by local authorities, at referenda and public meetings, may be the very reason for carrying out public examinations. Such examinations are conducted mainly by commissions, collectives, or ad hoc groups of experts. Members of public examination panels are responsible for the accuracy and validity of their expert evaluations in accordance with the legislation of the Russian Federation. A decision of a public environmental panel has an informative nature as a recommendation, but it becomes legally mandatory after its approval by the appropriate body of the State. Besides, the opinion of the public is taken into account when a project submitted for state environmental review has undergone public examinations and there are supporting materials.

Public environmental examination is supposed to draw the attention of state bodies to a definite site or facility and to disseminate well-grounded information about potential ecological risks. This important facet of public environmental organizations in Moscow and in Russia is very weak. To a large extent, it can be explained by an insufficient level of specific and general knowledge of ecology even on the part of the environmentalists themselves. Lack of knowledge on the part of ordinary citizens and public groups and inadequate information (for various reasons) produce alarm-motivated behavior by those who harm the organization of environmental activity in general and waste management in particular. There are nevertheless positive examples of public participation in designing policies of local authorities in the waste management sphere.

Speaking about the Moscow region we can point to the very productive work of the Public Ecological Commission attached to the Council of Deputies in Pushchino, in Moscow Oblast. The population of Pushchino is 21,000. The polygon for solid biological wastes (SBW) has practically exhausted its capacities. In 1996, in order to find a way out, the Administration of the town showed an interest in a proposal made by the Austrian firm FMW to support financially the construction of an electric power station in the vicinity of the town that would operate using both fuel briquettes and SBW of the town.

The briquettes would be manufactured in Turkey and would contain 70 percent Austrian industrial waste with added oil sludge. It was also envisaged that during the construction period of the electric power station, 300,000 tons of briquettes would be shipped and stockpiled. The original positive decision was annulled due to an independent evaluation of the project organized by the Public Ecological Commission.

The general public of Puschino put forward a counter proposal before the Administration in order to reduce volumes of SBW disposal at the polygon and to prolong its operation-segregation of SBW (food waste, paper refuse, fabrics, metal, glass, used car batteries).

As a result, a new scheme for sanitary measures in the town was worked out in 1998, which on the basis of segregation of waste provided for a considerable decrease in refuse flow to the polygon. Unfortunately, for lack of finances in the town budget, the scheme has not been introduced to the full extent. But in spite of severe shortages of special containers for segregated wastes, a network of receiving points for secondary materials was set up. One of the pressing tasks for greater public activity is wide popularization of environmental knowledge on waste management, especially among the young generation.

There is a very important role for public organizations to play in this domain when enlightenment and education are becoming a primary concern of nongovernmental organizations. Referring again to the example of the Public Ecological Commission in Pushchino, I have to underline that this organization is taking an active part in the enlightenment of the population through organizing exhibitions, placing publications in the press, and spurring school children into action to encourage cleaning of the town by means of environmental contests, seminars, and conferences. Children help the Commission organize mobile receiving points for secondary material. They even prepare announcements and post them around the town calling on the citizens to take valuable amounts of domestic wastes and car batteries to receiving points.

There are other examples of a growing influence of public organizations on the policy of administration in the sphere of waste management in the Moscow region. The Moscow Children's Ecological Center has worked out the Program "You, He, She and I-All Together Make Moscow Clean," which is being introduced with the support of the Moscow Government. In the framework of this program, children collect waste paper at schools, and they are taught how to be careful about the environment and material resources. The storage facilities agreed to support the initiative. They buy waste paper at a special price for school children. Then, the schools spend the earned money for excursions, laboratory equipment, books, and plant greenery.

Another example of an enlightened activity is a project realized in 1999 by the firm Ecoconcord on producing video-clips for TV about the adverse effects of waste incineration and the illegality of unauthorized storage of waste.

The name Ecoconcord speaks for the main purpose of this organization-to achieve mutual understanding between the general public and governmental organizations, to encourage public involvement in decision-making, and to promote the formation of policy bodies that would not let public opinion be ignored.

Proceeding from the global task of integrating the activities of interested parties in lessening adverse waste pollution, public organizations have to cooperate with authorities and not stand against them. Cooperation and consensus between governmental and nongovernmental organizations in working out strategies and tactics in waste management should become a prerequisite in successful realization of state policy in this sphere in the Russian Federation.

EMISSIONS OF POLLUTANTS INTO THE ATMOSPHERE AND HYDROSPHERE OF THE KUZNETSK COAL BASIN

The Kuznetsk coal basin (Kuzbass) is located largely on the left bank of the Tom River, the most urbanized part of Kemerovo Oblast. The main industries in this part of the Kuzbass territory are ferrous and nonferrous metallurgy, power engineering, machine building, construction, and chemical enterprises. Therefore, the general ecological condition of the Kuznetsk coal basin is determined not by the coal industry alone, with restructuring calling for liquidation of 35 coal mines by flooding, but also by other industries.

Given the geographical variance in environmental conditions and industrial impacts, several ecological-geographic districts can be distinguished. These are first of all the territories that have undergone the most intense industry-induced impacts: destruction and degradation of soil cover, disturbance of hydrogeologic conditions, pollution of surface and subsurface waters, atmospheric pollution from industrial emissions, and degradation of natural flora and fauna. These territories are in the Kemerovo and South Kuzbass ecological-geographic districts. Boundaries of the maximum industry-induced pressure on the biosphere coincide with the boundaries of these districts.

This pressure is present in about 30 percent of the territory within the limits of Kemerovo Oblast, where about 70 percent of the population lives and practically the entire coal industry of the Kuzbass is concentrated. The second group of districts (about 40 percent of the territory, 20-25 percent of the population) is subjected to a rather heavy industry-induced load from enterprises and from pollutant transport from adjacent territories, but the abundance of forests stabilizes to a large measure the ecological environment. And, finally, the third group of ecological-geographic districts (about 30 percent of the regional territory with 5-10 percent of the population) may be regarded as ecologically satisfactory. The atmospheric condition is an important ecological characteristic of the region. Air pollution still remains one of the most pressing ecological problems because the bulk of people live in districts where pollutant concentrations are often in excess of maximum permissible levels. The most polluted cities are Kemerovo and Novokuznetsk.

Air pollution in Kemerovo Oblast results from an extremely high concentration of various industries. Of 1,472 enterprises with pollutant emissions under the control of Goskomekologiya (State Committee on Ecology) of Kemerovo Oblast, the following are located on a small territory of 95,700 square kilometers: 21 enterprises of ferrous and nonferrous metallurgy, 126 coal-mining and coal- processing enterprises, 18 thermal-power engineering facilities, 10 chemical enterprises, 83 machine-building and metal-working plants, 184 construction- industry enterprises, and 308 enterprises of rail and motor transport and road services, as well as agricultural, food, light industry, and furniture enterprises and numerous steam heating plants.

The total pollutant emissions into the atmosphere in the populated areas of the region in 1999, including stationary and mobile (motor, rail, and air transport) sources, were 1,358,573 tons, including solid substances-235,899, sulfur dioxide-138,875, carbon dioxide-610,018, nitrogen oxides-143,282, hydrocarbons-211,916, other gases-18,486. Most of the total emissions are from pollutants from combustion of various fuels.

Emissions from mobile sources are 260,032 tons (19.14 percent), including the following: motor transport-239,595 tons, railroad transport-19,867 tons, and air transport-570 tons. The majority of emissions from mobile sources are exhaust emissions from motor transport amounting to 92.14 percent. The motor transport contribution to pollution is 19.14 percent in the region as a whole, while it is much higher in some towns, such as Anzhero-Sudzhensk-38.4 percent, Mezhdurechensk-40.1 percent, Kemerovo-44.1 percent. The exhaust emissions from motor transport have increased by 6.0 percent (or by 14,479 tons) as compared with 1998.

The stationary sources accounted for 1,098,541 tons of pollutants emitted into the atmosphere (the emission limit being 1,127,547 tons). Incomplete data indicate that around 200 substances enter the atmosphere. The majority are highly toxic and carcinogenic (3,4-benz(a)pyrene, various metal and silicon compounds, cyanides, fluorides, and a broad spectrum of hydrocarbons, including volatile organic compounds that enter into photochemical reactions in the atmosphere to produce ozone and other oxidants).

Enterprises of the following sectors are the main contributors to air pollution: metallurgy-421,706 tons, power engineering-206,170 tons, fuel-233,459 tons, chemical industry-5,209 tons, and other sectors-231,708 tons. The volume of recorded emissions into the atmosphere in comparison with 1998 has increased as follows: in the fuel industry-by 60,275 tons due to the more accurate accounting of methane emission sources; in electric power engineering-by 6,911 tons due to increased amount of burned fuel; in the chemical industry-by 1,952 tons due to a production increase; in metallurgy-by 29,346 tons due to a production increase. In 1999, 80 new enterprises were registered, while 115 enterprises were either liquidated or merged. The increase of emissions into the atmosphere throughout the region has totaled 98,309 tons. During the last five years (1995-1999), pollutant emissions from stationary sources have decreased by 7,004 tons, or by 6 percent, as a result of recession in the main sectors of the economy. Four million tons (79.4 percent) of pollutants were removed at the enterprises of the region in 1999. The highest level of removal was in the power engineering (92.3 percent) and chemical (87.4 percent) industries. A low level of pollutant removal was in housing-communal services-33.9 percent, at transport and road-service enterprises-30.5 percent, at trading enterprises-24.4 percent, and in public health services-6.6 percent. Noxious substances from the communication, educational, material, and technical supply enterprises go to the atmosphere without cleaning. The greatest volume of emissions is registered in the towns of Novokuznetsk, Kemerovo, Belovo, Leninsk-Kuznetsky, Myski, Prokopyevsk, Kiselevsk, Kaltan, and Mezhdurechensk. A great number of industrial enterprises are situated near residential districts. Recurrent weather conditions unfavorable for dissipation of emissions cause the high level of air pollution. This is confirmed by observations at the hydrometeorology and environment monitoring centers located in Kemerovo, Novokuznetsk, and Prokopyevsk. The pollution level in Kemerovo and Novokuznetsk, according to a generalized index developed by Rosgidromet (Russian Hydrometeorological Service), is estimated to be high.

Pollutant emissions into the city atmosphere in 1999, including stationary and mobile (motor, railroad, and air transport) sources, amounted to 117,777 tons. The main contributors to emissions from stationary sources are the enterprises of: power engineering-71.26 percent, ferrous metallurgy-7.15 percent, chemical processing-7.65 percent, housing-communal services-4.06 percent, and fuel industry-3.69 percent.

Pollutants removed at city enterprises amount to 588,245 tons, which comprise 90 percent. The level of removal is the highest in the power engineering industry-91.7 percent, in chemical industry-87.7 percent. It is low at the enterprises of housing-communal services-29.1 percent, machine building and metal plants-26.6 percent, transport and road services-4.3 percent. Emissions from trading and from material and technical supply enterprises go to the atmosphere without cleaning.

As compared to 1998, emissions from stationary sources have increased by 2,004 tons due to the production increase at city enterprises (Azot, Khimprom, Kemerovo State Regional Power Plant). Statistical accounts have been submitted by 140 enterprises for which MPE (maximum permissible emission) standards are established. In Kemerovo, regular observations of air pollution are performed using a network of eight stationary points of the state hydrometeorology and environmental monitoring committee.

Staff members of the Kemerovo scientific center have carried out work on the ecological zoning of the city territory based on investigations of sulfur accumulation by leaves of plants. Based on inventory data and the distribution of weather conditions (wind velocity, wind direction, and atmosphere stability), the average annual near-ground concentrations of the sum of sulfur-containing impurities have been calculated. Industrial processes associated with coal mining are sources of man-induced impacts on the environment. These sources are power plants, coal transportation, storage and loading, degassing and ventilating, burning spoil banks, maintenance- technological services, and motor transport. All possible sources of emissions and an assessment of their impact on the atmospheric pollution should be described in the design of a newly opened mine. Mine methane at operating enterprises goes to the atmosphere mainly from degassing and ventilating units.

According to the presently accepted documents, methane is one of the least harmful pollutants (maximum permissible concentration=50 milligrams per cubic meter). Today, the payment for one ton of methane emission is approximately 1,000 times less than for one ton of sulfurous anhydride. Therefore, the economic and administrative sanctions on methane emissions on the part of Russian territorial nature-preservation authorities are quite insignificant. However, the worldwide tendencies of recent years toward the limitation of greenhouse gases lead to greater attention to methane emissions. It is not unlikely, therefore, that the standards of payment for atmospheric pollution with methane will significantly increase in the near future, which, in view of the large emissions of this gas in the Kuzbass coal mines, may result in a substantial increase of nature-preservation payments and in a decrease of coal mining profitability.

A generalization of inventory data on the sources of harmful substance emissions into the atmosphere at the Kuzbass mines provides the ranges of total emissions per mine. Under the most unfavorable conditions, the payment of fines for methane emissions into the atmosphere does not exceed 6,450 rubles per year. A review of inventory data also shows that at Kuzbass mines, ventilation unit emissions at a height of 5-6 meters typically have a relatively high vertical velocity of gas-air mixture discharge (8-19 meters/second). This condition substantially increases the effective flare height and leads to a decrease in the near-ground concentrations at short distances from the source. With the indicated source parameters and the emissions at the upper boundary level, the maximum near- ground concentration is achieved at wind velocities of 3-5 meters/second at a distance of 50-300 meters and may be equal to 3-4 MPC (maximum permissible concentration). When a coal-mining enterprise closes, most sources providing loads on the atmosphere disappear. At the same time, state environmental control over the sources of pollutant emissions is terminated. But this does not mean that the closed mine completely ceases its negative influence on the atmosphere. Products of incomplete burning of spontaneously ignited coals and of mine equipment in the fire zone may be emitted. Spreading of dust from poorly controlled spoil banks also persists.

As to methane, after a mine is closed its ventilation ceases, and emissions of methane-air mixture are significantly reduced. But, as pumping of water also ceases, the water table rises, with the result that pressure in the mine grows and methane begins to escape to the surface and into the atmosphere. The rivers of the Kuzbass are polluted with waste waters disposed from numerous enterprises of different branches of industry. The quality of water bodies continues to be below standard specifications.

The most widespread pollutants of surface waters in the region are petroleum products, phenols, metal compounds, ammonium, and nitrites. The principal source is waste waters of industrial enterprises and housing-communal services. Four main water basins are in the region: the Tom, Inya, Chulym, and Chumysh Rivers basins. More than 32,000 rivers with a combined length exceeding 76,478 kilometers flow over the territory. Depending on local characteristics and relief, the rivers of the region are subdivided into plain- and mountain-type rivers. All of the rivers flowing over the territory of the region link to the Ob River basin and are tributaries of its upper reaches.

The main reasons for the increase in water consumption were an increase in output at some enterprises (West-Siberian Metallurgical Complex and

Kuznetsk Metallurgical Complex in Novokuznetsk, Azot and Khimprom in Kemerovo, Yurga Machine-building Plant in Yurga) and an increased use of water at coal-mining enterprises. The shrinkage of the irrigated land areas and the reduction of livestock populations have resulted in a decrease of water consumption for irrigation and agricultural needs.

Rivers of the Tom basin, where the main industrial potential of the Kuzbass is concentrated, are the most used and most subject to industry-induced impacts. According to the pH value, the Tom's waters are usually neutral or weakly alkaline. The contents of biogenic substances (Si, Fe, and compounds of N and P) show enhanced amounts of iron and ammonium ions, occasionally also of NO2. The concentrations of trace elements vary over quite a wide range, but the average level of their contents is not high. An examination of data has shown that the Tom's waters are polluted most with organic substances, with enhanced concentrations of petroleum products and phenols being most often registered throughout the length of the river. Identified in the Tom's waters (in the framework of experimental investigations) is an extensive list of various organic substances falling into the following classes of compounds: saturated and aromatic hydrocarbons (including those of petroleum origin), alkyl phenols, fatty organic acids and their ethers, alcohols, organic phosphates, and chlorine-organic compounds. Thus, based on the results of investigations in 1990-1993 along the

Tom River on the Kuzbass territory, the three most heavily polluted areas have been delineated: in the zones of influence of Novokuznetsk, Kemerovo, and Yurga. Among the most characteristic pollutants in surface waters of the Tom River, for which values exceeding MPC have been continuously or occasionally registered, are suspended solids, ammonium nitrate, heavy metals (Pb, Zn, Ni, Fe, Mn, Cr, Cd), petroleum products, highly volatile phenols, and other organic substances of different classes of hazard. The mode of distribution of hydrocarbons suggests their man-induced origin.

The presence of SAH (surface-active hydrocarbons) in nanogram quantities of lighter aromatic hydrocarbons (naphthalene and its derivatives anthracene, fluorene, fluorenthene, and pyrene) suggests that the enhanced concentrations of SAH in the Tom River are caused by the discharge of mine and subsurface waters contacting with coal rocks enriched in these compounds. The Inya River basin is second in importance and ecological loading. Sixteen million cubic meters of water were taken from water bodies of the basin in 1999, mainly for the needs of production (10 million cubic meters). Discharged into the basin's surface water bodies were 116 million cubic meters of waste waters from the towns of Belovo, Leninsk-Kuznetsky, and Guryevsk and from the

Promyshlennov, Leninsk-Kuznetsky, Guryevsk, and Belovo districts. Of 115 million cubic meters of waste waters needing purification, 104 million cubic meters (89.8 percent) have been treated, of which .01 million cubic meters have been purified to meet specified standards. Together with waste waters, 125,000 tons of pollutants are discharged into the rivers of the basin, including 249 tons of toxics and 20,562 tons of pollutants with reduced toxicity.

The source of the Inya River is located on the Taradanov ridge. The Inya is the right tributary of the Ob and flows through industrial and agricultural areas in the central part of Kemerovo Oblast. The river is 663 kilometers long, extending for 433 kilometers over the Kemerovo Oblast territory. The drainage basin area is 17,600 square kilometers. Within the region, the river is regulated by means of the Belovo Reservoir. The Inya is polluted mainly with waste waters from coal-mining enterprises and communal services, which is reflected in the chemical composition of water. A

total of 66 million cubic meters of waste waters have been discharged into the river, including 3,800 cubic meters without treatment. Together with waste waters, 81,000 tons of pollutants have been discharged.

The main pollutants of the Inya River and its tributaries are petroleum products, phenols, nitrogen- containing substances, and ions of heavy metals. Phenol pollution of the river averages 6-9 MPC. The one-time maximum concentration was registered in 1999:18 MPC in the summer low-water period. Average concentrations of petroleum products varied within a 3-6 MPC range. While the concentrations of petroleum products in the monitored section downstream from Leninsk-Kuznetsky remain within a 4.5-5.5 MPC range, in the section upstream from the town a decrease from 6 MPC in 1997 to 3 MPC in 1999 has been registered. In 1999, as compared with two previous years, the average concentrations of ammonium nitrates and nitrites decreased both upstream and downstream from the town.

Pollution of the Inya with organic substances, as judged from BOD5 (biochemical oxygen demand) and COD (chemical oxygen demand) indicators, is stable within a 1.5-2 MPC range, while average concentrations of total iron and zinc increased a little in 1999 (to 1-1.5 MPC) as compared with two previous years (0.5-1.0 MPC). The Chulym River basin includes the Yaya River and its tributaries, the Kiya and its tributaries, the Itatka, and others. About 33 million cubic meters of water were taken from water bodies of the basin in 1999, mainly for the needs of production.

Discharged into the surface water bodies of the basin were 61 million cubic meters. Of 55 million cubic meters of waste waters requiring purification,

49 million cubic meters (81.3 percent) were treated. Twelve million cubic meters (19.7 percent) were treated in accord with specified standards. Together with waste waters, 28,000 tons of pollutants were discharged into the rivers of the basin, including 87 tons of toxic substances and 4,400 tons of toxic sewage wastes.

The Chumysh River basin includes the Chumysh and its tributaries: Kara- Chumysh, Yegos, and others. Some 95 million cubic meters of water were taken from bodies of water in the basin, largely for the needs of production. Discharged into the rivers of the basin are waste waters from enterprises of Novokuznetsk Region and Prokopyevsk. A total of 23 million cubic meters of waste waters were discharged, including nine million cubic meters (40 percent) without treatment. Together with waste waters, 9,050 tons of pollutants were discharged, of which 21 tons were toxic and 1,600 tons were toxic sewage wastes.

Mining exerts an adverse effect on the water regime of Kemerovo Oblast. Dehydration of mining areas occurs and cones of depression form, with sizes depending on the geologic and hydrogeologic conditions and on the length of the mining period. An area of depression cones in the Kuzbass exceeds two thousand square kilometers.

The effect of mining on the river discharge is reflected in a decrease in the subsurface water discharge into the river due to drainage pumping in mines or quarries, by an increase in the river sedimentation caused by the same factors, and by a decrease in the subsurface water reserves. The daily flow from Kuzbass mines and open pits exceeds one million cubic meters. Drainage of deposits results in a decrease of water reserves in surface water bodies, drying up of wells and water supply wells, and exhausting of springs, streams, and small rivers. In the zone of mining, more than 200 rivers have disappeared or diminished, and a general degradation of the territories continues, which results in the destruction of habitat conditions and degradation of vegetation.

The coal industry is the second in importance for pollution of Kuzbass water bodies after power engineering, which discharges into the rivers 58.9 percent (1,515 million cubic meters/year) of untreated waters. The coal industry accounts for 14.6 percent (384 million cubic meters/year) of untreated waters. Coal enterprises discharge 34.4 percent of all suspended solids and 10 percent of petroleum products. Mines, per unit of output, discharge into water bodies 3.6 times more suspended solids, 5.2 times more chlorides, 2.6 times more easily oxidized organic substances, and 3.72 times more petroleum products than open pits. Suspended substances are the main pollutant of mine waters. Waste waters of some mines contain phenol, which forms as a result of pyrogenic decomposition of coal. Mine waters show strong bacterial pollution.

Closure of coal mines by means of flooding will lead to the contraction of their depression cones and to a change in the discharge directions of mine-polluted subsurface waters. The result may be that the subsurface waters previously discharged into mines will begin to discharge into surface water streams with pollutants from dumping grounds of various waste products (including dangerous chemical waste). The influence of waste waters on the surface water quality can be observed near the following mines: Pionerka-the Big Bachat River, Bungurskaya- the Bungurska River, Dimitrova-the Aba River, Shevyakov-the Olzheras River, Shushtalepskaya-the Kondoma River, Baidaevskaya-the Garshina River, Vakhrushev-the Aba River. An analysis of mine waters after they have passed treatment plants shows that the majority of solids analyzed exceed MPC. Thus, suspended substances in all of the mines analyzed exceed MPC from 2 to 34 times, BOD from 1.6 to 20.8 times, ammonia from 1.3 to 18 times, and so on. The discharges of waste waters from mines being closed have resulted in an increase of MPC in surface waters by a factor of 2 to 7 for a number of components.

The subsurface waters of the Kuzbass are of the infiltration type, with reserves formed due to atmospheric precipitation. The infiltration in the upper part of the geologic section varies, according to G.M.Rogov, from 200 mm (25 percent of precipitation) in the mountain-taiga zone to 85 mm (14 percent) in the low- mountain-taiga zone and to 35 mm per year (7-8 percent of precipitation) in the steppe zone.

According to Zapsibgeologiya (West-Siberian Production-Geological Association), traces of industry-induced pollution of subsurface waters have been recognized west of Myski and in the vicinity of Novokuznetsk. Pollution by a number of components (phenols, formaldehyde, COD, BOD) ranges up to 150 MPC. Much of the explored reserves in the Myski and Kiyzak areas are not exploited now because of the pollution with waste saline waters from a district steam heating plant over an area of four sq. km. and the liquidation of reservoir gravel by the Kiyzak building material quarry. On the territories of large livestock complexes and poultry plants the contamination of soil has resulted in the pollution of subsurface waters with nitrogen compounds and heavy metals. In some cases the subsurface waters under farming lands were found to have enhanced contents of pesticides (Kemerovo Region), nitrates-from 2 to 30 MPC (swine-breeding complexes in Chistogor and Tal), and organic compounds-phenols up to 3000 MPC (Kemerovo: Azot, Tokem).

Observations of the subsurface water regime under natural conditions conducted for many years show that the mode of ground and subsurface water table fluctuations depends most of all on the amount of precipitation and on the regime type. The wells under the riverside and terrace regime conditions clearly show a spring and autumn rise of the water table and its smooth recession in the course of winter. The minimum levels of summer-autumn low-water periods differ from those of winter low-water periods in both directions, but are most often lower or close to them.

The annual amplitude of water table fluctuations varies from 0.2 to 4 meters. Only the spring water table rise is registered (lagging in time, as a rule, in comparison with the riverside regime) followed by a smooth recession. Minimal levels in the summer-autumn low-water period are close to those in the winter low- water period. Annual amplitudes are insignificant, rarely exceeding one meter. The effect of the coal-mining complex on the hydrosphere causes a change of water regime of the territory-pollution of ground and waste waters with products of physical and chemical weathering of subsurface rocks. In every case, the zone of mining and the territories adjacent to it are drained by means of tunnels, pumping, and disposal of subsurface waters into the hydrological network beyond the mining area. The natural regime of subsurface waters becomes disturbed and their reserves diminish. In the process of both subsurface and open-pit mining, the lowering of the ground water table forms a cone of depression whose size depends on the geologic and hydrogeologic conditions of the mining area and on the duration of mining. One of the most adverse aspects of mine flooding is the possibility of polluting the subsurface waters, which are a source of drinking water. This will necessitate an urgent solution of the water supply problem for the populations of Novokuznetsk, Belovo, Kemerovo, and Anzhero-Sudzhensk.

Pollution of mine waters with metals is registered for zinc (up to 14 times background levels), copper (up to 270 times), lead (up to two times), manganese (up to 325 times), molybdenum (up to four times), arsenic (up to 100 times), vanadium (up to five times), fluorine (up to 5.9 times), and aluminum (up to 2.3 times). As is evident from an analysis of mine water pollution dynamics, the contents of nitrogen group compounds and petroleum products increase in spring, summer, and autumn and sharply decrease in the winter period. This means that an important role in the pollution of mine waters with these substances, particularly when water levels are extremely high, is played by snow-melt and storm waters bringing to the mines pollutants from petroleum products and household refuse accumulated on the territory allocated for mining. To help solve the large- scale problems of natural resource monitoring and environment protection in Kemerovo Oblast, an integrated information system based on the use of geoinformation technologies has been developed. Ecological Atlas of Kemerovo Oblast (ATLAS) is designed for the collection and storage of graphical and semantic information on the state of the environment and natural resources in Kemerovo Oblast, as well as for processing this information. The system provides support for the solution of a wide range of problems concerning monitoring, accounting, planning, distribution, and financial regulation in the field of natural resources usage and payment for environment disturbances and pollution. Besides, ATLAS can be used in higher and post-graduate ecological education. The system based on GIS-technologies is used as follows:

- To form electronic maps of localities using a base of graphic layers with a summary map of all semantic descriptions of objects available in each layer.
- To establish relationships between individual objects with semantic information stored in databases of the dBASE and PARADOX format.
- To create and/or attach cartographic-mathematical models of technical-natural phenomena with the visualization and saving of their results in a separate graphic base layer.
- To process and edit semantic and graphical data (in compliance with information security).
- To form, browse, and print out normative-reference information.

The aggravation of the ecological situation in Kemerovo Oblast in recent years is connected not only with the activation of production in heavy industry sectors, but also with the lack of ecological culture among the great majority of managers of all levels. At present, 12 public ecological organizations work in the Kuzbass. Among the most active of them are the following: Kemerovo Department of the All-Russian Society for Nature Preservation, Information Ecological Agency, Ecological Parliament of Children and Young People, Kemerovo Regional Society Social Health, Kemerovo Regional Department of the Russian National Organization Green Cross, and Ecological Movement Kuzbass. Scientists of the Kemerovo Scientific Center of the Siberian Branch of the Russian Academy of Sciences take an active part in the work of the majority of these organizations. The principal lines of activity of public ecological organizations are the following:

- Publication of Information Ecological Bulletin
- Ecological audit and consulting
- Public ecological expert examination

o Informational support and service in the environmental field

The regional Ecological Parliament of Children and Young People has adopted its own ecological code for children and young people in February 2000 on the basis of the recommendations of the UN Conference on the Environment and Development (Rio de Janeiro, 1992). Its fundamental principles are as follows:

o Destruction of the environment is a consequence of the destruction of personality, of a person's inner life, of his values.

o There is but one step from ecological ignorance to a crime against humanity.

o We have no right to enrich ourselves at the expense of nature; we must live in harmony with it.

o To preserve man as a species, we should preserve the natural environment; in order to preserve the environment, man should change himself, his attitude to it.

The Ecological Parliament of Children and Young people has concluded an agreement on cooperation to participate in the solution of regionally significant ecological problems with the Kemerovo Oblast administration in an effort to strengthen the interaction between the authorities and the ecological movement The Information Ecological Agency (IEA) may now be called a professional public organization. The agency collects and systematizes ecological information with special attention to regional ecological problems. The main emphasis is on involving the general public in the process of significant decisions and regulations in the field of environmental protection in the Kuzbass.

Information Ecological Bulletin is a monthly 24-page monthly publication with a circulation of 950 copies. The bulletin is intended for specialists, industry personnel, teachers, and representatives of public organizations. It covers the following issues: regional problems, projects, and public actions in the field of environment; ecological legislation, ecological audit, and ecological management; the environment, public health conditions, and the ecological rights of citizens; technologies in the field of environment; and ecological education. The IEA provides services for ecological audits, environmental impact assessments, ecological substantiation of business activity, valuation of maximum permissible pollutant emissions, waste disposition, permissible levels of environmental impact, and confirmation of limits on the use of natural resources. The IEA has appropriate licenses for all of the above-listed types of activity.

To realize these activities, the Agency forms temporary groups of specialists in different fields from IEA members. Since February 1998, the IEA has been affiliated with the Russian Network of Regional Centers of public ecological expertise in the context of a program realized by the Moscow public organization Ecoline and supported by the Institute for Sustainable Communities (USA). The Agency supports development of information and exchange of information. The scientists of the Kemerovo Scientific Center of the Russian Academy of Sciences take an active part in the popularization of ecological knowledge and of the problems of stable regional development by publishing popular scientific papers in the mass media and in the Information Ecological Bulletin. They participate in expert appraisals of regional legislative acts aimed at nature preservation and of regionally significant business projects.

Currently special attention is paid to the problems of ecological education and training. An analysis of the present situation shows an absence of multilevel ecological education as a system. The number of ecological schools in the region is far from sufficient. This is connected with the absence of ecological education programs, the lack of personnel, the complexity of curricula, and the lack of textbooks and training aids.

In schools of the region (mainly in the innovative educational institutions), attention is given to the scientific-research work of students in ecology. Their work is presented at scientific conferences, in the ecology sections. The Kuznetsk department of the Geographical Society together with the tourist station of Novokuznetsk has organized training on practical ecology for groups of students. Students become acquainted with methods for the observation and study of birds, with determination of water quality, and with the world of plants. They carry out ecological games and walking tours.

Additional ecological-biological education in Kemerovo Oblast involves the regional station of young naturalists as a coordination center of uninterrupted ecological education and ecological culture formation among pre-school children and among elementary and middle school students.

There are 15 scientific associations of pupils and students in the region established on the basis of young naturalist stations, ecological-biological centers, and children's and young people's centers. They include "Genetics of Animals," "Ecology of Plants," and "Biochemistry and Cytology" in Novokuznetsk; "Microbiology," "Young Forester," and "Fauna" in Kemerovo; and "Young Ecologist and Biologist" in Anzhero-Sudzhensk, and Myski.

Stations of young naturalists in Mezhdurechensk, Novokuznetsk, Anzhero-Sudzhensk, Topki, Kiselevsk, Prokopyevsk, Kemerovo, Yurga, and other towns, together with schools, are engaged in an integrated study of the ecological conditions of their towns, in the examination of large and small rivers, and in the investigation of flora and fauna of their native land. Various methods used in this study include ecological monitoring; bioindication of water bodies and air basins; and hydrobiological, zoological, and botanical investigations. It has become a tradition that the regional station of young naturalists, together with the regional Goskomekologiya and Kemerovo State University, conducts rallies/competitions of young ecologists, including defense of research works by the rally participants, and their demonstrations of ability to use the main methods of field ecology.

With active support from the regional Committee of Young Naturalists, the groups of young ecologists of the Kemerovo region participate in the realization of several Federal educational-research projects: "Phenology of Birds," "Life to Russian Waters," "Crane, the Bird of Peace," "Water on the Earth," and others. Ecological shifts at the stations of young naturalists continue in Kemerovo, Novokuznetsk, Mezhdurechensk, Yurga, Anzhero-Sudzhensk, and Myski. Pupils of School No. 62 in Kemerovo are engaged in the problem of potable water under the program "Clean Water of the Taydon-to the Kuzbass Towns." They report the results of their expeditions at Russian conferences and receive well-deserved diplomas and certificates.

The Kemerovo Scientific Center, with the participation of institutes of higher education and public ecological organizations, has conducted a number of international, all-Russian, and regional scientific-practical conferences and seminars. The most significant were the All-Russian scientific-practical conference "Ecology and Economy: Regional Problems of Transition to Stable Development. A Look into the Twenty-First Century," the international scientific-practical conference "Ecological Problems of the Regional Coal-mining Sector Under the Transition to Stable Development," the second international conference "Reduction of Methane Emission," and the scientific-practical seminar "Regional Problems in the Economical Education on the Eve of the Twenty-First Century." The aforementioned seminar discussed methodological approaches, standards, and training aids for a system of multi-level ecological education and training. The discussion demonstrated experience in the ecological education and training of the people. In the system of general secondary education, ecology is being introduced as an independent subject. In the higher schools, special courses of ecology, nature preservation, engineering ecology, and rational use of natural resources are being introduced. Several centers of ecological education work within the system of post- graduate professional development.

At the same time, the process of ecological education and training has not become continuous and obligatory, as is required by the Environmental Protection Law. A scientifically based system of ecological education and training is absent in the region, and the legal and normative foundation has not been formed. There are great difficulties in providing the material-technical and educational-pedagogical basis for carrying out practical expeditions. The difficulties in the dissemination of ideas and experience of Russian and foreign ecological education are aggravated by the absence of available information systems and periodicals.

To raise the level of ecological education, the following should be done:

- It is necessary to pass the law "On the Ecological Education and Training of Population in Kemerovo Oblast."
- A regional target program should be developed "Perfection of Ecological Education and Training in Kemerovo Oblast for the Years 2001-2005," with the specification of financial resources from the regional budget (via the Education Department and the Science and Higher School Department) and the regional ecological fund budget.
- A system of centers of ecological education and training should be established. They should have the following tasks: development of regional standards of different-level ecological education; assessment of the effectiveness of ecological education, expert appraisal, and certification of training aids; development of retraining and professional development programs for teachers in the ecological education system of the Kemerovo region; and assistance in the preparation and publication of training and methodology aids, including tutorial computer programs.
- The role of public organizations and the mass media in the process of ecological education should be increased. A standing seminar (school) for journalists and public activists is needed, together with a cycle of broadcasts and telecasts.
- Ethical and aesthetic education at each educational level should be improved and extended.

DYNAMICS OF RADIOACTIVE POLLUTION OF PRIMORYE TERRITORY AND THE NORTHERN SHELF OF THE SEA OF JAPAN

Investigations of the radioecological conditions in Primorye Territory and the Far-East region as a whole show that these conditions are closely connected to the radiation in the northern part of the Sea of Japan. Radiation contamination seems to be an acute problem in the Asia-Pacific region for three main reasons:

- o From almost the first years of the Soviet Union, this region has been completely closed to civilian organizations and individual researchers, inasmuch as intensive construction and development of military bases continued there for decades both before and after the Second World War.
- o The regional problem has caused public concern in the Russian Federation, Japan, Korea, the United States, and other states that have vital interests (fishery, aquaculture, recreation) that are potentially threatened by radioecological accidents and radioactive waste from Russia's Pacific Fleet.
- o The program of fleet reduction should have been completed in the region by 2000. During the last 10 years, 54 nuclear submarines have been taken out of commission, but only 10 were adequately salvaged with attention to wastes.

Governmental data and our own data were obtained and analyzed during long- term investigations of radiation conditions of the territories adjacent to submarine repair facilities and bases. Also, a study of radionuclide distribution in Peter the Great Bay was carried out.

On the basis of these studies, we reached conclusions about the relatively insignificant contribution of anthropogenic sources of radionuclides to radiation background levels of our region as a whole. Such sources average less than one percent of the total.

Besides local pollution sources from the fleet, we also investigated global sources. A comparison of the effect of the last Chinese atmospheric nuclear test in 1980 with the consequences of the Chernobyl accident showed that the nuclear test effects were longer (more than one year) and had a higher level of total beta-activity of the lower atmosphere in Primorye Territory. However, total beta-activity levels of the two releases were comparable.

Concerning probable radioactive environmental pollution of the south of Primorye Territory (in the opinion of experts of the Fleet's chemical service), the coastal facilities along the bays of Bolshoi Kamen, Sysoyeva, and Chazhma are sources.

These facilities deal with recharging nuclear reactors; replacement of filters; collection, temporary storage, and processing of radioactive waste; temporary storage of used nuclear assemblages; and repair and deactivation of contaminated equipment. Also potentially dangerous are the places where oil tankers with radioactive waste facilities were operating. The main components of radioactive waste are 137Cs, 90Sr, 60Co, and 144Ce.

Until 1993, burial of liquid and solid radioactive waste had been carried out in deep-water regions of the northwestern part of the Sea of Japan, 200-300 kilometers from the coastline. The spontaneous chain reaction on a submarine in Bolshaya Chazhma in August 1985 has remained the most severe nuclear incident. It preceded the accident at Chernobyl and belongs to the following class of incidents:

- o Uncontrolled reactor regime involving destruction of the active zone.
- o Release of fission products into the environment-the atmosphere and the seawater in the bay.
- o Wind transportation of aerosols of small dispersed particles through the industrial zone (the Navy ship repair works) and further, through the coastal part of the Dunai Peninsula with residential settlements. The difference between this nuclear incident and Chernobyl is that it took place with a reactor of a distinctly different design and with ten times less power. Its fuel assembly did not contain radioactive products accumulated during previous operation. Just before the accident, the reactor had been loaded with new fuel elements.

We have carried out the following studies as an independent expert examination of government activity in 1991-1994.

We obtained the following data about the probable damage of the environment by the accident:

1. The amount of radioactivity, its radionuclide composition, and its explosion potential were developed.
2. Models of atmospheric transport and gradual redirection of radioactivity in Ussurisk Bay were developed.
3. Numerical estimates of turbulent transportation of radionuclides in water and their release into the atmosphere were carried out.
4. The dynamic processes of redeposition of high-level radioactive pollution in the upper layer of seafloor deposits directly in the zone of the accident were studied experimentally.
5. Estimates were made of future conditions of the bodies of water with attention to long-lived radionuclides. Investigations of Ussurisk Bay in 1990- 1992, using tritium tracers and numerical modeling, were evaluated.
6. Evaluations of doses received by the population of Dunai as a result of the accident in Chazhma Bay were carried out. The population

received the heaviest radioactive doses during inhalation of iodine radioactive isotopes- 131I, 132I, 133I, 134I, and 135I.

7. The coefficients of risk for the population of Dunai were evaluated. The population of Dunai is 20,000. Twenty-two additional deaths caused by all forms of cancer and the same number of non-lethal cancer cases were predicted in Dunai.

The inhabitants who were up to 150 meters distant from the explosion along the trace axis received significant doses of external gamma-irradiation and external beta-irradiation of the skin. The analysis of bottom samples from Chazhma Bay has shown that the distribution of radioactivity, which depends more than 95 percent on 60Co, is non- uniform over the area and along the vertical. A large part of activity in the epicenter zone is situated at a depth of 15-20 centimeters from the bottom. Some solid grains were extruded from the bottom samples with the help of magnetic separation of highly-active samples. These "hot" particles from the fuel assembly contribute 50 percent to the total radioactivity of the sample.

The main processes influencing the space-time variations of radionuclides in bottom deposits in the region of the accident are radionuclide transport in water and radioactive decay. The flushing of radioactivity from the bay into Strelok Gulf reduces levels by about one percent annually. Radioactive decay of 60Co reduces levels each year by about 12 percent. This ratio is explained by the limited water dynamics, intensive sedimentation, concentration of most activity in larger "hot" particles with higher density, and low solubility of "hot" particles in seawater.

SOCIETY SHOULD BE PROTECTED FROM THE METAL THREAT

The Ecological Women's Assembly has been active since 1944, uniting within its membership women and youth of Russia and other former Soviet states. Among the many aspects of environmental protection of concern is the problem of chemical toxicants, including metals.

Listed in order of degree of human sensitivity to toxic metals, the metals are ranked as follows: Hg > Cu > Zn > Ni > Pb > Cd > Cr > Sn > Fe > Mn > Al. The sensitivity variations are not uniform.

Living organisms have special mechanisms of heavy metal detoxification. In response to the toxic action of Pb2+, Cd2+, and Hg2+, for example, the liver and kidneys increase the synthesis of low-molecular beta proteins, which contain cysteine in their structure. The high content of sulfhydryl groups in cysteine promotes the combination of metal ions into strong complexes, resulting in some level of detoxification. But it is clear that we must protect ourselves from this "metal" threat.

At one time the main anthropogenic sources of lead releases into the environment were lead-based paints, lead-containing pesticides (now forbidden), and lead in soils around some industrial enterprises.

Now the main source of lead pollution is automobile fuel. Vehicle exhausts account for up to 80 percent of the total lead content in the atmosphere. Using ethylized gasoline with a high lead content results in widespread heavy metal pollution of the atmosphere. In cities overloaded by motor transport, lead concentration in the atmosphere exceeds background values by 20 to 30 times. Street dust sometimes contains up to 1,000 milligrams of lead per kilogram. Oxides and heavy metal salts are almost indestructible, and they gradually accumulate in the environment in areas where people live.

Entering the atmosphere from exhaust gases of automobiles and then accumulating in the top layers of the soil, lead enters the human body through the gastro-intestinal path, as well as by inhalation. Lead is delivered by the blood and accumulates in bones, the liver, the kidneys, and the brain. Lead irreversibly affects the nervous system, impedes functioning of the reproductive system, affects the kidneys, and causes mental and physical retardation in children. Especially dangerous is the effect of lead on children, who, when inhaling dust, receive approximately five times more lead for their body weight than adults.

Also, lead assimilates in children at a level several times higher than in adults. According to the World Bank, lead pollution of the air from motor transport has become one of the three main risk factors for health in Central and Eastern Europe. The UN Committee on Sustainable Development considers a general prohibition of ethylized gasoline a primary health protection task for the global population.

The plan for complete cessation of leaded gasoline production was discussed at the Conference of the European Environmental Ministers in 1998 in Denmark. The parallel reduction of lead levels in human blood in the United States and the decreased use of leaded gasoline since the middle of the 1980s is clear. Also, it is interesting that in 1997, The Alliance to End Childhood Lead Poisoning (U.S.) issued a brochure entitled Myths and Realities of Phasing Out Lead Gasoline. The necessity and possibility of a complete change to unleaded gasoline are obvious.

When humans take in a combination of metals from the environment (during inhalation of polluted air, consumption of chemically contaminated food and water, and through the skin and mucous membranes), they are subjected to severe impacts of these toxicants. The combined effect of these toxicants is complicated because a living organism reacts to each toxicant differently: in some cases with adaptation (frequently temporary) and sometimes with sharp negative reactions. Frequently during medical examinations of people living in ecologically unfavorable regions, changes in the characteristics of blood are discovered. Also, the attributes of chemical intoxication are found (sometimes even exclusively) among children and older persons. Varying responses to the impact of chemical toxicants depending on sex differentiation have also been noted.

8

NGO Strategic Risk Management

These are hard, challenging times for NGOs around the world. Whether service or social change oriented, NGOs operate in dynamic economic, political, technological, and institutional environments. For NGOs devoted to development in both the North and South, with increasing frequency, their legitimacy is questioned and accountability demanded. Stakeholders and the broader society and governments are frequently asking NGO leaders about their impact on society? Ricardo Wilson-Grau is a management consultant and since 1993, a senior advisor with Novib, where he is responsible for researching and developing applications of strategic risk management.

These changes require that NGOs modify how they respond to the world and seek to shape it. Consequently, many development NGOs are altering their strategies, as the shift to rights-and results-based approaches exemplifies. Moreover, they are varying their strategies more frequently than in the past. Change, of course, has always been important in every organization's life. Indeed, for NGOs, change is absolutely essential; every NGO's mission statement commits it to improving some unacceptable aspect of the world. Change, however, brings with it uncertainty and risk.

Risk—The Simple and The Complex

The root word of risk, *risicare,* means "to dare." Daring to act audaciously is inherent to the lives of NGOs. Without taking risks, there is no innovation or social change. The nature of NGO work is to dare constantly to make decisions and act to achieve positive results, while daring to hazard bad outcomes. One of the beauties of the risk concept is its simplicity. As with anything occurring in the future, there is uncertainty about the results, desirable or undesirable; there are *consequences* of each good or bad result; and one needs to focus on the *probability* of positive and negative results. Of course, life cannot be so simple. There is an equally important and much more complex dimension to risk. Individuals, organizations, and societies are all unique. Thus, risk is rooted in specific historical contexts—from the political and psychological to the economic and environmental—that shape people's perceptions of the consequences and the probability of an uncertain event.

Business and local and national governments

Even in situations where there is a precise mathematical calculation of probabilities, people will act on their *beliefs* about the chances of good and bad results. Similarly, people take action based on their *preferences* for one result over another, even when they know precisely the potential benefits. Of course, when a judgment is about the uncertain future results of social change, the decision is especially subjective and risky.

Risk management is relatively new for NGOs. One reason is the ease NGO decision-makers have in confronting operational hazards that only one hundred years ago would have been terrifying. Insurance controls the damage caused by illness or accidents. Personnel access loans in case of personal or family emergencies.

The dangers of disaster that come with all new technology are more readily mitigated than ever before, as when NGOs use virus shields and back-up systems to protect computers against electronic attack or human error.. A second reason is that applying risk management to achieving upside results, and not solely avoiding the downside ones, is a recent innovation. In today's highly competitive and unpredictable environment, NGOs not only face major opportunities and new dangers to achieve their missions, but these positive and negative risks are arising much more rapidly than in the past and are becoming more complex. They must be managed as never before. Consequently, NGO decision-makers that use strategic risk management may actively nurture success and counter threats of failure.

Strategic Risk Management

In the last ten years, the concept of risk management has expanded from its origins in the insurance industry. It has extended into the fields of investment finance, medicine, environmental management, space science, and meteorology. Today, business and local and national governments apply risk management principles. The theory and practice has also grown from its original focus on exposure to negative risks to address positive risks as well. Building on traditional risk science, strategic risk management centres on a reinforcing, iterative process, a recycling sequence of steps for making and implementing decisions involving potential bad or good results.

- Clarifying what the organization seeks to achieve—*goals*.
- Identifying the principal opportunities and dangers that may affect achieving these goals—*uncertainties*.
- Assessing the likelihood that each opportunity or threat will materialize— *probabilities*.
- Calculating the extent of the resulting gain or loss to the organization from each opportunity or danger—magnitudes of the good or bad *consequences*.
- Weighing what the organization can do: 1) to increase the probability and the magnitude of the good consequences of each opportunity, and 2) to decrease the probability and the magnitude of the bad consequences of each danger—*risk management techniques* for each opportunity or threat.
- Deciding whether and how the organization is able to take these actions— *costs and benefits* of each technique.

This definition of risk is powerful. Instead of struggling to avoid all uncertainties— for that would be to avoid all chances of positive outcomes—an organization strives to increase the chances and size of positive outcomes while reducing the odds and magnitude of the negative outcomes. *This dual strategy is the essence of strategic risk management*. It contrasts with the narrow, negative traditional focus—merely preserving the organizations past achievements from future losses. While guarding against loss, the NGO that manages risk strategically takes carefully chosen chances, purposely mindful of the positive side of a potentially surprising future. An organization managing risk strategically dares to succeed.

A Tool for NGO Decision-makers

In recent years around the globe, NGO organizations that are committed to social change have strengthened their professional management to achieve their missions and long-term goals. NGO leaders once could safely assume that internal and external conditions with a potential major impact on their stakeholders, programs, property, income, and reputation would be stable for a year or two. No more. Currently and even more so in the future, the strategy is short term. For example, one major innovation in NGO management has been to introduce systems of strategic planning. Commonly, NGOs engage every three, four, or five years in this fundamental decisionmaking for achieving institutional goals. Increasingly, however, change is so rapid that managers at all levels of the organization must make decisions vital to achieving their missions outside the multi-year cycle. Now, monthly and even weekly, an

NGO's entire management must adapt to and participate in incisive strategic thinking and prompt strategic action. In fact, virtually everyone in an NGO must continually understand, accept, and participate in actions sharply focused on achieving their organization's fundamental purpose and goals.

This is easier said than done. Organization-wide involvement with uncertainty can create feelings of apprehension and insecurity. Strategic risk management offers a tool to build understanding and enthusiasm for change. From the broader perspective of risk as *risicare,* an NGO's staff comes to understand that changes— some bad, some good—are not only inevitable, but the organization can thrive with these changes. Everyone comes to recognize that change, properly anticipated and wisely managed, while still posing possible dangers, is a potentially positive force. Uncertainty becomes something with an upside and a downside, something that can be managed not just by decreasing the potential for losses, but also by increasing the potential for gains.

Empowered by this broadened approach to uncertainty and change, an NGO's personnel quickly think beyond the merely negative, accident-centred, insuranceoriented concept of risk. Recognizing that changes can be positive, even surprisingly good and certainly necessary, an organization's staff can come to work with risk as an opportunity to achieve positive outcomes, daring to succeed as well as to fail.

Capacity-building Through Strategic Risk Management

Strategic risk management can enhance but never replace a development decisionmaker's knowledge, field experience, cross-cultural skills, and other personal abilities. More specifically, strategic risk management enables NGOs to enhance their capacities in three areas.

Information. In management, the information function is vital. In today's "knowledge societies," decision-makers are flooded with data and ideas. The technological possibilities are a temptation to nurture a false sense of security by attempting to process all available information. Of course, managers must constantly observe, consult, read, and listen. Strategic risk management, however, offers NGO decisionmakers a methodology for rapidly sifting through and selecting the most relevant information.

Action. Today, NGO managers must combine hard, in-depth analysis with fast decisions. Risk management enables a decision-maker to act even as she or he thinks. Past successes and failures are analysed not so much to know what happened or to explain why things are as they are, but primarily to take the best decision about new activities. Exercising risk principles enables a decision-maker to identify what to change and innovate in order to maximize gains and minimize losses today, tomorrow, and in the future. For strategic decisions, certainly the search for truth must be rigorous. Strategic risk management incorporates the rational perspective of science, but the purpose is to understand in order to decide, to set objectives and make plans, but not at the expense of acting on them.

Delegation. Never before has the need for subsidiarity been greater for development NGOs. Strategic risk management facilitates delegation because risk principles are applicable at all organizational levels. Strategic risk management enables decisionmakers to spread authority and responsibility upwards, downwards, and across. Everyone can be engaged in taking risks responsibly to achieve their work units' "missions" or long-term goals. Thus, for instance, in an organization where everyone uses a risk approach, senior program managers with substantial field experience will be able to delegate with greater confidence to junior staff. In addition, a quicklearning, self-critical program staff will develop faster.

Strategic risk management can enhance but never replace a development decision-maker's knowledge, field experience, cross-cultural skills, and other personal abilities

In sum, traditional and strategic risk management both emphasize a proactive attitude towards risk-taking and employ similar methods of analysis and techniques for coping with risk. All risk-taking is based on logical analysis of essential information. Risk decisions also involve strongly reasoned beliefs and preferences about the probability and the importance of the desirable and undesirable outcomes. Thus, the advantages of both traditional and strategic approaches to risk combine art and science, integrating reasoning with intuition. The fundamental difference is that traditional risk management focuses on *only* threats of loss; strategic risk management encompasses *both* opportunities for gain and threats of loss. At best, traditional risk management can only keep an organization where it now is; strategic risk management enables an organization to advance and develop its potential.

STRATEGIC RISK MANAGEMENT AND GRANT-MAKING AT NOVIB

Founded in 1956, the Netherlands Organization for International Development Cooperation (Novib/Oxfam Netherlands) is a non-governmental foundation funded by the Dutch government and public. Novib's purpose is to encourage a world community in which socio-economic contradictions between rich and poor are eradicated, the wealth of the world is more justly divided, and people and population groups can learn about and come to respect each other's cultures, and in the interest of their own development, cooperate on the basis of shared responsibility and mutual solidarity. Furthermore, Novib is a member of Oxfam International, a confederation of 12 organizations working together with over 3,000 counterpart organizations in more than 100 countries to find lasting solutions to poverty, suffering and injustice. As do all the Oxfams, Novib takes a rights-based approach to achieve structural, enduring improvement in the quality of life of people. Every NGO must customize its use of strategic risk management in accordance with its mission and long-term goals, which pose special challenges for an organization that approaches grant-making from highly political and normative perspectives.

Grant-making Guided by Organizational Values Rather than by Partisan Ideology Novib works for changes in policies and their corresponding practices to modify the structures and relations of power that are obstacles to people exercising their political, civil, economic, social, and cultural rights. In every society and community, access and control of resources are structured in ways that benefit some individuals and groups and discriminate against others. Thus, the key to success of a rights based-approach to development and social justice is empowerment. Citizens and social organizations obtain the capacity to be significant actors in a process to change the structure and relations of power to benefit the many and not just a few dominant sectors. To contribute to these ends, Novib applies three institutional strategies.

Every NGO must customize

First and foremost, Novib is a donor to approximately 850 local organizations in more than 50 countries in Africa, Asia, Latin America, the former Soviet Union, and Eastern Europe. These grantees are NGOs who work directly with and for the poor and disenfranchised. The aim of this cooperation is to increase the capacity of people to exercise their individual and collective rights and to make decisions about control and use of material, human, intellectual, and financial resources. The support, however, is purely financial. Novib believes that because of the power of money, a donor-recipient partnership may be undermined if the grant-maker also attempts to provide these organizations with professional or technical assistance on ways and means to improve their performance. It can easily lead to dependence, disempowerment of the grantee, and strategic or organizational problems.

Second, Novib strives to inform Dutch public opinion. It educates the Dutch public about the non-Western world by challenging conventional images and encouraging deeper insights concerning development. Novib also tries to make the cultures of the South accessible to the Dutch public through, for example, publishing books written by southern writers. Novib promotes the personal involvement of Dutch individuals and organizations in actions such as fair trade aimed at a more equitable distribution of the world's resources. Third, with the other Oxfams, Novib defends the interests of developing countries in the political and economic power centres of the West and tries to influence policy decisions in favour of the world's poor. Novib bases its core work of grant-making on a strongly normative approach to development as cooperation between independent social actors. Institutional autonomy, mutual accountability, consultative decision making, and transparency between donor and grantee are the four pillars of Novib's relationships of development cooperation. Novib channels well over 80 percent of its annual budget of US$170 million to fund like-minded counterpart organizations. Novib does not make grants to individuals. The average annual value of a grant is around US$150,000, and Novib is highly flexible in its funding. Grantees largely decide where Novib's donation can do them the most good. In addition, Novib strives to fund its grantees in three-year cycles and frequently, for nine or more years. In the rapidly shifting environment of international development cooperation, however, throughout each year staff increasingly face strategic choices about what grantees to fund.

Changing Political Environment

As is the case with NGOs around the world, Novib's stakeholders increasingly expect to know what has been achieved with their support and involvement. Furthermore, Novib now competes for funding from its principal donor, the Dutch Ministry of Development Cooperation, based on the quality of results and not solely on professional grant-making. Consequently, since 2000, Novib has given much more emphasis than before to the results it strives to achieve. To this end, Novib is applying strategic risk management in a variety of areas of operational decisions. The principal area is grant appraisal. Novib realized that if grantees and Novib itself only practice traditional risk management, then Novib's grants might be relatively safe, but the potential for more significant impact in a rapidly changing environment would be limited.

In 1980s and 1990s, the quality of the partner organization was the guarantee of positive results. Novib approached this challenge with a checklist of what it considered good grantee practice. That instrument was designed to provide a reading of the health of an organization and the quality of the project it proposed that Novib fund. Novib's rationale was that the closer a grantee was to standards of organizational excellence, the more likely the grant would be used wisely and the project successfully implemented. Solidarity, the right strategy, and excellent management continue to be important but are no longer sufficient.

Novib and its grantees must demonstrate impact. Committed to this demanding task in often volatile circumstances, Novib realized that if grantees and Novib itself only practice traditional risk management, then Novib's grants might be relatively safe, but the potential for more significant impact in a rapidly changing environment would be limited.

To increase the magnitude of the results, Novib understood that it must dare to manage risks strategically and not bureaucratically if it were to contribute to development. Novib decided that the emerging concept of strategic risk management would offer an especially appropriate tool for managing its grant-making. This methodology permits holistic, non-linear and dynamic analysis and decision-making about the potential for results. Consequently, from 2001 to 2003, Novib researched and developed a grant appraisal methodology grounded in risk management science. From August 2003 through February 2004, Novib field-trained over one hundred of its grant makers and managers in the new methodology.

THE APPRAISAL PRODUCT—JUDGMENTS

In Novib, a team of two to three program officers, a financial officer, and a team secretary are responsible for the Novib portfolio in a country or region. They use an appraisal manual, the "Toolbox," to support them in formulating their risk judgments. The product—their strategic risk appraisal—is a narrative document of four to eight pages with three components.

The upside risks: the opportunity for cooperation

The starting point is the congruence between the positive *results* a grantee wishes to achieve and one or more strategic objectives of Novib for the country or region. The Novib team identify and interpret what the grantee wishes to achieve that will improve the quality of life of sectors affected by economic, social, and political inequality. In particular, the team explains what it believes is the potential contribution to changes in policies and practices. They also identify other positive *consequences* or "added social value" of the grantee's activities. The positive consequences are the most important but not the only element of the opportunity for cooperation and for Novib to provide funding. The amount and duration of the grant also depends on the *probability* of success. Thus, the team looks hard at the counterpart organization's resources and track record and at the environment in which it operates. It identifies the capacity that the grantee has demonstrated to achieve similar results and to manage change. Furthermore, the team takes into account favourable external social actors and factors. With this foundation, the team formulates its judgment about the probability of this organization achieving its results.

The downside risks: the principal dangers to success

The second component of the appraisal is the down-side risks or threats that endanger the success of the opportunity. Novib calls these "principal dangers." They are the risks in which the probability of occurrence and potential negative impact could undermine a grantee's ability to achieve the results. Equally important, the team explains how the grantee proposes to manage these "mortal" risks to success.

The upside-down risks: changing opportunities and dangers

Risk exposure to both positive and negative results must be managed into the future and this, of course, is the grantee's responsibility. The project proposal is essentially a plan for the management of the positive risks. The grantee informs Novib how it will manage the negative risks. Together, they agree on an agenda to monitor and review progress towards the results and the control of the principal dangers. This annual reflection analyzes how the opportunity and dangers may have changed, but also identifies new opportunities and emerging threats for the coming year. In sum, the content of the appraisal highlights the positive risks and the opportunity to contribute to significant social change. The negative risks are those that endanger success.

ENGAGEMENT AND DIALOGUE

Novib's grant appraisal methodology is based on mutual respect between Novib and its grantees and a sound understanding of each other's expectations and needs. A program officer and the officer's team quickly confirm a promising opportunity (and weed out others). They analyse only the important obstacles to success and make decisions using judgment and reflection, as well as facts and figures, all in consultation with the grantee. The risk appraisal enables Novib staff and grantees to negotiate agreements about enhancing the opportunity to cooperate and mitigating the dangers to the success of that cooperation.

The pre-assessment team meeting

First, Novib communicates to all applicants that Novib supports grantees that take risks in seizing new opportunities to achieve their social change goals. Upon receiving a project proposal, one team member, usually a program officer, decides or confirms in the case of a current grantee if the project proposal meets Novib's minimum criteria.

- Fits within Novib's grant-making strategy for the country or region.
- Is compatible in terms of organizational purpose and values.
- Fulfills minimum administrative and financial standards, such as being a legally constituted NGO organization with a bank account.

If the team agrees in principle to appraise the organization and its proposal, the program officer in the lead prepares a draft appraisal for discussion by her team with the information at hand. This includes the grantee's proposal and for current grantees, evaluations, annual reports, audits, and field visit notes. Experience to date is that key additional information is always required. For example, usually there is a lack of clarity about the intended results of the grantee's activities. In Novib's case, this is especially true concerning potential policy and practice changes. Of course, the use of a risk appraisal methodology also requires a change in mindset within the Novib team. For instance, the previous appraisal methodology was calibrated to identify problems and set conditions, not embrace positive and negative risks.

Visit to the grantee

Generally, not all the missing information can be obtained through correspondence. The customary emphasis by donors is on what the grantee is going to *do* with their grant. Novib's new focus on what is to be *achieved* and on the results represents a new dimension to the donor-grantee relationship and requires face-toface dialogue. Therefore, the team crafts the questions that one or two program officers, sometimes accompanied by the financial officer, pursue during the visit to the organization. They begin with a morning or afternoon of questions and answers to gather information. The grantee's director, senior management team, and board members, occasionally, are present.

In the following day or two, the program officer (and other team members if present) completes the draft appraisal and presents it to the grantee. The grantee reads and discusses internally the appraisal before another session with the program officer(s). In the second half-day meeting, it is the grantee's turn to ask questions, correct misinformation, and comment on the analysis in the risk appraisal. They wrap up discussing how the grantee will manage the negative risks.

The visit is the central event in the appraisal process. The face-to-face critical dialogue is sharply focused on the political dimension of the cooperation—what both NGOs aim to change in society. In the first year, Novib applied the risk appraisal methodology to project proposals from almost 200 NGOs in countries with a wide range of political, economic, and cultural diversity. Around the world, grantees and Novib staff alike consistently consider this respectful, transparent discussion in a spirit of conscious risk-taking and mutual accountability to be the most valuable part of the new methodology. They are able to counter together the pressures for donors to subcontract for results and for grantees to play cat and mouse in order to preserve their institutional integrity. Grantees learn why Novib is supporting (or not funding) a project, as well as Novib's hopes for and concerns about their projects. Novib learns about the fundamental challenges the NGO counterpart faces in achieving significant social change.

Team discussion and decision

The program officer responsible submits to the team the appraisal and a ten to twenty page description of the grantee. The two documents—one part analysis and the other part facts and figures—complement each other. The program officer has sifted through considerable amounts of information, has analysed that which is essential to understand the opportunity for cooperation, and made judgments about the impact and likelihood of both success and failure. All of this has been done in consultation with the NGO grantee. Therefore, the team does not repeat or simulate the process of appraisal. Instead, colleagues enrich the quality and coherence of both products.

In making their decision to fund, the team members go beyond examining the probability and the importance of potential structural, sustainable changes in the lives of people represented by the project to be funded. They strive together to strengthen, integrate, respect, and accept responsibility for Novib's and the grantee's necessarily different but convergent views.

Follow-up and review

The Novib methodology stipulates a review of the opportunities and dangers at least once a year. The grantee and program officer discuss the grantee's experience in the past twelve months in working towards achieving the results and managing the principal dangers and the implications for opportunities and dangers in the second year. The review also looks forward:

How has the opportunity changed? Are there new opportunities that may deserve higher priority? How have the threats changed? What new action is required to manage them?

NGO PARTNERSHIPS FOR GLOBAL HEALTH PROMOTION

The role of civil society organizations (CSOs) has received increasing importance in public policy and health policy over the past decade. As more financial and other resources were invested in this sector, the profile of its constituent groups changed. Different agencies define CSOs and NGOs differently. There is need for clarity in understanding the heterogeneity of this sector, and to recognize the unique roles of different constituents for global health promotion. NGOs in the 1960s and 1970s were largely not –for – profit voluntary organizations working towards integral development. In health they included medical service through hospitals, health centres, and mobile clinics run by charities, missions and philanthropic organizations. With experience and reflection this group developed a deeper community based understanding of the dynamics of health, health care and development in different socio-cultural situations.

They were often able to achieve what governments in resource poor situations could not. With professional and social skills developed through working in difficult circumstances they became alternative experts, and the sector soon became an additional policy option. With growing recognition, money and influence, the profile of NGOs and new entrants to the sector changed. NGOs now include corporate NGOs, with companies setting up Trusts and Societies, building brand images, obtaining tax benefits and blurring the profit and not for profit sector. Government NGOs (GONGOs) and other new entities developed to overcome the bureaucracy of government. Professional associations' and research bodies with a high degree of knowledge and expertise, such as the International Union for Health Promotion and Education comprise another important section. NGO networks developed at national and global levels with a specific focus on health. During the past decade a global people's health movement emerged with a strong focus on health determinants and a right's based approach to health care. The potential for partnerships are thus many. Including those that can impact on health determinants provide a strategic option to global health promotion.

NGO coalitions for health promotion

The Millennium Development Goals (MDGs) provide a renewed framework for partnerships between governmental and nongovernmental organizations to create an environment conducive to development and elimination of poverty. Investment in health is critical for development and achievement of the MDGs. Through advocacy for healthy public policy, NGOs increase community health literacy and knowledge. NGOs with diverse structures and functions are the *sine quo non* in health promotion due to their grass roots presence and closeness with communities, which enables them to respond to people's health needs, concerns and aspirations.

NGOs understand that health is produced not just by hospitals and health professionals, but by individuals and families in the context of their daily lives and by influencing health determinants. NGOs are a positive force through direct health empowerment and action with people, as well as by working on the deeper issues. They apply the principles of health promotion including capacity development, knowledge transfer, community participation, empowerment, intersectoral collaboration, equity and advocacy for sustainable development.

The agenda for health promotion involves tackling multiple determinants of health. No single governmental or nongovernmental organization can deal with the multiplicity of issues. This is a sound rationale for NGOs to establish networks and alliances between themselves and with academia, governmental and other organizations to maximize their resources and achieve better outcomes. Partnerships provide an opportunity to make best use of the strengths and comparative advantage of each organization. However NGO coalitions do not occur by chance. To be effective partnerships must be planned, fostered and managed. Partnerships can be focused and time bound to achieve defined outcomes or work through long-term commitments. An example is the Geneva based NGO Ad Hoc Advisory Group on Health Promotion.

NGO Ad Hoc Advisory Group on Health Promotion

Born as an outcome of the WHO 4th International Conference on Health promotion in Jakarta in 1997, the Group supported implementation of its recommendations, and worked in partnership with others towards the Global Conference on Health Promotion in Mexico City, 2000.

The Group comprises several NGOs whose activities include health promotion and education, health co-operatives, nursing, rural women; social welfare, women's health and those whose main mandate may not be "health". Member's commitment to health promotion helps pool resources and expertise in tackling health determinants. For example, Associated County Women of the World (ACWW) partners with local NGOs, and Governments to provide literacy centres in Mali. ACWW provides partial funding and expertise to help local NGOs achieve their goals with community ownership and ongoing monitoring.

The wide diversity of activities, international structures and grass root involvement give the NGO Ad Hoc Group its richness of approach, experience and expertise. Working collectively and individually, and in close partnership with WHO headquarters, the Group has kept the Jakarta and Mexico agendas in the forefront of the NGO community. The Group hosts briefings at the World Health Assembly on NGO and government partnerships in health promotion. This would not have been possible for any single NGO. By their work and commitment, the Ad Hoc Group contributes to the attainment of the Millennium Development Goals.

Capacity Building

Human resources are the lynchpin to achieve health and development goals. Distortions in health care priorities hinder progress in health promotion. Major distortions include concentration of health facilities and personnel on urban populations rather than rural, on tertiary care rather than primary, on curative care rather than on promotive and preventative services and on the middle-class and better off rather than on the poor. Though the primary health care strategy promoted by WHO was designed to achieve greater equity and universal coverage, health reform and economically driven models of care reduced public spending on health and social services leading to growing inequities.

Besides misallocation and mal-distribution of resources, access to health care is hampered by shortage of competent health professionals capable of providing comprehensive health care. Poor investment in training, recruitment and retention, force health care workers to look for 'greener pastures' leading to brain drain. Nurses and physicians trained at public cost migrate from poorer countries to the developed world, leaving health care facilities in a state of collapse.

Nursing staff shortages cause closure of essential health care facilities, including emergency rooms. Serious shortages in all health professional categories in Zimbabwe resulted in closure of health facilities and reduced access to services. The New York Times reported, *"the nation is currently engulfed in a huge nursing shortage which is going to get worse"*. In the United Kingdom there is concern that: *"the National Health Service (NHS) does not have enough pairs of hands to deliver the care that the nation needs... and hospitals are turning abroad to find staff'*.

Shortages of doctors are reported in several countries including Botswana, Ghana and Guinea Bissau. In some developing countries, shortage of nurses and doctors often results in staffing rural clinics by poorly trained personnel ill-equipped to provide comprehensive services including health promotion. In these circumstances, it is likely that investment in health promotion will continue to be eroded and neglected. NGO coalitions and all stakeholders need to address this issue on priority.

Health promotion strategies draw upon multiple actors and stakeholders including multilateral organizations such as UN agencies; development banks; national and local governments; faith-based groups, citizen's organizations; international, national and local NGOs; WHO collaborating centres; academic institutions; trade unions; the arts and entertainment industry; the private sector and others. Collaborative efforts by stakeholders who promote the public good in health is crucial for success. For example, the progress made in onchocerciacis control was only possible with committed partnerships. While reducing under-nutrition and universalizing access to water and sanitation attract less attention, regressive policies of some organizations also reverse health gains.

Community Empowerment

Different stakeholders, working with empowered communities can become a powerful voice, lobbying governments to invest in human resources particularly for health promotion training and capacity building. NGO networks have a convening power and a large outreach capacity enabling them to bring about a "paradigm shift" from the curative to the preventive, promotive and social health model. Training and capacity building by NGOs are characterized by active community participation, empowering individuals and families to increase control over the determinants of their health, and to demand universal access to health care. NGOs and health profession associations should be enabled to become "social health activists".

Coalition building

Strengthening NGO coalitions for health is necessary in the current landscape characterized by declining development resources, increasing privatization of services, and reverse transfer of resources from developing countries. Coalitions need to be built with skill, care and mutual trust using strategies that include identifying opportunities and partners with shared goals; reaching agreements; maintaining and evaluating partnerships. This takes time and resources.

Challenges faced include selecting partners, working with communities, defining partnerships goals, setting time frames, mobilising resources and keeping long term commitments to meet complex evolving needs. Often unequal distribution of power and decision-making within NGO groups or between NGOs and governments can negatively impact outcomes and sustainability of partnerships. Corporate interests working through governments and international bodies can be counterproductive. Lack of trust and suspicion between NGOs and governments is a potential threat.

Coalitions can multiply actions outlined in the Ottawa Charter: building healthy public policy, creating supportive environments, strengthening community action, developing personal skills, and reorienting health services. Mutual commitments to engagement between governments, civil society and NGOs would help achieve better health. Governments need to see beyond their term in office and to see the long-term role of health promotion. NGOs and civil society need to be rooted in their reality, and to see beyond that reality and their own constituencies to engage with a wider spectrum of stakeholders. Both need to recognize barriers that prevent the realization of health promotion in the community and to undertake cooperative measures to tackle this. As an intergovernmental agency, WHO has a long history of working with NGOs In health promotion WHO – NGO partnership from decision making to evaluation has been fruitful. While partnerships are strong at WHO headquarters, there is scope for improvement at country and regional levels.

GLOBAL COALITION'S PROMOTING HEALTH, ADDRESSING DETERMINANTS

Concern about the social determinants of health, and the difficulties faced by governments and international bodies to effectively work on their own towards Health for All goals, resulted in the emergence in the late 1990s of a much broader global coalition, the Peoples Health Movement (PHM). Unlike the 1970s, health groups and NGOs are now joined by women's movements, the science and literacy movement, the environment movement, trade unions, development groups and many community based organizations, all of whom recognize that better health is a common concern.

Collective analysis, planning, action and reflections with affected communities build solidarity. Groups from varied backgrounds and cultures have become connected locally and globally through horizontal and vertical linkages. This awakening culminated in the first Peoples Health Assembly (PHA 1) in December 2000 in Savar, Bangladesh, wherein 1493 persons from

75 countries debated health related issues over five days and adopted the Peoples Charter for Health.

Through thousands of prior community, village and town meetings, the Charter built on perspectives of people, whose voices are rarely heard. It clearly addresses health determinants, namely:

a) economic challenges posed by the global trading system, third world debt, intellectual property laws, speculative international capital flows;
b) social and political challenges, including the right to work and livelihood, gender issues, rights of expression, political participation and religious choice, the weakening of public institutions and services;
c) environmental challenges including water and air pollution, climate change, ozone layer depletion, nuclear energy and waste, toxic chemicals and pesticides, loss of bio-diversity, deforestation and soil erosion ;
d) war, violence, conflict and natural disasters.

Action points concerning these issues, and for developing a people-centred health sector with people's participation resulted in much follow up. Spontaneously translated into 50 languages the Charter has become one of the largest consensus documents on health providing a framework for action. Since 2000, country, regional and issue based circles evolved leading to specific action such as the right to health care campaign in India; advocacy regarding global public private initiatives; policy dialogue with the WHO; a global campaign on patents; the Peoples Charter on HIV/AIDS and Asian People's Alliance for Combating HIV/AIDS; the first Global Health Watch report; International Health Forums; state national and UNESCAP health policies; a Tsunami Watch; and most importantly advocacy, street action and community work, including training thousands of community health workers.

Media strategies resulted in greater national and local reporting of health issues and controversies, including corruption. In some countries health moved higher on the public and political agenda with commitments to increase budgetary allocations. There has been support for the peace movement in the USA, Europe and Asia, and a PHM response to disasters in Iran, Sri Lanka, and India. The second Peoples Health Assembly in Cuenca, Ecuador in July 2005 raised issues and concerns of the Americas and reviewed progress since PHA I.

9

Credibility Among NGOs

Credibility is the quality of being believable or trustworthy. It refers to whether or not a person or a statement is believed or trusted. Sometimes leaders or experts are not considered by the public to be credible because they have a personal interest in the outcome of a situation or a conflict which would likely influence their views and/or statements about that situation or conflict.

For example, a salesperson's "believability" is established through empathy, willingness to listen to specific needs, and continual enthusiasm toward his or her work and the customer's business. It is the quality of being plausible, believable, dependable, or worthy of confidence. An improvement of credibility is considered to be the same as confidence building or providing quality to the user. Thus, a "credible" communicator is perceived as both expert and trustworthy. Credibility is one of the most critical factors that affects an NGO. Being credible is simply the perception of being trustworthy and believable. Why do people buy brand name goods and services? One of the key reasons is that the brand represents a level of quality that they know and trust. So how can an NGO build credibility? A key factor is being consistent, with reference to the work being done, the message being disseminated, or the concepts being advocated. Sharing knowledge is a useful way to build credibility. This helps in building the intellectual base of the NGO, and its ability to articulate the views of the people it is speaking for. And obviously, telling the truth is always the best way. Good testimonials can also be a powerful way to generate trust. A number of strategies can be seen being used by NGOs to build their credibility:

- Use of academics and experts to evaluate NGO projects and activities
- Associating with national or regional associations, alliances, or forums
- Obtaining UN accreditation
- Finding credible spokespeople

- Speaking and publishing regularly
- Seeking awards and prizes as recognition for work done
- Partnering with key community, governmental and industry entities
- Writing case studies that tell compelling stories from people and communities they serve
- Geting some good press stories
- Understanding an NGO's strengths and larger connections, communicate the strengths and connections consistently
- Keeping a significant presence online-both web and email
- Generating a good image through newsletters, bulletins, press releases etc.

Ultimately, building good credibility builds trust and confidence-which not only strengthens staff morale, but enables an NGO to garner resources to be more effective in its programmes and projects.

The Power Shift and the NGO Credibility Crisis

World politics has undergone a radical and often-overlooked transformation in the last fifteen years, resulting neither from the collapse of the Soviet Union nor the rising tide of fundamentalism, but from the unprecedented growth of non-governmental organizations around the globe. NGOs or Civil Society Organizations (CSOs) have moved from backstage to centre stage in world politics, and are exerting their power and influence in every aspect of international relations and policy making. NGOs have been a positive force in domestic and international affairs, working to alleviate poverty, protect human rights, preserve the environment, and provide relief worldwide. Few, therefore, have felt the need to take a critical look at the effectiveness and accountability of these organizations. After 9/11, however, the specter of terrorists using NGOs as a front for their operations and some highly publicized cases of abuse have made this a critical issue that needs to be addressed by the NGO community. In addition, the increasing power of NGOs has prompted scholars, governments, and the media to raise questions about the roles and responsibilities of these new global, non-state actors. Fundamental questions include: how many NGOs actually exist, and what are their agendas? Who runs these groups? Who funds them? And, perhaps most significantly, to whom are NGOs accountable, and how and what influence do they actually have on world politics? This article will attempt to address these questions and suggest some ways in which NGOs can become more transparent and accountable as a means of protecting the credibility and independence of these vital organizations.

New Actors and Agendas

Organizations such as Amnesty International, Green peace, and the International Campaign to Ban Landmines have helped bring non-governmental organizations the international recognition that has made "NGO" a household word. Some NGOs gained notoriety by organizing large-scale protests that captured international headlines due to the violence and disruption they caused. Still others have organized meetings to coincide with the official gatherings of the G-8, the World Trade Organization, the World Bank, and the International Monetary Fund with the intent of challenging their legitimacy.

Milestones in this largely non-violent NGO revolution include the Solidarity Movement's role in the 1980's political transformation in Poland; the influence of environmental activists on the outcome of the 1992 Earth Summit in Rio de Janeiro; the international coalition of groups led by the South Council that developed the 1994 "Fifty Years is Enough" campaign directed at the World Bank and International Monetary Fund; and the labour, anti-globalization, and environmental groups that derailed the 1999 Seattle WTO meeting. The effectiveness of these efforts stunned the major multilateral institutions and governments worldwide and forced them to develop ways to engage and involve NGOs in their deliberations and decision making. With their place in world politics now firmly established, the majority of NGOs have moved from protesting on the streets to contributing to policy making in the boardrooms of the United Nations, World Bank, World Trade Organization, and the International Monetary Fund.

International relations were once the exclusive domain of diplomats, bureaucrats, and states; however, today's policy-makers must consider a diverse set of international actors when formulating policy, including organizations as varied as CNN, al-Jazeera, the International Campaign to Ban Landmines, al-Qaeda, the Association of Southeast Asian Nations (ASEAN), and the Organization of Petroleum Exporting Countries (OPEC). While these actors were not born of globalization, they have been empowered by it. The diffusion of information, technologies, and power have leveled the playing field and enabled NGOs large and small to organize locally and have a global impact.

Jessica Mathews, Lester Salamon, and others have written extensively about the dramatic proliferation of NGOs and the impact these institutions are having on world politics. The current body of literature, however, has not examined the problems created by what can be called a crisis of transparency and accountability, an issue that looms on the horizon for the entire NGO sector. As we will see, NGOs as an international community lack the transparency and accountability in terms of finances, agenda, and governance necessary to effectively perform their crucial role in democratic civil society.

NGO Proliferation and Power

The term "non-governmental organization" describes a wide variety of organizations variously known as "private voluntary organizations," "civil society organizations," and "non-profit organizations." The dramatic proliferation in the number of NGOs and the growth in public and private grants and contracts flowing to these organizations have enabled them to become a powerful force in world politics. Because so many types of organizations are subsumed under the acronym NGO, the scope and breadth of this sector's typological landscape is lost. Our inability to accurately gauge the size and range of this sector is one of the critical problems that needs to be addressed jointly by the public (first sector), private (second sector), and NGOs (third sector) around the world. Despite these limitations, a variety of efforts at estimation provide a glimpse into the scope of NGO proliferation.

The Economist estimates that the number of international non-governmental organizations rose from 6,000 in 1990 to 26,000 in 1996. According to the 2002 UNDP Human Development Report, nearly one-fifth of the world's thirty-seven thousand INGOs (international non-governmental organizations) were formed in the 1990s. The Independent Sector, a non-profit organization that serves and tracks developments in the third sector of society, estimates that there are currently 1.5 million non-profit organizations in the United States. Similarly, India was estimated to house more than one million NGOs. NGOs have not only increased in numbers but also in membership, with many organizations more than doubling their member base at a steady rate.

Recent figures from the United States Institute of Peace (USIP) emphasize the growth of NGO budgets, many of which have reached millions of U.S. dollars. USIP states that the 160 INGOs associated with Inter*Action* have a combined annual revenue of $2.3 billion, almost all of which comes from private donors. USIP also echoes the point that "sheer growth in the number of INGOs in recent years has been dramatic," noting that more than 1,500 INGOs are registered observers of the United Nations.

The real story is not the proliferation of NGOs, but how these organizations have effectively networked and mobilized their members to reshape world politics. This point was graphically illustrated by the significant NGO presence at the 1992 Earth Summit in Rio, where 17,000 NGO representatives staged an alternative forum to the UN-sponsored meeting, while 1,400 were involved in the official proceedings. Emboldened by their success, an even larger group converged in Beijing for the Fourth World Conference on Women in September 1995. There, an astonishing 35,000 NGOs organized an alternative forum and 2,600 NGOs participated in the official multilateral negotiations.

Understanding the Paradigm and Power Shift

The growth of non-state actors has in large part been fuelled by the perceived inability of both domestic and international institutions to respond to the social, economic, and political consequences of rapid advances in science and technology, growing economic interdependence, and political fragmentation. In addition, a growing number of transnational threats (pandemics, global warming, and the proliferation of WMDs) that require a coordinated response have created a need for new partners and approaches to solving global issues. As the NGO sector grows, however, it is also facing a new array of organizational challenges that it must address. We have identified six interrelated forces that we believe have propelled the remarkable growth of NGOs, and here look at both the problems and possibilities that each of these represents:

1. increased democratization, and recognition of the importance of civil society in promoting democracy;
2. an increased demand for independent information and analysis;
3. the growth of non-state and inter-state actors;
4. improved communications technologies;
5. the globalization of NGO funding, especially from North to South; and
6. what can be called "a crisis in confidence."

Democratization and the Civil Society Ideal: The addition of more open societies has been a necessary condition for the creation of an environment conducive to the proliferation of independent, issue-driven, and action-oriented NGOs. The emergence of the civil society movement has put political pressure on governments, which in turn have created the space and demand for NGOs in the political landscape.

The work of civil society theorists, such as Robert Putnam of Harvard University, and the dramatic social labouratories of Poland, the Philippines, and South Africa have served to advance the perception that democracy cannot prosper unless a society contains an extensive network of organizations that promote civic engagement, dialogue, and trust among both acquaintances and strangers. NGOs are perhaps the most natural and effective response to this need. Furthermore, according to civil society proponents, such organizations are critical to promoting the protection of freedoms and social needs as well as the quality of public information and political interaction.

It is important to remember that many NGOs do not fit the mold of the grassroots, mass-participation vehicles idealized by many theorists. However, NGOs often come the closest to engaging directly with those citizens most affected by but least heard in policy decision-making. The growth in interest in civil society has thus stimulated interest in NGOs as an alternative source of information on issues of national and international concern and as a potential critic of government policy that can, in theory, speak with a uniquely objective voice independent of either governmental or business interests.

Growing Demand for Information, Analysis, and Action: In an increasingly interdependent and information-rich world, governments, policy makers, and citizens face the common problem of bringing expert knowledge to bear on decision making. Policy makers need basic information about the societies they govern—about how current policies are working, possible alternatives, and their likely costs and consequences.

Citizens increasingly demand the same, and NGOs have grown to be an integral part of the response to this increased demand for information.

Both policy makers and the general public, however, are often besieged by more information than they can possibly use. The problem is that this information can be unsystematic, unreliable, and/or tainted by the interests of those who are disseminating it.

NGOs have an important role to play in monitoring and facilitating the collection of reliable data needed to make informed decisions – a role that is particularly important in developing and transitional countries, where such information often does not otherwise exist.

Furthermore, NGOs, which tend to focus on a relatively narrow range of issues, are often much more expert on a given topic than a general policy maker could possibly be and therefore provide a bank of experience and knowledge to which officials can turn.

Even when providing reliable information, however, NGOs are hardly neutral on issues of policy formation.

Due to their varied nature, NGOs often play the interesting dual role of providing information and acting as an agent of political pressure on the government, leading to potential conflicts of interest. Transparency and the disclosure of interests and funding sources here are crucially important, but there are often few mechanisms to ensure compliance, especially on an international scale.

Growth of States, Non-state, and Inter-state Actors: The latter part of the twentieth century has seen unprecedented growth in the number of nation-states, as well as in governmental and non-governmental organizations. In 1950 there were only fifty nations and approximately sixty inter-governmental organizations. We now have four times as many nation-states and inter-governmental organizations and, as noted earlier, an almost exponential growth in the number of NGOs.

The forces that drove the expansion of all non-state actors also led to the astounding proliferation of NGOs. No factor is as significant as the global trend toward increased democratization and decentralization, which began with the increase in the number of nation-states after World War II, and the creation of a host of inter-governmental organizations (such as the UN, World Bank, and WTO) to which certain powers and functions were delegated.

While the grand vision of a world government was never fully realized, a seamless web of organizations and activities, most notably in the areas of low politics, has helped reduce conflict and facilitate bilateral and multilateral relations.

In our current system of global governance, inter-governmental institutions work with what *The Economist* identifies as "an enormous weakness"—they are limited by the treaties and states that created them, and therefore subordinated to the national interest of states, making decisive and responsive action difficult.

The embattled public image developed by these large, centralized bureaucracies has made them easy targets of "NGO swarm," as NGOs eagerly move to fill the vacuum in global governance. Partly in response to the mass meetings and protests described earlier, World Bank president Jim Wolfensohn gave some of the Bank's harshest critics a role in the majority of the Multilateral Development Banks' work.

Over half of World Bank projects are currently executed in partnership with NGOs. This move, however, has not only "co-opted" some of the Bank's former critics but also created a situation in which "NGOs are at the centre of World Bank policy, and moreover often determine it. While the current World Bank is more transparent, it is also more beholden to a new set of special interests."

The ultimate legitimacy and impact of NGOs, therefore, even in work with institutions such as the World Bank, are still compromised by the lack of transparency that exists in the NGO community today.

This translates into an increased incentive for organizations such as the World Bank and the United Nations, which work extensively with NGO partners, to support the development of a set of standard policies and best practices to improve third sector transparency and accountability.

Improved Communications Technologies: Extraordinary changes in the technology of communication have also helped transform the world of NGOs.

The widespread diffusion of knowledge made possible by improvements in information and telecommunications systems, plus the near-ubiquity of electronic facsimile machines by the early 1990s, made it possible to transmit documents almost instantly to virtually anywhere in the world. The growth of the Internet has furthered an instant, inexpensive, and almost entirely unregulated flow of information.

NGOs, whose goals for impact often outstrip their budgets, have benefited greatly from the information age and have found that they can have a tremendous impact with a small staff.

Leaders in the NGO community agree that NGO growth has been greatly facilitated by the increased ease in collaborating, and the dissemination of information across vast distances. International consortia of like-minded NGOs have sprung up across cyberspace to share ideas and coordinate efforts to push for their adoption into policy.

Contributing to the growth of NGOs has been the fact that the nature of the present information age makes it increasingly difficult for authoritarian governments to restrict the inflow of information and opinions they would prefer to exclude. Increasingly, the only options are to allow untrammeled access or to bar access to the Internet entirely. However, the issue of accountability rises again when discussing NGOs' increasing reliance on cyberspace, a forum in which there is almost no means for quality control of information. Sham NGOs can easily be created online and disseminate their views at low cost in a manner that might prove convincing to an unsophisticated viewer. Thus, in the cyber-age as in the age of NGOs, the caveat emptor principle is more appropriate than ever before for those seeking reliable information.

Globalization of NGO Funding: Although the market for ideas is well established and expanding, even the most prominent NGOs require constant inflows of money in order to operate. In both Western countries and the developing world, many organizations operate with small budgets and minuscule staffs.

Thus, the issue of funding trends and sources is crucial to the discussion of trends in the development of NGOs because it is the globalization of funding that has helped create and sustain many of these institutions.

In Africa, Asia, and Latin America, particularly, NGOs often lack critical tax incentives for donors that foster philanthropic traditions and in turn encourage local support. As a result, much of the impetus for NGO activity growth in developing and transitional economies has been the flow of money from industrialized countries. Many donors have chosen to work through NGOs out of a concern that their funds may otherwise be misused.

While international funding has dramatically increased the resources available to NGOs, it clearly poses problems of its own.

Foreign funding can raise questions about the credibility of an organization's activities: if foreign donors are providing money for an NGO, might they be dictating its goals as well? This can be distorted and exploited, and may even serve as an excuse for an authoritarian leader to shut down organizations, which was the experience of some East European affiliates of the Open Society Institute in the 1990s. Less extreme controversies have also occurred in industrialized nations. Critics have expressed concern that the use of foreign money to support the work of U.S.-based NGOs may come with strings attached, or at least cause institutions that accept money from foreign corporations and foundations to mute any criticism of the donor country's foreign or domestic policies.

The issue of funding and accountability becomes even more complex when an NGO operates across national boarders, at which point the need for NGO transparency and accountability becomes most clear. It is often almost impossible to accurately track the funding of NGOs based outside the United States, Europe, Japan, and Australia.

Most NGOs in the developed world have at least achieved financial transparency as a result of a mix of public and private oversight, regulation, and accreditation.

Every NGO in the United States, for example, must file its finances annually with the Internal Revenue Service (IRS), the federal agency in charge of taxation. Once filed and processed, these reports are accessible to the public. In addition, every U.S. NGO must register with the state in which it is resident and is required to publish an annual report.

Charitable organizations throughout Europe, Japan, and Australia are also required to register with their governments; beyond registration, however, further accountability in terms of governance and programs is not uniform, and in many cases is not required. Given the current concerns about security, it is essential to understand where international NGOs get their funding in order to understand exactly whose interests they may be, even inadvertently, promoting. This lack of transparency in the NGO sector is perhaps their greatest vulnerability, and must be addressed internationally in order to ensure the integrity and continuity of the work of NGOs. Unlike a true democratic mandate, however, funding for NGOs is almost impossible to track.

Echoing Steve Rudolph, Peter Tavernise points out that many foundations do not probe deeply into what exactly is being done with grant funds in both developed and developing countries. Grant makers' trustees, who are volunteers, often do not even read grant proposals, and program officers are often "too busy" with grant applications to read reports on projects' impact. Thus, while funders are in a prime position to demand accountability from NGOs, this opportunity is often lost.

Paralysis and Poor Performance of the Public Sector: While the challenges to the governments in Eastern Europe and the former Soviet Union were swift and dramatic, there has been a more gradual erosion of confidence in the leaders and institutions of governments across the globe.

The paralysis and poor performance of policy makers as well as the seemingly endless stream of scandals involving public officials and a bloated, unresponsive bureaucracy have led the public to question the very legitimacy of their governments. We live in a period when the nation-state is distrusted, or more precisely, its institutions are considered ineffective and unreliable. Similar to their role in international governance, NGOs operating on a local level have emerged in an effort to address the deficiencies of nation-states and the lack of leadership shown by government officials.

It is important to note, however, that the rapid proliferation of NGOs has not always resulted in a clearer policy making scenario. Rather, as John Paul Lederach, director both of the International Conciliation Service of the Mennonite Central Committee and the Conflict Analysis and Transformation Program at Eastern Mennonite University points out, NGO proliferation has resulted in the development of myriad qualified institutions to focus on issues in "hitherto inaccessible and neglected parts of the world."

While this is positive, Lederach also points out that this "has also complicated relief efforts by creating an extraordinarily complex system which makes medieval Europe look centralized and ordered by comparison."

REVERSING ACCOUNTABILITY

True international accountability is for the moment an elusive goal, one that first requires a comprehensive definition and an answer to the complicated question, accountability to whom? There is no global method to ensure that NGOs are accountable to anyone, a fact that leaves their mandate compromised if NGOs do not as a sector prioritize the achievement of transparency and accountability.

There is a need, therefore, at the very least, for committed action on the part of NGOs towards organizational and systemic transparency that is in line with their role in impacting policy and engaging the public in dialogue on the challenges facing our world. In a period of intense scrutiny of governments and corporations, it is only logical that NGOs should be closely examined.

NGOs have proven their effectiveness in holding large institutions and governments accountable and exposing them to public scrutiny. In terms of accountability from the reverse perspective, however, neither the policy nor academic communities have systematically analysed the funding, transparency, and accountability of NGOs. No international mechanism currently exists in which a meaningful dialogue about these critical NGO components can take place.

This fact both weakens the credibility of NGOs that, as a sector, cannot claim to be anything close to models for transparency, and also leaves NGOs as a group vulnerable as no "industry-wide" standards for transparency and accountability are in place. Kumi Naidoo, president of CIVICUS, a civil society advocacy group, captures the importance of this issue when he addresses civil society organizations (CSOs):

In seeking to improve our accountability and transparency, we need not be defensive or apologize for our work. [CSOs must] think critically about long-term viability, especially when some government and business leaders are questioning the legitimacy of CSOs, and when CSOs operating in new conditions of political instability are increasingly being asked to be transparent, legitimate, and accountable.

Civil society organizations must meet this challenge head on by making themselves more accountable and transparent. Maintaining public trust in CSOs is critical for ensuring active, participatory democracy, which can enrich our public life at the national and global levels.

We should not be afraid to ask who holds groups working in the public interest accountable or, as a *New York Times* article put it, "Asking Do-Gooders to Prove They Do Good." In the final analysis, the NGO community must be willing to practice what they preach or they will risk losing both their credibility and their independence. The diversity of the NGO sector is, in many cases, a source of disorganization.

Observations such as John Paul Lederach's thus represent a further call to NGOs to ensure that their work is not jeopardized by weaknesses in their sector. The kind of dialogue and coordination that would be necessary for NGOs to achieve significant advances in terms of the creation of norms for transparency and a framework for discussion of accountability would also have the attractive benefit of creating an NGO sector that is more self-aware, cohesive, and therefore effective.

BRIDGING THE CREDIBILITY GAP

The proliferation of NGOs is challenged by the fact that the impact, nature, and interests of these organizations can each become almost impossible to measure.

Despite the fact that NGOs have always played a role in "sustaining an independent civil society," their proliferation and the increased scope of their role in every aspect of society now requires better monitoring and regulation so that they can function effectively and protect the integrity and independence of the entire third sector. The NGO community holds one of the most significant roles internationally in maintaining accountability in the private sector, public sector, and international bureaucracies. It is therefore vital that the NGO community commit itself to developing a set of credible and verifiable standards that can be universally applied.

The path toward achieving increased transparency must begin with systematic international dialogue on the topic within the NGO community. A primary objective of such dialogue would be a consensus regarding the state of transparency in the NGO community and the establishment of realistic goals for the sector on this issue.

These goals must include an approach that focuses on making the finances, governance, and programs of NGOs more transparent. These recommendations will take skill to craft, given the great diversity that exists in the third sector, but proactive steps in this area are necessary and can serve as a prudent safeguard against the potential loss of the public's trust.

Private donors, national governments, and international organizations should actively encourage this effort and provide the resources necessary to help the NGO community define and implement the principles of transparency for NGOs worldwide.

Bibliography

Ann M. Florini : *The Third Force: The Rise of Transnational Civil Society,* Washington, DC: Carnegie Endowment for International Peace, 2000.

David Hulme: *Beyond the Magic Bullet: NGO performance and accountability in the post-cold war world,* West Hartford, Kumarian Press, 1996.

Drewes, Jeanne : *Computers: Planning for Disaster,* Law Library Journal, Winter, 1989.

Fox, Lisa L. : *Management Strategies for Disaster Preparedness,* Chicago, American Library Association, 1989.

Harry J. Steiner: *Diverse Partners: non-governmental organizations in the human rights movement,* Cambridge, Harvard Law School and Human Rights Internet, 1990.

John Boli and George Thomas: *Constructing World Culture: International Nongovernmental Organizations Since 1875,* Stanford, Stanford University Press, 1999.

John Clayton Thomas: *Public Participation in Public Decision: New Skills and Strategies for Public Managers,* San Francisco, Jossey-Bass Publishers, 1995.

Jonathan A. Fox and L. David Brown: *The Struggle for Accountability: The World Bank, NGOs, and Grassroots Movements,* Cambridge, Mass.: MIT Press, 1998.

Julie Fisher: *The Road from Rio: sustainable development and the nongovernmental movement in the Third World,* Westport, Praeger, 1993.

Kahn, Miriam B. : *Disaster Response and Planning for Libraries,* Chicago, American Library Association, 1998.

Kees Biekart: *The Politics of Civil Society Building: European Private Aid Agencies and Democratic Transitions in Central America,* Utrecht, International Books, 1999.

Keyes K.E. : *Emergency Management for Records and Information Programs,* ARMA International, Kansas, 1997.

Leon Gordenker: *NGOs, the UN & Global Governance,* Boulder, Lynne Riener, 1996.

Mary Anderson: *Managing Global Chaos: Sources of and Responses to International Conflict,* Washington, DC: United States Institute of Peace Press, 1996.

Matthias Finger: *Environmental NGOs in World Politics,* London, Routledge, 1994.

McPhee, John : *The Control of Nature,* New York, Farrar, Straus, Giroux, 1989.

Michael Edwards and David Hulme: *Beyond the Magic Bullet: NGO performance and accountability in the post-cold war world,* West Hartford, Kumarian Press, 1996.

Norris, Debra Hess : *Disaster Recovery: Salvaging Photograph Collections,* Philadelphia, PA, 1998.

Paul J. Nelson: *The World Bank and NGOs: The Limits of Apolitical Development,* New York, St. Martin's Press, 1995.

Paul Wapner: *Environmental Activism and World Civic Politics,* Albany, SUNY Press, 1996.

Peter Willetts: *Pressure Groups in the Global System*, London, Francis Pinter, 1982

Stommel, Elizabeth : *Volcano Weather: The Story of 1816, The Year Without a Summer*, Newport, Seven Seas Press, 1983.

Thomas Carroll: *Intermediary NGOs: the supporting link in grassroots development*, West Hartford, CT: Kumarian Press, 1992.

Thomas G. Weiss & Leon Gordenker: *NGOs, the UN & Global Governance*, Boulder, Lynne Riener, 1996.

Thomas Princen and Matthias Finger: *Environmental NGOs in World Politics*, London, Routledge, 1994.

Varley, Anne : *Disaster, Development Environments*, New York, J. Wiley, 1994.

Walker, Bridget : *Women and Emergencies*, Oxford, Oxfam, 1994.

Watson, Lyall : *Earthwork: Essays on the Edge of Natural History*, London, Hodder and Stoughton, 1956.

Yolanda N. Kakabadse and Sarah Burns: *Movers and Shapers: NGOs in International Affairs*, Washington DC, World Resources Institute, 1994.

Zenaida, D. : *Women and Children During Disaster: Vulnerabilities and Capacities*, Elaine Enarson and Betty Hearn Morrow, 1995.

Index

❑❑❑